W9-CES-837

JUDICIAL POWER
AND
RECONSTRUCTION POLITICS

THE SUPREME COURT 1865–1869

Left to right: David Davis, Noah H. Swayne, Robert C. Grier, James M. Wayne, Chief Justice Salmon P. Chase, Samuel Nelson, Nathan Clifford, Samuel F. Miller, and Stephen J. Field.

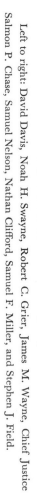

JUDICIAL POWER
AND
RECONSTRUCTION
POLITICS

STANLEY I. KUTLER

THE UNIVERSITY OF CHICAGO PRESS
CHICAGO AND LONDON

Library of Congress Catalog Card Number: 68–16702

THE UNIVERSITY OF CHICAGO PRESS, CHICAGO 60637

THE UNIVERSITY OF CHICAGO PRESS, LTD., LONDON WC I

To my wife, SANDY

PREFACE

A few years ago I initiated research on a long-range project concerning judicial power and legislative responses beginning with the last third of the nineteenth century. For background, I had intended to treat the Supreme Court during the Civil War and Reconstruction era in a perfunctory manner and briefly demonstrate what everyone conceded: that the Court's "self-inflicted wound" in the Dred Scott case impaired its prestige and effectiveness, that the Republican-dominated Congress represented a threat to judicial independence, and that, in general, the period marked the nadir of judicial power and influence. But the details of that traditional account, I soon discovered, bore little relation to reality.

What follows is a number of discrete yet related essays, illustrating what I believe are more plausible themes. First, I would suggest that congressional Republicans were not united or dominated by a hostile attitude toward the federal judiciary but, in fact, contributed significantly to the expansion of its powers. In addition, despite the furor over the Dred Scott decision, the Supreme Court exhibited a remarkable tenacity and toughness which resulted in the perpetuation and then the enlargement of its powers. Considered together, these themes lead to my conclusion that the period represented continuity, not a lapse in judicial development, and thus form a more meaningful backdrop for understanding the later character and uses of federal judicial power.

This period of judicial history should not be viewed as an isolated episode, or as exclusively connected with the phenomenon of southern military reconstruction. Much of the congressional attitude toward the Court can be explained and understood in the light of prewar events and political drives. Similarly, what happened in the immediate postwar period was vitally relevant for the development of judicial power and its applications over the next century. Furthermore, the judicial history contributes to the larger meaning of the so-called Era of Reconstruction. The pattern of congressional judicial legislation, combined with the Court's responses and decisions, reflected the basic impulse of the period—to reconstruct the nation in order to insure constitutional and political hegemony for the politically and physically dominant elements of the nation.

The essays are arranged topically. I have found this the most useful approach to counterpoint the standard interpretation and to illustrate my own theses. Finally, I do not claim to have written an exhaustive study of the judicial and legal history of the period. I could have elaborated more on the doctrinal quality of judicial decisions and detailed all the jurisdictional changes of the period. I think, however, that this would have been too much a detour from my primary concern with the Court's institutional and political status during a time of tension and upheaval.

It always is a pleasant task to acknowledge the aid of various individuals and institutions. Willard Hurst, Vilas Professor of Law at the University of Wisconsin, offered a detailed critique of my manuscript which saved me from errors of fact and judgment and enlarged my view of the subject and the subtleties of legal history. Three other very kind and tolerant friends took time from their own busy lives to read earlier drafts. Richard N. Current of the University of North Carolina, Martin Ridge, Editor of the *Journal of American History,* and my colleague, Richard H. Sewell, generously provided significant suggestions regarding content and style. Harold M. Hyman of the University of Illinois offered substantial aid at a crucial time; as always, I deeply appreciate his encouragement of my work. Arthur Bestor, William Hanchett, Alan D. Harper, and, particularly, Donald M. Roper, contributed their counsel during various stages of the work. My Wisconsin students, Michal Belknap, George M. Curtis, Miss Terry Keister, George Parkinson, and William M. Wiecek, assisted me with research materials from time to time.

The American Council of Learned Societies, the American Philosophical Society, and the Louis M. Rabinowitz Foundation provided travel funds for various phases of my research. The Research Committee of the University of Wisconsin Graduate School helped in numerous ways. The staffs of the archival depositories and libraries cited in my notes offered their usual efficient services, but I am especially grateful for the courtesies extended by the late Helen Newman, Librarian of the United States Supreme Court, and Buford Rowland of the National Archives. Portions of this book appeared in different form in the *American Historical Review* and the

Journal of Southern History; I am grateful for permission of the respective editors to reproduce those materials.

My debts to my wife, Sandra Sachs Kutler, are simply too numerous and varied to catalog here. Finally, Jeff and David, too, helped in their unique ways.

Madison, Wisconsin

CONTENTS

1

Traditions and Alternatives

The historical accounting of the Reconstruction era has gone through remarkable transformations. Until recently, historians have shrouded the post–Civil War decade with a darkness-at-noon quality; it was known as the "tragic era" and was supposedly marked by a "blackout of honest government." And yet, contemporaries had recognized an obligation to the newly freed Negro, had regarded Andrew Johnson as a stubborn and possibly disloyal obstructionist, and had accepted the prominent Republicans and their works as faithful reflections of Lincolnian ideals. In recent years, interpretations have been coming back full circle to many of the contemporary evaluations. A new generation of historians, experiencing its own milieu of wars, social conflicts, and political tensions, has approached the Reconstruction period with a fresh spirit.

The sources and evidence now being explored are, of course, not new; they were readily available to earlier generations of scholars. The difference in their use is merely one of emphasis. Thus, Andrew Johnson was not necessarily a harassed, persecuted figure who clung to the flag and the Constitution and, in the long run, upheld the "right" positions. Eric McKitrick has argued, just as plausibly, that he was an inept, blundering, obstinate, even obtuse man whose thinking never came abreast of reality and the open character of constitutional questions. An Englishman, W. R. Brock, has offered a persuasive interpretation of the congressional Republicans and their program by relying primarily on the congressional debates, a source as old as the events themselves. In similar fashion, La Wanda and John Cox have demonstrated that concern for the Negro and civil rights was not a sham issue advocated exclusively by"Radical" Republicans.[1]

This new scholarship demonstrates that the story is by no means one-dimensional. No longer may we ascribe all good motives to Andrew Johnson and his supporting cast and all bad impulses to Radical Republicans and their ilk. Nor can we polarize the politics of the time and speak, on the one hand, of those who sought to undo everything of ante bellum America, and, on the other, of those who sought the preservation of all the best in American life, government, and institutions. In short, the story cannot be related as a simple contest between black and white—no matter how, without punning, one identifies the black and white.

Through the decades the history of the Supreme Court during Reconstruction has had a singular consistency, and this remains even now unchanged. Its origins can be traced as far back as the rantings of the outraged and isolated Democratic minority of the 1860's. William A. Dunning, one of the first serious students of the period, embellished the account with scholarly trappings at the turn of the century. Then Charles Warren, in his history of the Supreme Court, enriched the tale. And from these twin founts, writers on the Supreme Court during Reconstruction have uncritically drawn their facts and interpretations.[2]

[1]A number of excellent articles have called attention to shortcomings in the established accounts of Reconstruction. The pioneering ones were Francis B. Simkins, "New Viewpoints of Southern Reconstruction," *Journal of Southern History*, 5 (February, 1939): 49–61, and Howard K. Beale, "On Rewriting Reconstruction History," *American Historical Review*, 55 (July, 1940): 807–27. The outstanding recent essay is Bernard Weisberger, "The Dark and Bloody Ground of Reconstruction Historiography," *Journal of Southern History*, 25 (November, 1959): 427–47. The bibliography of the "new revisionist" works is growing rapidly. The bibliographical sections in John Hope Franklin, *Reconstruction after the Civil War* (Chicago: University of Chicago Press, 1961), La Wanda and John H. Cox, *Politics, Principle, and Prejudice, 1865–66* (Glencoe, Ill.: The Free Press, 1963), and Harold M. Hyman, ed., *The Radical Republicans and Reconstruction: 1861–1870* (Indianapolis: Bobbs-Merrill, 1967), list some of the newer materials. The complexity of the struggles over particular issues and the corresponding group alignments are illustrated in W. R. Brock, *An American Crisis: Congress and Reconstruction, 1865–1867* (New York: St. Martin's Press, 1963), Eric L. McKitrick, *Andrew Johnson and Reconstruction* (Chicago: University of Chicago Press, 1960), and David Donald, *The Politics of Reconstruction* (Baton Rouge: Louisiana State University Press, 1965).

[2]William A. Dunning, *Essays on the Civil War and Reconstruction and Related Topics* (New York: Macmillan, 1898), pp. 121–22, 136–38; Dunning, *Reconstruction, Political and Economic: 1865–1877*, Torchbook ed. (New York: Harper & Row, 1962), pp. 94, 256–58; Charles Warren, *The Supreme Court in United States History*, 3 vols. (Boston: Little, Brown & Co., 1922), 3:1–219.

The long-accepted story has an alluring simplicity that neatly dovetails with the traditional image of the grossness and cynicism of the so-called Radical era. Two themes have dominated the historiography. There is, first, the notion that the Supreme Court was left as a weakened, if not impotent, institution in consequence of its disreputable Dred Scott decision of 1857, which denied Congress the power to prohibit slavery in the territories. Beyond this, the second view concedes an attempt, albeit feeble, by the Court to exert some influence over events but then finds the justices meekly retreating before threats of annihilation or reprisal from vindictive, determined, or even demonic Radicals. Claude G. Bowers, the politician-historian, conveniently summed up the story for a vast audience: "Never has the Supreme Court been treated with such ineffable contempt, and never has that tribunal so often cringed before the clamor of the mob." The concurrent ideas of intimidation and impotence thus form the bedrock for the traditional history of the Supreme Court from 1857 to about 1873. A survey of the relevant events which have substantiated these themes is in order as a point of reference–and then departure.[3]

Charles Evans Hughes's description of the Dred Scott decision as a "self-inflicted wound" has been used to dramatize the Supreme Court's error and its sharp plunge in public esteem. However noble its intentions, the Court seemingly had acquired an affinity for the southern cause. Its image of impartiality now apparently melted in the heat and passion of the sectional conflict. Its dominant membership of southerners and "doughfaces" contributed further to its unpopularity. In short the Court had forfeited its credibility and moral authority in the North. When secession became a reality, the Court—so the story goes—lingered on as a decrepit relic of evil days gone by. Shorn of its prestige and respect, it had an ignominious part in the Civil War and Reconstruction. It was unable to "play anything like its due role of supervision, with the result that during the [war] . . . the military powers of the President underwent undue expansion, and during [Reconstruction] . . . the legislative powers of Congress" similarly enlarged.[4]

[3]The following summation represents a composite from many of the standard political and constitutional studies of the period, which are discussed in the Bibliographical Essay.

[4]Edward S. Corwin, "The Dred Scott Decision in the Light of Contemporary Legal Doctrines," *American Historical Review*, 17 (October, 1911): 68–69. Incident-

Supposedly, then, the Court was an object of suspicion and distrust when it was confronted with the great constitutional crisis and the highly explosive politics of Reconstruction. A band of "vindictive" men in Congress, frustrated by the loss of prerogatives to the wartime executive, were apparently determined to achieve their own reconstruction program without interference from an obstinate president or from a fussy judiciary insistent upon traditional constitutional limitations and niceties.

According to the traditional accounts, the President nevertheless tried to thwart the congressional will, and so, at first, did the Supreme Court. It interposed its authority against such excesses as the use of military tribunals for civilians and punitive, restrictive legislation against former Confederates. The Court's decisions in the *Milligan, Cummings,* and *Garland* cases usually are described as eloquent testimony in behalf of traditional values of American liberty and freedom against violations bred by a wartime environment. But as the nation was not inclined to heed fundamentals, these decisions merely served as grist for the Radical Republican mill. The Radicals bracketed the Court with the rapidly discredited Andrew Johnson and argued that both were seeking to deny the North the full fruits of its triumph. Thaddeus Stevens, in particular, railed against the *Milligan* decision, asserting that it was "far more dangerous" than even the infamous Dred Scott decision.[5]

Stevens's outcry presumably struck the keynote for a wholesale assault on the Court's institutional functions, its independence, and its membership. Indeed, Professor James G. Randall found that "the annihilation of the Court itself was talked of by Republicans." In July, 1866, the Radicals had already reduced the size of the Court over Johnson's veto, supposedly to prevent the President from making undesirable appointments and to manifest their contempt for the Court.

The tumult in Congress apparently was not without effect in the highest judicial councils. The justices ceased to speak out with the courage, boldness, and forcefulness that had characterized their

---

ally, Corwin's statement offers an amusing insight into his value system. Although he usually deplored judicial interference with legislative policy, he seems to have regretted the Court's "inability" to deal with congressional reconstruction.

[5]*Ex parte Milligan,* 4 Wallace (71 U.S.) 2 (1866); *Cummings* v. *Missouri,* 4 Wallace (71 U.S.) 277 (1867); *Ex parte Garland,* 4 Wallace (71 U.S.) 333 (1867). Stevens's remarks are in the *Congressional Globe,* 39th Cong., 2d sess., p. 251 (January 3, 1867). Hereafter cited as *Cong. Globe.*

stands on military tribunals and test oaths. In *Mississippi* v. *Johnson* and *Georgia* v. *Stanton*,[6] for example, the Court "evaded" and "dodged" opportunities to answer fundamental questions touching on the congressional program of military reconstruction. Although the Reconstruction Acts of 1867 were "palpably unconstitutional under the *Milligan* doctrine," the Court declined to offer a definitive constitutional ruling. At this point, however, the oft-told story loses its customary unity. Some writers have charged the Court with cowardice: "the judges turned their backs on the brave argument of . . . *Milligan* . . . and retreated behind technicalities to keep from handing down a decision." Other writers, recognizing the fearsome power of the Radicals, have said that the Court acted with great "prudence." Still others have approved the Court's self-restraint and denial of jurisdiction on the ground that the problem was "political" and beyond the purview of judicial authority.

Suspicion of judicial intentions supposedly persisted in certain congressional quarters, despite the Court's reticence in the Mississippi and Georgia cases. In late 1867 and early 1868, some Republican congressmen attempted to forestall a judicial veto by requiring a two-thirds or unanimous vote of the Court. Some members even sought to abolish judicial review altogether. When the justices accepted jurisdiction in *Ex parte McCardle* in February, 1868, and heard arguments on the constitutionality of the Reconstruction Acts, they confirmed the worst fears of the extreme Radicals and alarmed the Republican rank and file. Riding roughshod over Democratic opposition and a presidential veto, Congress withdrew appellate jurisdiction from the Court for cases such as McCardle's. One historian has excoriated this action as an "abominable subterfuge" and "a shameful abuse" of power. Former Justice Benjamin R. Curtis, of Dred Scott fame, wrote that Congress, "with the acquiescence of the country, conquered one President, and subdued the Supreme Court."[7]

Finally, in *Texas* v. *White*,[8] the Court adopted the "orthodox view" and again refused to interfere with congressional policy. Chief Justice Salmon P. Chase's opinion in this case has been de-

[6]*Mississippi* v. *Johnson*, 4 Wallace (71 U.S.) 475 (1867); *Georgia* v. *Stanton*, 6 Wallace (73 U.S.) 50 (1868).

[7]*Ex parte McCardle*, 6 Wallace (73 U.S.) 318 (1868); 7 Wallace (74 U.S.) 506 (1869). Curtis's quote is in Benjamin R. Curtis, *A Memoir of Benjamin Robbins Curtis*, 2 vols. (Boston: Little, Brown & Co., 1879), 1: 421.

[8]*Texas* v. *White*, 7 Wallace (74 U.S.) 700 (1869).

scribed as "probably better as politics than as law" and as a "major victory for the Radicals." *Texas* v. *White* is often seen as the high-water mark of respectability for the Radical program and the ultimate in judicial compliance and quiescence.

By almost all accounts, then, despite some variance on details, the Supreme Court during Reconstruction was discredited, intimidated, and impotent. The period represented the nadir of judicial power, influence, and prestige. Recent revisionism of the period has failed, thus far, to alter the story. One revisionist work, summing up much of the new interpretation, dismisses the Court with a brief footnote which states only that the Court "played a passive role" and that "its prestige declined considerably."[9]

Evidence is available, however, for presenting a very different account, one that drastically alters the major interpretations. Some of the new themes might be suggested here. The Dred Scott decision did not absolutely shatter the Court's political standing and public prestige. There was no single-minded, overriding attitude of hostility toward the Court within the Republican party, and at no time was the Court in danger of "annihilation." A broad spectrum of views prevailed within that group on judicial as well as other issues during Reconstruction. Actually, there was a positive thrust to congressional legislation during the Reconstruction period, a thrust which actually expanded judicial power in a significant manner.

As for the Court's functions during the postwar decade, a closer attention to the Reconstruction cases again calls for a different conclusion. Furthermore, an examination of the broader range of judicial decisions adds another dimension to its status and power. In short, the Court in this period was characterized by forcefulness and not timidity, by judicious and self-imposed restraint rather than retreat, by boldness and defiance instead of cowardice and impotence, and by a creative and determinative role with no abdication of its rightful powers.

A clue to these ideas is to be found in the contemporary remark that the Supreme Court under Salmon P. Chase was of only "little less importance" than that under John Marshall. A search through the rich but prickly thicket of historical evidence leads to a similar conclusion.

[9]Kenneth M. Stampp, *The Era of Reconstruction, 1865–1877* (New York: Alfred A. Knopf., 1965), 146n.

2

The Healing Wound:
The Supreme Court and National Politics
1857-1866

More attention has been lavished on the political and public reaction to the decision in the Dred Scott case than on the actual opinions of the Supreme Court justices. There is good reason for this. No judicial decision prior to 1857 had touched so vitally on the country's political nerves. Naturally, there has been concern with what the nation thought of the "final" constitutional solution to its nagging problem of slavery and the territories.

Historians have found little difficulty in discerning and summing up that reaction. Simply stated, the consensus is that the Dred Scott decision set off an eruption of anger and criticism throughout the North, for the majority justices, whatever their good intentions, had sorely misgauged the North's willingness to acquiesce in a judicial settlement that countenanced slavery in the territories. No doubt the Court suffered a loss of prestige as a result of its "self-inflicted wound."

But what was the extent of the damage? According to the usual diagnosis, the popular hostility generated in 1857 persisted for the next decade and a half.[1] This handicap of suspicion and distrust forms the basis for the conclusion that the Court had little influence in the nation's affairs during the Reconstruction era.

Reaction against the Dred Scott decision was, indeed, hostile. There was sharp, at times vicious, criticism of the ruling and of Chief Justice Taney and his colleagues. Moreover, political and public memories of the decision and the "wicked" Chief Justice lingered through the Civil War and beyond. But is it possible that one de-

[1]Charles Evans Hughes, *The Supreme Court of the United States, Its Foundation, Methods and Achievements: An Interpretation* (New York: Columbia University Press, 1928), pp. 50-51. Corwin, "The Dred Scott Decision in the Light of Contemporary Legal Doctrines," *American Historical Review,* 17 (October, 1911): 68-69.

cision could spend completely the fund of respect that the Court had accumulated for itself? Or can a useful distinction be made between the reaction to the *decision* and the contemporary appraisals of the *institution?* Possibly, the failure to make this distinction has unduly blurred the Court's image after its Dred Scott decision. Hughes's diagnosis might be probed somewhat further: was the "self-inflicted wound" massive and paralytic, or was it perhaps only local in character, and the "victim" still ambulatory?

There should be little need to detail the negative reaction to Dred Scott; there is no question but that the decision evoked almost unprecedented debate and anger.[2] Though many Americans denounced the decision, many others agreed with it and welcomed it, in the North as well as the South.[3] The Democratic party, although seriously disrupted, still commanded vast and loyal numbers in the North, and Democrats generally endorsed the decision.

The Democratic sentiment, of course, represented the luxury of the victors and the fickleness of the Court's support. Historically, the Democratic party had opposed national judicial power and particular Supreme Court decisions on philosophical and political grounds. Yet, in the decade or two before the Dred Scott decision, much of the Jefferson-Jackson tradition of antagonism and distrust had spent its force. Indeed, just prior to 1857 the Supreme Court was probably at the peak of its prestige and power. The vitality of the American judiciary, which De Tocqueville observed in the 1830's, certainly had been strengthened by the 1850's. George Ticknor Curtis, brother of one of the Dred Scott dissenters on the Court and himself one of the losing lawyers in the case, later recalled that for nearly seventy years the Court "had been looked to as the final arbiter on constitutional questions, with a confidence such as has not been reposed, on so great a scale and upon such important subjects, in any other human tribunal." Curtis added that the Supreme Court "constituted one of the dearest treasures of this nation." The late Justice Robert H. Jackson regarded the Court's

[2]See, for example, *New York Daily Tribune,* March 7 and 11, 1857; *Chicago Tribune,* March 11 and 12, 1857; *Cong. Globe,* 35 Cong., 1 sess. (March 3, 1858); Theodore Parker, *The Present Aspect of Slavery in America and Immediate Duty of the North* (Boston: Bela Marsh, 1858). Also see Stanley I. Kutler, *The Dred Scott Decision: Law or Politics?* (Boston: Houghton Mifflin & Co., 1967).

[3]See, for example, *Washington Daily Union,* March 11, 12, 1857; *Charleston* [South Carolina] *Daily Courier,* March 9, 1857; *Cincinnati Daily Enquirer,* March 8, 1857; *Detroit Free Press,* March 14, 1857.

decision as frivolous or rejected it outright while tempering their criticism of the judiciary itself. On the whole, the *idea* and the *image* of the Supreme Court persisted with great vitality. To be sure, some disaffection carried over into the wartime and postwar period. Yet most Republicans continued to view the Supreme Court as an indispensable part of the American constitutional system, though they desired a Court more receptive to their own interests and desires. Creative reform, not denunciation or destruction, proved to be the Republican antidote to the Dred Scott decision.

The election of Abraham Lincoln in 1860 seemed to augur ill for the Supreme Court's future. During his famous campaign debates with Stephen A. Douglas in 1858, Lincoln steadfastly rejected the Dred Scott dictum denying congressional authority over slavery in the territories, and he promised that the Republican party would strive to reverse that decision. The warmest advocates of judicial power, well aware of the judiciary's dependence upon executive and legislative cooperation, must have shuddered at the Court's prospects after 1860. Sharpening the attack in his inaugural address, Lincoln insisted that a judicial decision bound only the parties to a suit, and he denied that the "policy of the government, upon vital questions affecting the whole people, is to be irrevocably fixed by the decisions of the Supreme Court of the United States." If the nation were to be forever bound by the Dred Scott decision, then, he warned, "the people will have ceased to be their own rulers, having to that extent practically resigned their government into the hands of that eminent tribunal."[8]

To use Lincoln's position on Dred Scott as clear evidence of his hostility to judicial power and the Supreme Court is, however, quite misleading. He directed those remarks to a particular issue and case. As a young man in 1838 speaking on the perpetuation of our political institutions, he had advocated respect for and reliance upon the courts. He had deplored "the increasing disregard for law which pervades the country, the growing disposition to substitute the wild and furious passions, in lieu of the sober judgment of Courts." Later he acknowledged the Supreme Court as the "tribunal which the

[8]Basler, ed., *Collected Works*, 2:494–96, 4:268. The *Chicago Tribune,* March 8, 1861, was delighted to reprint the *Louisville Democrat's* approval of Lincoln's remarks: "Some may censure the general remarks about the decisions of the Supreme Court; but the intelligent reader will see that it is but the old Democratic doctrine of Jefferson and Jackson. If it be a heresy, it is not Lincoln's."

Constitution . . . established to decide Constitutional questions" and as "the most enlightened judicial tribunal in the world."[9] As for the Dred Scott decision, it is most revealing of Lincoln's fundamental attitudes that he did not persist in exploiting it as a political issue. After his inaugural statement, he never again directly attacked the Court or the decision.

Lingering bitterness and the heady air of power nevertheless prompted many Republican pressures to do something about the Court. The *Chicago Tribune* came perilously close to a root-and-branch position: "That bench-full of Southern lawyers, which gentlemen of a poetical temperament call an 'august tribunal,' is the last entrenchment behind which Despotism is sheltered." The newspaper proposed a constitutional amendment reducing the Court's power, or simply dropping some of the justices and appointing "better men." The *New York Tribune* preferred the simpler expedient of increasing the Court to thirteen men.[10]

Lincoln kept his silence on judicial matters until his first annual message to Congress on December 3, 1861. He then proposed long-sought reforms that in no way altered the nature of judicial power. He directed his attentions instead to improving the efficiency of the judicial system, particularly the circuit courts. Characteristically, he offered several alternatives: first, the reorganization of the circuits into "convenient" size, the courts to be served by Supreme Court justices and independent circuit judges; second, the option of relieving the justices from all circuit duty; and, third, the possibility that circuit courts be abolished altogether. Lincoln's opening remark on judicial reform was the only one that touched on Supreme Court organization. He urged that the Court "be of convenient number in every event," a suggestion that seems prophetic in view of the increase to ten members in 1863. But it is not altogether clear or definite that Lincoln had a membership increase in mind in 1861. The statement preceded his alternatives on circuit matters, and it seems more plausible Lincoln was suggesting that the size of the Court be convenient, or compatible with, whatever Congress chose to do regarding the circuits. Finally, Lincoln even urged Congress · to expand the appellate jurisdiction of the Supreme Court. To clarify and enhance the authority of the Court of Claims, he recommended

[9]Basler, ed., *Collected Works*, 1:109, 312.
[10]*Chicago Tribune*, March 4, 1861; *New York Tribune*, June 10, December 12, 1861, December 3, 1862.

that appeals to the Supreme Court be allowed on questions of law.[11] He proposed nothing that touched on the basics of judicial power; his proposals were mild, indisputably constitutional, and hardly original. There were, however, advocates of more radical measures. Following the President's message, Senator John P. Hale of New Hampshire, offered a resolution instructing the Judiciary Committee to inquire into the "expediency and propriety of abolishing the present Supreme Court" and instituting another such tribunal in its place. Hale's reckless and extreme proposal received only slight consideration and, a few weeks later, was quietly buried by Lyman Trumbull's Judiciary Committee.[12]

It is surprising, therefore, to find historians attaching great symbolic import to Hale's scheme. James G. Randall considered the resolution and its reception quite ominous. "Forfeiture of respect for the court," he wrote, "seemed to be implied in the whole debate." Actually, there was a brief debate, and moderate Republican leaders such as Lafayette S. Foster, Orville H. Browning, and Jacob Collamer led a successful assault upon Hale's resolution. They not only derided his proposal but emphasized the importance of the Supreme Court as a coordinate branch of the government.[13] Since Hale received no support from his fellow partisans, it is difficult to understand how this proposal could stigmatize his whole party.

In any event, Hale's remarks constituted a purely partisan attack, not an institutional one. He complained that the present justices had been appointed as politicians rather than as lawyers, and that the Supreme Court had been made "a part of the machinery of the old Democratic party." Hale later lamented that the Republicans had neglected their "obvious duty" to the nation, humanity, and God, "to drive a plowshare from turret to foundation stone of the Supreme Court of the United States."[14] His fellow Republicans obviously felt no such obligation to the nation, or for that matter, even to God. The Court survived and functioned, and no one was more painfully aware of this than the Court's archfoe, John P. Hale.

[11]Basler, ed., *Collected Works,* 5:42. See chap. 7, *below.*

[12]*Cong. Globe,* 37 Cong., 2 sess., pp. 8, 26–28 (December 4 and 9, 1861). See Richard H. Sewell, *John P. Hale and the Politics of Abolition* (Cambridge, Mass.: Harvard University Press, 1965) for a penetrating account of Hale's career.

[13]James G. Randall, *Constitutional Problems under Lincoln,* rev. ed. (Urbana: University of Illinois Press, 1951), p. 9n; David M. Silver, *Lincoln's Supreme Court* (Urbana: University of Illinois Press, 1956), p. 43. *Cong. Globe,* 37 Cong., 2 sess., pp. 27–28 (December 9, 1861).

[14]*Cong. Globe,* 38 Cong., 1 sess., p. 753 (February 11, 1864).

The defeat of Hale's resolution did not foreclose Republican attempts to make the Supreme Court more responsive to the party's will. But the character of reform hardly followed an extremist pattern. The seemingly prosaic Judicial Reorganization Act of 1862, for example, truly marked a substantive change, while conceived within a traditional framework. There can be little quarrel with either the necessity or the propriety of such legislation. The malapportioned judicial circuits, before 1862, probably constituted the most blatant "rotten borough" of American governmental institutions.

The Republican reorganization act of 1862 equalized the circuits and brought the newer states into the judicial system. This measure had some partisan and sectional motivation, for it was one of many Republican attempts to reduce the South's, and hence the Democratic party's, domination of the national government. It also served as a device to insure the appointment of loyal, northern men to existing and future vacancies on the Supreme Court. This had little to do with hostility to the institution as such. On the contrary, it secured and enhanced Republican confidence in the Supreme Court. While the legislation served the Republicans' crasser motives, it also created a more effective system for the administration of justice.

For decades before the Civil War, non-Democratic elements in the North and West found themselves frustrated by southern control in Washington. Congressional over-representation in proportion to the rest of the country and an informal seniority system operated to preserve southern power. The judicial system, as it existed prior to 1862, reflected the disproportionate southern influence. Since 1837 the nation had been divided into nine circuits.[15] Five of these consisted exclusively of slave states, with a population of a little over eleven million, while the remaining four contained over sixteen and a half million. The Ninth Circuit, embracing Mississippi and Arkansas, had little more than a million people; the Seventh consisting of Ohio, Indiana, Illinois, and Michigan, had over six million. Eight of the newer states, six of them free states, were not assigned to any circuit.

The Republicans long had expressed a legitimate concern with the sectional imbalance of the circuits and of the Supreme Court. Two months before the Dred Scott decision, Representative Benjamin Stanton of Ohio proposed a reorganization of the circuits,

[15]5 Stat. 176 (March 3, 1837).

but to no avail. Stanton advocated reform primarily on practical grounds, pointing out, for example, that the Second Circuit (New York, Connecticut, and Vermont) had more business on its docket than the five southern circuits combined. Given the vast litigation in commercial, admiralty, and patent law in the Second Circuit, Stanton probably was correct.

He pressed for change so that the Supreme Court, which he significantly acknowledged as the "ultimate arbiter of all questions arising upon the Constitution," could be reconstituted so "as to command the confidence of the whole people in all sections of the country." He warned that because of the inequities of representation, judicial decisions would have no moral force and little popular support. If southerners should seek to preserve the existing sectional organization of the Court for their own political advantage, they might "destroy the court without aiding the party or section" in whose favor it decided.[16] Stanton did not speak disparagingly or disrespectfully of judicial power; rather he insisted on reform in order to preserve that very power.

Three years later, Representative James M. Ashley, also from Ohio, delivered a slashing attack on the incumbent Supreme Court. Ashley pointed to the successful "Calhoun Revolution" which had secured southern dominance of the Supreme Court and the circuits. He hinted at dark, conspiratorial forces that long had operated to assure a federal government favorable to slavery interests. He contended that, in certain instances, southern senators had blocked appointments for northern circuits when they believed the nominee antagonistic to the expansion of slavery. With the Dred Scott experience fresh in mind, Ashley may well have spoken for many Republicans when he exclaimed that he had "lost all confidence in, and veneration for" the Supreme Court.[17] He promised that reorganization of the circuits and of the Court itself ranked high on the agenda of Republican plans. Here, again, was the implication that reform was the key to a restoration of Republican confidence in the Supreme Court.

The *New York Tribune*, in 1859, now somewhat more subdued and rational in its criticism of the judiciary, well realized the issues at stake. The South, it charged, had long been alert to its weakening

---

[16]*Cong. Globe*, 34 Cong., 3 sess., pp. 300–301 (December 12, 1857).

[17]*Ibid.*, 36 Cong., 1 sess., Appendix, pp. 365–68 (May 29, 1860). Ashley also noted the disparity in business between each circuit.

grip on the executive and legislative branches of government and looked to the Supreme Court "as its final hiding-place from the avenging spirit of Freedom." Calhoun, in particular, had "fixed his eagle eye upon it and resolved to make it the subservient hack of the negro propaganda." The *Tribune* pinpointed the South's dominance of the circuits as the source of its control of the Supreme Court, and it properly traced this to the Judiciary Act of 1837 which had created two new southern circuits. Consequently, the Supreme Court, as constituted on the basis of the existing circuits, was "scandalously sectional, grossly partial, a mockery of the Constitution, a serf of the slave power, and a disgrace to the country." The *Tribune* promised that a "truly national administration" would reform it and so "regain for it the confidence of the people by adapting it to the ends for which it was created."[18]

This was precisely Lincoln's objective and, once attained, undoubtedly served to restore such confidence. The Republican party, now in power and out of the political wilderness, wasted little time in recasting the judicial dice. The legislation as finally passed in July, 1862, incidentally, may profitably be viewed as one of the first substantive achievements of Republican Reconstruction—reconstruction, that is, to make national institutions more responsive to the needs of the dominant section.

After disengaging themselves from Hale's resolution, responsible Republican leaders began consideration of Lincoln's suggestions for circuit reform. On December 18, Trumbull favorably reported a bill to equalize the circuits in consideration of population and business needs. Legislation, however, is not the exclusive fruit of principle, party or otherwise. Personal interests or ambitions regarding the spoils always loom large and indeed figured prominently in this bill's history. Trumbull presented a fairly equitable arrangement for the circuits, but the Senate soon bogged down on the particular state alignments within each circuit.[19] The dissatisfaction with Trumbull's original bill, and the subsequent jockeying, stemmed from a fear that one's state would be attached to others which had many prominent candidates for the pending vacancies on the Supreme Court. For example, a senator who desired to push one of his favorites for the high bench, assiduously worked to prevent his state's being placed in the same circuit with Illinois. Obviously, the

[18]*New York Tribune*, March 26, 1859.
[19]*Cong. Globe*, 37 Cong., 2 sess., pp. 124 ff. (December 18, 1861).

President desired to make an appointment from his own state, where he had political associates of long-standing. Hence the very capable Iowa delegation, in both the Senate and the House, managed to detach their state from Illinois, as had been provided in the bill originally reported. Future Supreme Court appointments hinged on

TABLE 1

Circuit	1860[a]	1862[b]
1st	Rhode Island, Massachusetts, New Hampshire, Maine 2,360,038	Rhode Island, Massachusetts, New Hampshire, Maine 2,360,038
2d	New York, Vermont, Connecticut 4,655,980	New York, Vermont, Connecticut 4,655,980
3d	Pennsylvania, New Jersey 3,578,250	Pennsylvania, New Jersey 3,578,250
4th	Maryland, Delaware, Virginia 2,395,583	Maryland, Delaware, Virginia North Carolina 3,388,205
5th	Alabama, Louisiana 1,672,203	Alabama, South Carolina, Florida, Mississippi, Georgia 3,656,924
6th	North Carolina, South Carolina, Georgia 2,753,616	Louisiana, Texas, Arkansas, Kentucky, Tennessee 4,013,152
7th	Ohio, Indiana, Illinois, Michigan 6,151,003	Ohio, Indiana 3,689,939
8th	Kentucky, Tennessee, Missouri 3,447,497	Michigan, Wisconsin, Illinois 3,236,945
9th	Mississippi, Arkansas 1,226,775	Missouri, Iowa, Kansas, Minnesota 2,136,154

[a]. Circuits according to Judiciary Act of 1837, with 1860 population census.
[b]. Circuits according to Judiciary Act of 1862, with 1860 population census.

many factors, but the make-up of the circuits may have been most crucial; Trumbull, in fact, acknowledged there would be no presidential nominations until some bill passed.[20] The bill cleared Con-

[20]*Ibid.*, pp. 187–88, 288, 469, 2675, 2914, 3089 (January 6, 13, and 24, June 12 and 25, July 3, 1862). Senator James R. Doolittle, a Wisconsin Republican,

gress in its final form in July, 1862. The Republicans had achieved their avowed purpose of equalizing the circuits, as evidenced by a comparison of the 1860 and 1862 circuits. Some imbalance persisted. The three northwestern circuits contained nine million people, while the newly devised southern ones served eleven million. But surely this was more realistic than the prewar pattern, which seemingly reflected an application of Calhounian concurrent majority principles. (See table 1.)

Representative John A. Bingham of Ohio, a prominent and responsible party spokesman on constitutional and legal questions, summarized the 1862 legislation as essentially principled and proper. The reorganization, he said, before the final alterations were made, "merely consolidates the southern circuits and makes an additional circuit in the Northwest, where an additional circuit is needed, by reason of the great increase of population . . ., and reduces the number of circuits in the extreme South where they are not needed." Population of the South was only one factor; the inability of the federal government to function in the South in 1862, of course, further lessened the need. Bingham went on to point out to the House that the bill did not alter the number of judges on the Supreme Court.[21] But if the Republican party were to fulfill its avowed purpose to provide a more representative judicial system, and one more responsive to its needs, then such a measure was both necessary and desirable.

The reorganization of 1862 retained the existing separate circuit arrangement for the Pacific coast states of California and Oregon.[22] Given the circumstances of travel, it was absurd to expect one of the existing Supreme Court justices to travel a circuit across the continent in conjunction with his other responsibilities. Moreover, by 1862, the Court still had five men—Taney, Nelson, Grier, Wayne, and Catron—who had supported the pro-slavery position in the Dred Scott case. In addition, Justice Clifford, appointed to replace Benjamin Curtis in 1858, long had been regarded as a "doughface."

ultimately voted against the reorganization bill because of personal and state considerations. He was anxious for judicial office himself and was bitterly disappointed when Wisconsin and Illinois were joined in the same circuit. See his correspondence with his wife, January 24 and March 17, 1862, James R. Doolittle MSS, State Historical Society of Wisconsin.

[21]*Cong. Globe*, 37 Cong., 1 sess., p. 173 (December 23, 1861).

[22]In 1855 Congress provided a separate circuit for California, with a separate circuit judge (10 Stat. 631 [March 2, 1855]). Similar provision was made for Oregon after it became a state.

In short, the Court still was quite a way from being made safe for Republicanism.

For these reasons, then, an increase of the Court, including a new circuit, appeared logical and inevitable. It has been argued that "it was no coincidence" that Congress proposed an increase of the membership of the Supreme Court during the hearing of the *Prize Cases*.[23] But it is difficult to discern a direct causal connection; the timing of the two events was coincidental. Before the bill passed, and before Lincoln made his appointment, the Court already had heard arguments in the cases. The barn door, so to speak, had already been locked. Moreover, there is no evidence that the Court's nine members at the time were so impressed by an increase proposal as to allow their judicial opinions to be influenced by it. The line-up undoubtedly would have been the same if there had not been such a measure pending.

The most striking thing about the congressional plan to increase the Supreme Court to ten members was the total absence of debate in Congress. When, in 1937, Franklin D. Roosevelt proposed adding up to six new members to the Court, the Republican party, then in a position analogous to that of the Democrats in 1863, united and fought tenaciously against the bill, albeit with crucial support from disenchanted elements of the majority party. Curiously, the Democratic party in Congress remained quiescent in 1863. While the *New York Times* applauded the measure and acknowledged that the new member would "speedily remove the control of the Supreme Court from the Taney School," Democratic newspapers, usually quick and vociferous in their response to Republican measures, withheld comment. Perhaps remembering that they, too, had adjusted the Court to party needs in 1801 and 1837, the Democrats found it expedient to remain silent.[24]

The reorganization of 1862, and the increase of the following year, offered Lincoln and his party the opportunity to destroy the pattern of southern dominance. This reform reflected the essentially conservative nature of Republican feeling toward the judiciary.

[23]Silver, *Lincoln's Supreme Court*, p. 105.
[24]*Cong. Globe*, 37 Cong., 3 sess., pp. 1121, 1178, 1300, 1454, 1490, 1499 (February 20, 23 and 26, March 2 and 3, 1863). *New York Times*, March 4, 1863. The 1863 enactment also altered the peculiar arrangement for the West Coast. The new Supreme Court justice was meant to be a representative of that circuit. The process of circuit adjustment was not completed until the postwar period. See chap. 4, *below*.

Above all, it reflected the prevailing belief that there was nothing wrong with the constitutional and institutional status of the Court. And thus it incidentally reflected a realistic faith that constitutional decisions are brought by men, not storks.

The President turned to the delicate task of Supreme Court appointments once Congress had released him from southern geographical considerations. Until this time, members of the Court traditionally had matched the circuits; the justice for the First Circuit, for example, usually was a native of that area. It was no wonder, then, that Republican politicians and newspapers had deplored the Dred Scott decision as a product of a biased tribunal at a time when five of the nine justices were southerners.

A few months after assuming office, Lincoln faced the pleasant but important prospect of filling three Supreme Court vacancies. Peter V. Daniel of Virginia, a conservative southerner, had died in 1860. President Buchanan had attempted to fill his place with Attorney-General Jeremiah S. Black. The Republicans, sensing the opportunity for themselves, successfully blocked the nomination. Venerable John McLean of the Seventh Circuit died in April, 1861. Shortly after secession, Justice John Archibald Campbell resigned his seat and returned to his native Alabama. Replacing McLean was no problem, and in January, 1862, before the passage of the reorganization measure, Lincoln named Noah H. Swayne of Ohio to McLean's place. The vacancies left by the southerners Daniel and Campbell was another matter. Before replacing these two, Lincoln waited until Congress had acted.

Since Congress had left the South with only three circuits, and since there were three southerners remaining on the Court, Lincoln found himself freed from the previous dictates of geography. The two vacancies covering the new northwestern Eighth Circuit and the trans-Mississippi Ninth, he filled with loyal Republicans from those regions. To the first of these places, he named David Davis, an old friend and colleague from Illinois circuit-riding days. To the other, he appointed Samuel F. Miller of Iowa, thus yielding to the insistent Iowans in Congress. He gave the position representing the newly created Tenth Circuit to Stephen J. Field of California.

There are countless and diverse considerations which dictate presidential appointments to the Supreme Court. Politics, friendship, geography, and religion (probably not very much in Lincoln's time) have been most dominant. No doubt each of these figured in

Lincoln's actions, but he concerned himself primarily with a nominee's attitude toward the war and its purposes. When he later appointed Salmon P. Chase to the chief justiceship, Lincoln allegedly told George S. Boutwell that "we wish for a Chief Justice who will sustain what has been done in regard to emancipation and the legal tenders."[25] Surely the variables of geography and, in one notable instance, personal friendship partially motivated Lincoln, but it is difficult to avoid the conclusion that political factors dominated his thinking.

Lincoln's appointments received overwhelming editorial support. Republican newspapers welcomed each Republican justice as bringing the Court closer to political reality and popular sentiment. Even the lone Democratic nomination of Field failed to stir partisan discord. His vigorous activities in securing California's loyalty to the Union, and his well-known family connections, undoubtedly enhanced his standing with the Republicans. Lincoln's choices truly bridged the partisan gap, for even the hypercritical Democratic newspapers rarely objected to the new jurists. Actually, little was known of these men and their public records. For example, the first reports of Miller carried his first name as Daniel, confusing him with a more prominent Iowan of that name. One Democratic midwestern newspaper declared that Lincoln's appointment of "Judge Swan" evidenced the President's "conservative disposition" and his "determination to keep the Government out of the control of the fanatical Abolitionists," a judgment that may have been true regarding a "Judge Swan," but one that hardly reflected any knowledge of Judge Swayne.[26]

The death of Chief Justice Roger Brooke Taney in October, 1864, presented the crucial opportunity and challenge for Lincoln and the Republican party. Here was the chance to alter decisively the balance of power on the Court and convert it into a favorable one. Charles Sumner sensed the moment with unbounded glee. "Providence has given us a victory," he told the President. "Thus far the Constitution has been interpreted for Slavery . . . . It may now be interpreted wholly for Liberty."[27] But here, too, was the moment of

[25]George S. Boutwell, *Reminiscences of Sixty Years in Public Service*, 2 vols. (New York: McClure, Phillips, 1902), 2:29.

[26]Charles Fairman, *Mr. Justice Miller and the Supreme Court, 1862–1890* (Cambridge, Mass.: Harvard University Press, 1939), pp. 50–51; *Pittsburgh Post,* July 23, 1862; *Cincinnati Daily Enquirer,* July 25, 1862; *Dubuque Herald,* July 25, 1862.

[27]Sumner to Lincoln, October 12, 1864, Robert T. Lincoln Papers, Library of

making one particular appointment which more than any other would symbolize Lincoln and his party's attitude toward the Court. Republicans responded to Taney's passing with a mixture of relief, nostalgia, and persistent vindictiveness, and Democrats with regret. Ben Wade provided a bit of morbid humor: "In the early winter of 1861, when Chief Justice Taney was ill, I used to pray daily and earnestly that his life might be preserved until the inauguration of President Lincoln, who would appoint a Republican Chief Justice, but when I saw how complete his recovery was and how his life was prolonged, *I began to fear that I had overdone the business.*" A northern citizen is reputed to have remarked that Taney had "earned the gratitude of his country by dying at last. Better late than never."[28]

Most of the commentary, however, graciously took note of Taney's whole judicial career and contrasted it favorably with the Dred Scott decision. But for that single exception, the *New York Times* editorialized, "the soundness and impartiality of his judicial decisions have always been respected by the bar and conceded by the public." Attorney General Edward Bates, who worked quite well with Taney, came right up to the mark of what is probably the current historical consensus on Taney. "The lustre of his fame, as a lawyer and judge," Bates wrote in his diary, "is for the present, dimmed by the bitterness of party feeling arising out of his unfortunate judgment in the Dred Scott case. That was a great error, but it ought not and will not, for long, tarnish his otherwise well earned fame,"[29]

Although Charles Sumner and others pressed for an immediate appointment, Lincoln waited until after the November election to select Taney's successor. While other names were suggested, Salmon P. Chase's supporters exerted great pressure from the outset. Sumner, for one, vigorously pushed Chase's name almost immediately after Taney's death. The prominent spokesman for the party's radical element, the *Chicago Tribune,* similarly wasted little time. "We are sure that we express the views of a majority, both in numbers and

Congress; Sumner to Francis Lieber, October 12, 1864, *The Works of Charles Sumner,* 15 vols. (Boston: Lee & Shepard, 1872–83), 4:207–8.

[28]Hans Trefousse, *Benjamin Franklin Wade* (New York: Twayne, 1963), p. 235; Thomas G. and Marva R. Belden, *So Fell the Angels* (Boston: Little, Brown & Co., 1956), p. 136.

[29]*New York Times,* October 14, 1864; Howard K. Beale, ed., *The Diary of Edward Bates, 1859–1866* (Washington: American Historical Association, 1933), p. 418.

in intelligence, of the American people," the paper editorialized, "when we say that the President could perform no act which would confer more honor upon his administration, give higher satisfaction to its supporters and less offenses to its reasonable opponents, or better serve the cause of freedom of all men under our constitution, than by the appointment of Salmon P. Chase."[30] Lincoln did not disappoint Chase's admirers and, on December 6, 1864, he submitted the Ohioan's name to the Senate.

Lincoln's motivation for naming Chase is shrouded in typical Lincolnian ambiguity. It has been suggested that the President sought to appease the growing radical segment of his party. There also is the notion that Lincoln, in effect, kicked Chase upstairs in the hope of forestalling the latter's political intriguing. In any event, the consideration that Chase would be right on emancipation and legal tenders (which Lincoln supposedly mentioned to Boutwell) must have been in Lincoln's mind. Moreover, he must have been aware of the likelihood that Chase would be a popular choice. The Republican press, moderate and radical alike, heartily supported the President's decision. Even the *New York World,* probably the most prominent anti-administration newspaper, praised Chase's nomination and called the new Chief Justice "the ablest man in the Republican party." The *New York Times* perceptively contrasted the reception of Chase's appointment with the storm evoked by Andrew Jackson's nomination of Taney in 1835. The *Times* duly noted the momentous issues that Chase and his colleagues would soon face; yet Chase apparently was a great comfort, for, as the *Times* noted, "almost everybody trusts him."[31]

The nation's most radical newspapers, many of which had campaigned for Chase's appointment, regarded the nomination as a symbolic triumph of liberty over slavery. The *Chicago Tribune,* for example, confidently predicted that Chase's constitutional construction would be rooted in "an enlightened devotion to liberty tenfold more powerful for good than has been Roger B. Taney's worship of slavery, potent for evil." The *New York Independent* quite simply visualized Chase's appointment as an opportunity for a "righteous reversal" of the "unrighteous" Dred Scott decision. With a final parting shot of contempt for Taney, the *Independent*

---

[30]*Chicago Tribune,* October 15, 1864.
[31]Boutwell, *Reminiscences,* 2:29; *New York World,* December 7, 1864; *New York Times,* December 8, 1864.

concluded that it was "a fit season for the Dwarfs to go out and the Giants to come in."[32]

The symbolic and substantive meaning of Chase's appointment cannot be overestimated. Taney's passing, first of all, marked the disappearance of the last vestige of southern power in the national government. And what a vivid contrast offered by the new Chief Justice! Chase, perhaps as much as any other one man, had formulated the basic constitutional arguments against slavery. As an attorney in the *Van Zandt* fugitive slave case of 1847, and as a United States Senator, Chase had challenged the South's basic constitutional assumptions. Now, as northern armies insured the triumph over slavery, Chase fittingly succeeded the man who naïvely believed that he had secured permanent constitutional protection for the peculiar institution.

Taney's death did not, however, altogether erase the bitter memories of 1857. These came out again in the row that erupted over an attempt to appropriate government funds for a marble bust of the late Chief Justice. Republicans now vented anew some of their persistent ill-feeling toward the old Jacksonian. Pettiness and vindictiveness were the dominant tones, yet some significant attitudes toward the Supreme Court also were revealed.

In February, 1865, Senator Trumbull reported a bill providing a $1,000 appropriation for a bust of Taney for the Supreme Court Library. A similar honor had been accorded Taney's predecessors. Trumbull acknowledged the tradition, but he sensed some difficulty. Anticipating the furor that followed, he conceded the late Chief Justice's error in Dred Scott, but added: "No man is infallible. He was a great and learned and an able man". Charles Sumner, however, who had rejoiced at the opportunity presented by Taney's death, was not content, as he said, to speak only well of the dead, and proceeded to turn Trumbull's routine courtesy measure into a substantive issue. Taney's name, Sumner said, "is to be hooted down the page of history . . . . Senator [Trumbull] says that he for twenty-five years administered justice. He administered justice at last [i.e., in Dred Scott] wickedly, and degraded the judiciary of the country, and degraded the age." Rather than appropriating money for a commemorative bust, Sumner countered that there should be "a vacant space in our court-room [to] testify to the justice of our

---

[32]*Chicago Tribune*, October 15, 1864; *New York Independent*, December 8, 1864.

Republic. Let it speak in warning to all who would betray liberty."[33]

Sumner's assault upon Taney was personal and partisan; at no time was he critical of the Supreme Court. While he lambasted Taney—for one decision only—he still extolled the virtues and greatness of Marshall and Story, contrasting Taney unfavorably, of course, with those judicial heroes. Sumner often talked the language of concurrent review during the later heyday of Reconstruction, but he rarely failed to pay his respects to the Court as a vital institution; whatever objection he had against it rested exclusively upon the one transgression of Dred Scott. Moreover, with his friend Salmon P. Chase as Chief Justice of a court containing four other Lincoln appointees, Sumner probably had few qualms about the Supreme Court of 1865. It is unlikely that Chase had a more ardent booster than Sumner. Sumner's harangue against Taney, while at the same time evincing respect for the Court and its traditions, may well have been a microcosm of the national attitude. In all probability, there was little inclination to honor Taney in 1865. Congress withheld funds for the bust until 1873—with Charles Sumner then in isolated opposition.

During the 1865 debate, Reverdy Johnson, Taney's fellow Marylander, successful counsel in the Dred Scott case, and a leading figure of the bar, shrewdly nailed down the Republican opposition as only personal and partisan. He reminded his fellow senators that the Dred Scott decision had been concurred in by other justices who were still alive and who were not being subjected to such criticism and defamation. For example, there was Justice Wayne, "whose purity no one will dare to question," Johnson said; Catron, whose loyalty the senator contended was as great as Sumner's, and more serviceable; and Grier, whose opinion in the *Prize Cases* Sumner and other Republicans greatly treasured. None of the Republicans who had led the onslaught against Taney responded to Johnson.[34] Quite simply, Wayne, Catron, and Grier had redeemed themselves by outward manifestations of loyalty to the Union; Taney's stance on the suspension of the writ of habeas corpus in *Ex parte Merryman,* and his anti-administration vote in the *Prize Cases,* among other items, only compounded his original sin.

In a larger and more practical sense, Taney's replacement by Chase decisively altered the character of the Court, at least on paper.

[33]*Cong. Globe,* 38 Cong., 2 sess., p. 1013 (February 23, 1865).
[34]*Ibid.,* pp. 1014–15.

The new Chief Justice, with Swayne, Davis, Miller, and Field, represented a solid bloc of Lincoln appointees. True enough, Wayne, Catron, Nelson, Grier, and Clifford remained from the prewar days, but in the *Prize Cases,* a crucial test of sentiment toward administration policies, Grier and Wayne sided with the majority. And of these latter five, only Clifford was under seventy, indicating the likely possibility of further changes in the near future.

Chase's appointment certainly had a beneficial effect upon popular views of the Supreme Court. The *Chicago Tribune,* a persistent critic of the Taney Court, recognized, with remarkable prescience, how important a favorable Court would be to the North after the Civil War. It predicted that the rebels, "with brazen front," would still do battle in the judicial arena over the right of secession, presidential powers, confiscation, reconstruction, and the formation of new governments in rebellious territory. The *Tribune,* however, seemed smugly confident of the outcome, and significantly acknowledged that "the Supreme Court will sit in the final earthly judgment upon the rebellion and its authors *and upon the Government and its upholders.*"[35] The fact that Chase and some of the other Lincoln appointees proved disappointing to some Republicans after 1865 is immaterial here; *before* that disenchantment set in, it is clear that the Republicans respected the Court as an institution, recognized a place and function for it in the scheme of government, and seemed confident of the kind of role it would play. When the Republican "ox" was gored—that is, when the optimism of 1864 was shattered by two decisions in 1866 and 1867, many Republicans changed their tune. Then, admittedly, in some quarters it sounded like 1857 all over again; but surely there was no constant hostility, and there was no constant image of judicial disloyalty and inadequacy projected from 1857 through Reconstruction.

The alteration of the judicial system and reconstitution of the Supreme Court may have offered the Republicans adequate assurances against a repetition of the conditions that had worked against their interests at the time of the Dred Scott decision; there remained, however, the necessity of altering the decision itself. Ultimately, of course, the Thirteenth Amendment marked the death-knell of the pro-slavery doctrines, but in June, 1862, the Republicans moved to redeem their pledge to undo the decision, at least in its immediate

[35]*Chicago Tribune,* October 15, 1864. Emphasis added.

effects. By a simple statute Congress declared the territories to be forever free of slavery.[36] This expressed the party's oldest and most basic tenet, that, as Lincoln expressed it, the territories were places for *free* people. But the congressional action can also be seen as a direct repudiation of the Supreme Court's ruling. This was not the first or the last time that a coordinate branch of the government directly challenged a Supreme Court decision. Andrew Jackson, in his Bank Veto Message, for example, made it quite clear that the Supreme Court was not the sole, final authority on constitutional questions. During the New Deal period, Congress repeatedly passed laws which, if one relied on precedents, were blatantly unconstitutional; in 1938, for example, Congress passed a child labor law that almost precisely echoed one which had been declared void in 1918.

But it is most interesting that the passage of the 1862 act was almost completely unaccompanied by critical commentary on the Dred Scott decision or the Supreme Court. One looks in vain to find the congressional Republicans using the measure as a vehicle for a wholesale assault upon the justices or the decision. At no time was the case mentioned; at no time was there a direct attack upon Taney and his colleagues; at no time was there evidence offered of a marked disrespect for the Court as an institution. The prominent Republican newspapers were similarly subdued.

During the brief debate on the bill Representative Samuel C. Fessenden perhaps best expressed what really lurked in the minds of the Republican legislators when he said that he refused to have his vote controlled on any issue because of "the opinion of this chief justice or that." This is the closest the Republicans came to an attack upon Taney. More significantly, Fessenden expressed some of the older Jeffersonian-Jacksonian notions of concurrent review, probably much to the embarrassment of the Democrats. "I shall vote," he said, "on what I understand to be in accordance with the Constitution of the United States."[37]

Representative William D. Kelley of Pennsylvania also had Dred Scott in mind, as indicated by his reference to the South's deployment of "enigmatical legislation and judicial chicanery" to support its system of slavery. But while Kelley spoke of "judicial chicanery," he evinced respect for judicial power in the scheme of

[36] 12 Stat. 432 (June 19, 1862).
[37] *Cong. Globe*, 37 Cong., 2 sess., pp. 2050–51 (May 9, 1862).

American government and, incidentally, a great deal of confidence in what court decisions would be. Responding to Democratic charges that the people of fifteen states, that is, the border and seceded slave states, could not stand such legislation, Kelley offered an eloquent peroration on the role of the Court: "If the Union is to stand, if the Constitution is to be the supreme law of the land, the people of fifteen States, and of thirty-four States, will stand such and all other legislation *until it can be tested before the Supreme Court of the United States;* and if sustained as constitutional law by that court, the people of all the States will be made to stand by it by the power that is now crushing out the great rebellion that was to have overthrown the Constitution and put the advancing civilization of the age on the countermarch towards barbarism."[38] Kelley said nothing about the possibility that the Supreme Court would reject such legislation; given the pending changes in its membership, he could well afford to ignore such an alternative.

After 1857 memories of the Dred Scott decision somewhat tarnished the Court's prestige. But criticism and some hostility are inherent in the nature of the Court through its entire history. Constitutional decisions rarely satisfy all the contending parties; yet the dissatisfaction that results is usually confined to the specific issue and context.

The Supreme Court after the Dred Scott decision was not the first or the last to experience the menace of legislative and political reprisal. To be sure, the Court often has shifted direction as a result of outside pressure, membership changes, internal reconsideration, or a combination of these. But the substance of the Court's form and function has remained unaltered despite attacks or hostility. The Court's absorption of slings and arrows following the Dred Scott decision is a case in point of its capacity for survival.

There nevertheless has been an insistence upon viewing the post–Dred Scott Court and the Republican party as bitter antagonists in a morality play. Within such a conceptual framework one has to find the administered "punishment" that rectified the "crime." Usually, the Judicial Reorganization Act of 1862 and the increase legislation of the next year are tagged with such a dubious label. On the contrary, these measures in no way altered the Court's functions or powers. More positively, they had the virtue of satisfying long-

[38]*Ibid.*, pp. 2049–50. Emphasis added.

standing and relevant regional, as well as Republican demands— demands that antedated Dred Scott's case—as minimal gestures to restore confidence in the Court. If one considers the sectional imbalance that had existed in the federal judiciary for a quarter century, the wartime legislation was reasonable, just, and obviously quite politic. Moreover, the Republicans' attitude toward the Court once they achieved power had implicitly recognized the judiciary as a desirable prize. Their preoccupation with reorganization amounted to creative reform, reflecting a practical regard for the Court's potentiality as a power phenomenon.

Whatever the error of its ways in Dred Scott, the Supreme Court had cultivated and secured a firm place for itself in the American system of government. The labors of John Marshall, Roger Taney, and their colleagues molded a hardy institution with a reservoir of strength sufficient to overcome even self-impairment. The Court's political situation after 1857 simply was not as precarious as is often assumed. Furthermore, there is the important fact that the Court functioned in a "business as usual" fashion throughout the period in both public and private controversies.[39] The eight volumes of court reports from 1857 to 1865 clearly reflect the Court's continuing utility.

In 1864, it may be recalled, the *Chicago Tribune,* one of the most vocal critics of the Court and the Dred Scott decision, conceded the importance of the Court when it recognized that the justices would sit in final judgment of the rebellion and acts of the Union government. More specifically, in early 1866, the *Nation,* similarly hostile to what it considered the Court's deviation from the line of duty in the Dred Scott case, paid the ultimate tribute to the Court's power. Contemplating the possibility that President Andrew Johnson would veto the Civil Rights Bill, the *Nation* instead urged that he "leave the question of its constitutionality to the Supreme Court, which only is competent to decide it."[40] As the nation came to the end of the Civil War and faced the momentous questions of its aftermath, the old wound of 1857, although it remained a convenient and useful symbol from time to time, seemed to be well healed.

---

[39]Fairman, *Mr. Justice Miller,* pp. 97–98.
[40]*Nation,* 2 (March 22, 1866): 353; cf. *ibid.,* 4 (January 10, 1867): 30.

3

Reconstruction Politics and the Supreme Court

  While the Supreme Court played only a peripheral role in the main drama of Reconstruction, it represented a brooding omnipresence to the parties most immediately involved. The Court found itself precariously perched between the stated policies and goals of the Republican party and the rising expectations of the Democrats and the South. The very wonder is that the justices managed to do as well as they did. In many ways, the Court could thank its alleged defenders, the Democrats, for such an unenviable position. The minority party, frustrated in its attempts to stem the tide of Republican Reconstruction, chose to rely on the rubrics of "constitutionality" and judicial determination as a last-ditch defense. Confidently, the Democrats predicted judicial nullification of the Republican legislation and the vindication of their own opposition. Thus the Supreme Court, probably in spite of itself, was intimately bound up in the partisan political struggles of the late 1860's.

  The Democrats' attitude toward the Court during the Reconstruction era shattered the party's historical tradition. Frantically, the legatees of Thomas Jefferson and Andrew Jackson scrounged for every scrap of evidence left by the Masters to forge an impregnable ideological shield for "state sovereignty" and "states' rights." But the party's great spirits must have writhed in agony to witness the "party of the people" calling forth the judicial host to batter down the works of the new Republicanism.

  Until about 1850, a suspicion of the federal judiciary had been a cardinal article of faith for the Democratic party. Although he had leaned in the other direction in the 1790's, Jefferson laid down the first commandments of hostility after his election to the presidency in 1800. Seeing his Federalist enemies in the "stronghold of the judiciary," prepared to break down "all the works of Republicanism," and then being rapped by John Marshall in *Marbury* v. *Madison,* instilled Jefferson with a life-long distrust and animosity toward the Supreme Court. In his later years, and after a number of clashes between his native Virginia and the United States Supreme Court, Jefferson became particularly vitriolic on the subject. "The judiciary of the United States is the subtle corps of sappers and miners constantly working under ground to undermine the foundations of our confederated fabric," he wrote in 1820. A year later, he complained to Spencer Roane, a Virginia Supreme Court judge, that "the great object of my fear is the federal judiciary. That body, like gravity, ever acting with noiseless foot, and unalarming advance, gaining ground step by step, and holding what it gains, is ingulphing incidiously the special governments into the jaws of that which feeds them." Jefferson's fanaticism knew no bounds: "The germ of dissolution of our federal government is in the constitution of the federal judiciary; an irresponsible body."[1]

Andrew Jackson, almost from necessity, had sustained the party's tradition. His alleged remarks concerning Marshall's inability to enforce the Cherokee Nation decision ("John Marshall has given his decision, now let him enforce it.") at least indicates a popular climate of opinion regarding the Court. Equally well known was the theory of constitutional interpretation he had expressed in his Bank Veto Message of July 10, 1832. Here he picked up the idea, earlier formulated by Jefferson, that each branch of the government was competent to determine for itself the constitutionality of a particular measure. Whatever the Court had said in *McCulloch* v. *Maryland* regarding the validity of a national bank did not necessarily bind and control the president or Congress. The Court's

[1]Jefferson to Thomas Ritchie, December 25, 1820, and Jefferson to Spencer Roane, March 9, 1821. Paul L. Ford, ed., *The Writings of Thomas Jefferson,* 10 vols. (New York: G. P. Putnam's, 1892–99), 10:170,189. Jefferson to Charles Hammond, August 18, 1821, Albert E. Bergh, ed., *The Writings of Thomas Jefferson,* 20 vols. (Washington, D.C.: Thomas Jefferson Memorial Association, 1904–5), 15:331. For conflicting interpretations of Jefferson's shifting views on judicial review, see Samuel Krislov, "Jefferson and Judicial Review: Refereeing Cahn, Commager and Mendelson," *Journal of Public Law,* 9 (Fall, 1960):374–81; Wallace Mendelson, "Jefferson on Judicial Review: Consistency through Change," *The University of Chicago Law Review,* 29 (Spring, 1962):327–37; and the debate between Krislov and Mendelson in *Journal of Public Law,* 10 (Spring, 1961):113–24.

authority, he declared, could not "control the Congress or the Executive when acting in their legislative capacities."[2]

Nothing alters attitudes toward the Supreme Court more than changes and shifts in political power. From the end of the Jackson administration to the Civil War, two such factors had influenced the Democratic party. First, after years of unremitting hostility to their old Federalist foe, John Marshall, the Democrats finally had awakened to the reality that the federal judicial system was theirs. The Judiciary Act of 1837, along with Supreme Court appointments of men whose views on federalism would have made even Jefferson blush, had secured control of the judiciary for the Democrats. Second, as Democratic dominance, and particularly the political position of the South, deteriorated in the 1850's, the party increasingly turned to the Supreme Court for confirmation of its cherished constitutional values. Declining majorities or entrenched minorities, until recently, have found the Court to be a useful ally.

Two incidents of the 1850's epitomize the Democrats' shifting attitude which paved the way for their ultimate reliance upon the Court during the next decade. In 1855, a North-South Democratic coalition had proposed implementing federal judicial power to overcome state resistance to the fugitive slave laws. The Toucey Bill, following a section of the 1833 Force Act, provided for the removal of cases from state to federal courts in causes where federal officials acted under the color of the authority of federal law. After Senate passage, the bill died in the House; in the former, however, the measure provoked a bitter, yet historically comical, debate. Disgorging their pet "state sovereignty" theories, southerners boldly proclaimed the virtues of national acquiescence in national policy. The Free Soil opposition naturally found itself in the uncomfortable position of decrying national power and denouncing the federal judiciary as a threat to rights and liberties. But in the next two decades, like Hamlet and Laertes, the combatants exchanged weapons, and with equally devastating results. In the postwar period, the Republicans regularly resorted to removal procedures

[2]James D. Richardson, comp., *A Compilation of Messages and Papers of the Presidents* (New York: Bureau of National Literature, 1896–1922), 3:1139–54. Jefferson had inserted the concurrent review theory in his first inaugural message but then discarded it. He did, however, often refer to the idea. See, for example, Jefferson to Spencer Roane, September 6, 1818, Ford, ed., *Writings of Jefferson*, 10:140. Incidentally, the Jacksonians were quite capable of utilizing federal judicial power when it was in their interest. See chap. 8, *below*.

to protect particular, substantive federal laws and, finally, to enhance materially the scope of federal jurisdiction.[3]

More revealing of the relationship between political power and attitudes toward the federal judiciary was the Democrats' willingness to permit a judicial solution of the nagging problem of slavery in the territories. Beginning with the abortive Clayton Compromise of 1848, extending through the Compromise of 1850 and the Kansas-Nebraska Act of 1854, the party had consciously sought to facilitate a judicial settlement by liberalizing jurisdictional avenues. As the stalemated political system made a political settlement of the issue almost impossible, leading party spokesmen expressed a desire for an authoritative judicial decree on the constitutional issues. President Buchanan's inaugural message on the forthcoming Dred Scott decision symbolized the change which had taken place in a representative party figure. Just fifteen years earlier, Buchanan had qualified the force of a judicial decision as limited only to the issue before the Court: "I should never hold myself bound by their decision, whilst acting in a legislative character . . . . I cannot agree that 'its judicial expositions are of equal authority with the text of the Constitution.' " Yet in taking his presidential oath, Buchanan solemnly proclaimed that the great political problem was "a judicial question which legitimately belongs to the Supreme Court," and that he would "cheerfully submit" to its decision—a decision, of course, which he already knew.[4]

Following the Civil War, the political strength of the Democratic party on the national level was about on a par with that of the Federalists after the election of Thomas Jefferson. Accordingly, the Democrats assumed the classic stance of a minority group, arguing for traditionalism and stability within a constitutional framework which they themselves had advocated and had worked under in their own days of power. They found a compatible, useful ally in President Andrew Johnson—the "Last Jacksonian," as he recently has been characterized. In addition, they *thought* that their versions of constitutional sanity and correctness were the same as those harbored by the justices of the Supreme Court of the United States.

[3]*Cong. Globe*, 33 Cong., 2 sess., Appendix, pp. 211 ff. (February 23, 1855).

[4]Wallace Mendelson, "Dred Scott's Case—Reconsidered," *Minnesota Law Review,* 38 (December, 1953): 16–28; Stanley I. Kutler, *The Dred Scott Decision: Law or Politics?* (Boston: Houghton Mifflin Co., 1967); *Cong. Globe*, 27 Cong., 1 sess., Appendix, pp. 161–69 (July 7, 1841); Richardson, *A Compilation of Messages and Papers*, 7:2962.

The *Milligan* decision in late 1866 particularly stimulated Democratic hopes for judicial salvation. In the few years prior to that decision, however, Democrats seemed confused about what the Court's future course might be. The *New York World,* for example, recognized that Lincoln had appointed four "dyed in the wool" Republicans and one "weak-backed" Democrat, and the Court now was a "valuable party machine." The *World* well remembered its history, labelling the Court as always being an opponent of "the strict constructionists." The Democrats' change in attitude toward the Court during the 1850's nevertheless had left its mark, as the *World* considered it necessary to have a judicial arbiter and would "rather submit even to a prejudiced arbiter than not have any at all."[5]

Professor Eric McKitrick has demonstrated convincingly that Democratic and southern opponents of Reconstruction relied upon the strategy of "deadlock" to frustrate Republican aims. Briefly stated, the idea was that the cumulative force of presidential resistance, public opinion, the Constitution, and the Supreme Court would stall and, ultimately, defeat the Republicans' schemes. Obviously, the judiciary was the last link in the chain and, as the other barriers crumbled, the opposition's faith in the Court's powers became almost religious.

Throughout late 1866 and early 1867, the Democrats had regularly predicted that the Court would save the Republicans from themselves and the nation. "We advise the Radicals," warned the *New York World,* "to give due weight to the fact that the Supreme Court is an insurmountable barrier to their unconstitutional designs." But as events moved on—with the Republican triumph in November, 1866, the passage of the Reconstruction Acts in March, 1867, and the overriding of more Johnson vetoes—the Court (read Constitution) became the last refuge for opposition hopes.[6] Imagine

---

[5]*New York World,* March 11, 1864. The *World's* remarks were in response to Senator Hale's diatribe against the Court in February, 1864. See chap. 2, *above.* See the Washington, D.C., *National Intelligencer,* December 20, 1866, for typical Democratic praise of *Milligan.*

[6]Eric L. McKitrick, *Andrew Johnson and Reconstruction* (Chicago: University of Chicago Press, 1960), pp. 464–66. For some representative newspaper quotes, see *New York World,* December 19, 1866, January 11, 1868; *New York Herald,* January 5, 1867. Interestingly enough, the conservative *New York Times* (April 21, 1867) warned the Democrats and the South that it was folly to rely on a court which had neither the force nor the will to enforce a political decree. Moreover, such appeals to the Court were "unwise" because they turned "the Southern mind from the only remedy—the development of its own natural resources."

then the paroxysms of rage which gripped the Democrats as the ruling congressional forces worked to secure guarantees against judicial intervention in Reconstruction policy.

In January, 1868, the Republicans first sought such insurance with a proposal requiring a two-thirds vote of the Supreme Court to invalidate laws of Congress. The measure passed the House of Representatives, but died in the Senate.[7] While pending, however, the bill had provoked prolonged debate and outrage from the opposition. After all, with President Johnson neutralized, the Court was the last obstacle to overcoming "constitutional government" and now, as the Democrats saw it, the Republicans literally were going to stuff the ballot box to have their way. The Democratic defense of the Court had no limits on unctuousness and sanctimony.

The *Detroit Free Press*, a particularly vitriolic Democratic organ, accused the opposition of laying "sacrilegious hands upon the Supreme Court . . . —that Judiciary Department which had remained free from political mutations." The Republicans' maneuver constituted an attempt to destroy the judiciary and consolidate all power in the hands of Congress, the newspaper warned. "Congress," it concluded, "has lost its sense of shame. The Supreme Court bills show it." Yet in a perverse way Democratic newspapers, with their congressional counterparts, had welcomed the two-thirds proposal, for they saw it as a "confession" by the majority that the Reconstruction Acts really were unconstitutional.[8]

The two-thirds proposal thoroughly alarmed the Democrats. They repeatedly and confidently had asserted that five of the eight justices would invalidate the Reconstruction Acts. Obviously, if the proposed bill passed, the number would be inadequate. Suddenly the Democrats discovered the virtues of the common law principle that a majority vote determined the action of a judicial tribunal. The *New York World* complained that the bill was "the most dangerous assault that by *any* possibility can be made on the Constitution [and] . . . lays the axe at the very root of American institutions."[9]

The Democratic defense of the Court wreaked havoc upon the party's historical view of the judiciary. Now, whatever the majority

[7]See chap. 5, *below*.

[8]*Detroit Free Press*, January 16, 26, 30, 1868; *New York World*, January 13, 1868.

[9]*New York World*, January 21, 1868. Interestingly, Justice David Davis did not seem very excited or concerned over the congressional activity (Davis to Mrs. Davis, January 15, 1868, Davis Papers, Willard King Collection, Chicago Historical Society).

will as reflected by legislative determination, "the constitutional validity of laws passed by Congress [should be] . . . submitted, when contested, to the decision of that Court." The *New York World* expressed the conviction that the two-thirds proposal would be declared unconstitutional if enacted, for the Court was "just as competent to declare *this* law unconstitutional, as to pronounce *any* law unconstitutional; and there ought to be no question that it will vindicate its rights and dignity by doing so." Jeffersonian fragments constituted the authoritative source for Democratic constitutional theory during this period. But the images and metaphors could be abused: using the same words that Jefferson had employed to condemn the Court some four decades earlier, the *World* referred to the Republicans as "a diligent body of sappers and miners, to subvert the Constitution by undermining its palladium in the Supreme Court."[10]

A particularly illustrative incident portraying the Democrats' departure from their historical traditions came during the impeachment trial of Andrew Johnson. On April 11, 1868, Representative George Woodward of Pennsylvania, introduced a bill "to test the constitutionality of questionable acts of Congress." Woodward's bill provided that whenever Congress overrode a presidential veto, the president could bring a fictitious case before the Court to test the constitutionality of a statute.[11] The new Democratic scheme neatly dovetailed with Johnson's constitutional defense of his flouting of the Tenure of Office Act.

Woodward's proposal naturally had no chance of passage in the Republican-dominated Congress. Yet the bill offered the Republicans a splendid opportunity to scoff at the opposition's lack of faith in representative government. John Broomall, also of Pennsylvania, labeled the measure as a "monstrous proposition," which would "create a third branch of the national legislature." Broomall argued that because the Court rarely had voided congressional laws, there was nothing to justify the creation of such an extraordinary jurisdiction. It did not take Broomall long to recognize Woodward's desperate purpose: to secure a Court test of the Reconstruction Acts.[12] Woodward's ingenuity, incidentally, had been prompted by

[10]*Detroit Free Press,* January 22, 1868; *New York World,* January 14, 17, 1868; *New York Times,* January 14, 1868.
[11]*Cong. Globe,* 40 Cong., 2 sess., p. 2291 (April 10, 1868).
[12]*Ibid.,* p. 2430 (May 12, 1868).

the Republicans' recent successful drive to withdraw Supreme Court jurisdiction in the *McCardle* case.

After the Supreme Court accepted the congressional will and declined jurisdiction in the *McCardle* case, Democratic bitterness toward the justices returned in all its atavistic forms. Publicly and privately, Democratic spokesmen alternately denounced and bewailed the Court's lack of courage. Thus, the Democrats once again viewed the Supreme Court as a political instrument working to frustrate their will and the Constitution. Even before the Court acted, however, some Democrats demonstrated the fragility of their new alliance. Senator Garrett Davis of Kentucky bitterly denounced Justice Swayne and Chief Justice Chase in early 1868 because they had upheld the Civil Rights Act in separate circuit court opinions and had done so on the basis of the "meretricious" Thirteenth Amendment!

Davis's anger, plus an obvious distaste for federal power in any form, led to an interesting proposal on his part. In late 1867, he introduced a constitutional amendment quite similar to the "Court of the Union" scheme of disgruntled conservatives a century later. Davis suggested the formation of a tribunal, composed of one member from each state and appointed by the states, with jurisdiction to decide questions of federal constitutional power and to settle conflicts between the state and federal governments. The Kentuckian of course stood almost alone in support of his idea, but nevertheless his thoughts and words reflected certain basic party instincts. He lamented the character of judicial appointments since 1789, although he thought that six of the nine justices (i.e., Democrats!) as of 1861 were "eminently conservative and true to the Constitution." In sum, however, Davis believed that the Supreme Court had failed in its original purpose and should be abandoned: "Experience . . . has demonstrated both the insufficiency and the unfitness of the Supreme Court to answer those great ends, for which it in part, but largely, was designed."[13]

[13]*Ibid.*, pp. 492–99 (January 14, 1868). Davis's resolution died in committee but was introduced again in 1871 (*ibid.*, 42 Cong., 1 sess., p. 120 [March 16, 1871]). Davis may well have been the most anachronistic man in Congress, and the Republicans treated him accordingly. Alluding to the "era of good feeling" following Appomatox, Senator James W. Nye (Rep., Nev.) suggested that "it was a great pity that [Davis] . . . did not surrender at the time that Lee and his army did. [Laughter]" (*ibid.*, 40 Cong., 2 sess, p. 499 [January 14, 1868]). The modern "Court of the Union" idea calls for a tribunal of the state chief justices to review United States Supreme Court decisions affecting federal-state relations. See *New*

Generally speaking, the congressional Democrats mirrored aspirations and expectations expressed in the party's organs. During the heated debates over passage of the two-thirds proposal and the repeal of habeas corpus jurisdiction affecting the *McCardle* case, the Democrats had passionately defended the powers and authority of the Supreme Court. Regularly, they mourned the loss of constitutional liberty and respect for constitutional limitations upon governmental power. Reverdy Johnson of Maryland, a former attorney-general and confidant of Taney, best summed up the party's position: "A latitudinarian construction of the Constitution, the absorption of nearly all the power into the legislative department . . . , an unwillingness to submit to the judiciary, an interference with . . . the legitimate powers of the President . . . —these are the symptoms of the times."

For Johnson and his fellow partisans, the Court was the Great White Hope. True, it had erred, they acknowledged; yet it discharged its high judicial functions "from a pure sense of what the laws and the Constitution . . . require." The Democrats believed that the Court had some mystical hold on the nation which would not allow "absolutism" in Congress to "trample it down and crush it out of existence." There was, one representative proclaimed, an abiding national "reverence for that tribunal, for its justice, its learning, its conservatism, its ability, its adherence to the great principles of our Government, and its protection of the rights of the citizens."[14]

The Democratic ambivalence toward the Supreme Court is nowhere more striking than in the attitudes of Andrew Johnson. It certainly was a curious twist of events which brought Johnson to seek the Supreme Court as an ally in his struggle with Congress. Unlike others in his party, Johnson's historical instincts persevered throughout much of Reconstruction.

York Times, April 14, 1963; Charles L. Black, Jr., "The Proposed Amendment of Article V: A Threatened Disaster," *Yale Law Journal,* 72 (April, 1963): 957–66. An undated clipping from the Washington *National Intelligencer* in the David Davis papers reveals the perceptive insight that the *McCardle* appeal, followed by the Court's reticence, aroused the anti-court extremists in both parties. Justice Davis attributed the unsigned editorial to the conservative lawyer, James G. Carlisle (Davis to Julius Rockwell, April 29, 1868, Davis Papers, Chicago Historical Society).

[14]*Cong. Globe,* 39 Cong., 2 sess., pp. 462, 588 (January 15, 19, 1867); *ibid.,* 40 Cong., 2 sess., p. 480 (January 13, 1868). See chap. 5 for detailed Democratic reactions to various Republican drives to limit judicial power.

Andrew Johnson naturally desired, and probably expected, the Supreme Court to override the congressional will. Yet, this was the same man who, as a young congressman in 1848, had blunted Whig assaults on the presidential veto with a vigorous counterattack on the judicial power to void legislation. The judiciary, he said, "is irresponsible to the people," but nevertheless had a deplorably absolute and final veto power. On two occasions, he unsuccessfully had attempted to implement his ideas by proposing a constitutional amendment to limit federal judges to twelve-year terms.[15] This was not an isolated effort on Johnson's part. As governor of Tennessee in 1853, and again in 1855, Johnson had recommended that the Tennessee General Assembly address a joint resolution to Congress urging passage of such an amendment. Near the end of his presidential term, in July, 1868, he advanced a remarkable set of constitutional amendments which provided for the direct election of presidents, a limit of one six-year presidential term, cabinet succession to the presidency in event of an absence of both a president and vice-president and, again, a twelve-year term for federal judges. On the last point, he was of the strong impression that life tenure was "incompatible with the spirit of republican government."[16]

Johnson's one significant defense of the judiciary came in the *McCardle* controversy, but only as a matter of mere expediency. Early in 1868, Congress frankly sought to thwart a judicial threat, real or imagined, to the Reconstruction Acts of 1867. Under its constitutional authority to determine appellate jurisdiction, Congress had repealed provisions giving the federal courts authority to hear further habeas corpus appeals arising from violations of the act. Apparently relying on Johnson's well-known attitudes toward judicial power, Justice David Davis and others on the Court had recognized the possibility of presidential acquiescence.[17] Johnson,

[15]*New York World,* January 20, 1868. *Cong. Globe,* 30 Cong., 1 sess., Appendix, pp. 853–54 (August 2, 1848); *ibid.,* 31 Cong., 2 sess., p. 627 (February 21, 1851); *ibid.,* 32 Cong., 1 sess., p. 443 (February 2, 1852).

[16]Robert H. White, ed., *Messages of the Governors of Tennessee, 1847–1855,* 6 vols. to date (Nashville: Tennessee Historical Commission, 1952——), 4:558, 587–88, 648–51. Richardson, *A Compilation of Messages and Papers,* 8:3837–41. Johnson's desire for cabinet succession surely reflected the effects of the recent impeachment crisis. Incidentally, while operating in his "treason is odious" syndrome, Johnson got off a choice remark at the time of Taney's death: "Taney is dead! And let freedom and justice rejoice. He has gone into his tomb, remembered only to be despised" (*New York World,* October 25, 1864, quoting *Nashville Times*).

[17]Davis to Julius Rockwell, April 22, 1868, Davis Papers, Chicago Historical Society.

however, vetoed the repeal, and Congress promptly overrode his action.

The President predictably pitched his veto message to constitutional objections, but he had to resort to abstract conceptions rather than concrete clauses. Such legislation, he said, affected "most injuriously the just equipoise of our system of Government; for it establishes a precedent which, if followed, may eventually sweep away every check on arbitrary and unconstitutional legislation." Johnson's consecration of judicial authority and power hardly befitted his Jacksonian past: "Thus far during the existence of the Government the Supreme Court . . . has been viewed by the people as the true expounder of their Constitution, and in the most violent party conflicts its judgment and decrees have always been sought and deferred to with confidence and respect. In public estimation it combines judicial wisdom and impartiality in a greater degree than any other authority known to the Constitution."[18]

As always, Johnson claimed to have a strong grasp of what the "people" desired. In March, 1868, he was confident that the "people" saw the Court as the "true expounder" of the Constitution. Four months later, with equal certitude, he could assert that "popular judgment" demanded a restriction on the life tenure of the true expounders of the faith. The expediency of a veto in the McCardle affair notwithstanding, Johnson's public positions and statements during his presidency hardly indicated a reluctance to curb judicial power. It is significant, for example, that he *signed* the 1866 legislation which reduced the size of the Court and prevented him from gaining any appointments. On one occasion, moreover, he staunchly had opposed any further increases in federal court jurisdiction.[19] Quite simply, Johnson's "marriage" to the Court on the Reconstruction Acts was a self-imposed shotgun affair.

The Democrats' reverence for the Supreme Court can be explained only on the basis of their expectations for its treatment of Reconstruction legislation. They confidently expected the justices to invalidate the Republican program at the first opportunity.

[18]*Cong. Globe,* 40 Cong., 2 sess., pp. 2128, 2170 (March 26, 27, 1868); Richardson, *A Compilation of Messages and Papers,* 8:3845. Johnson also found kind words for the Supreme Court when he expressed the desire to have the "final arbiter fixed by the Constitution" decide the validity of the Tenure of Office Act (Richardson, *A Compilation of Messages and Papers,* 8:3823, 3825).

[19]See chaps. 4 and 8, *below,* for details of the court-reduction legislation and removal statutes respectively.

Isolated, and decisively routed in Congress, the Democrats soon saw the presidential veto become a useless weapon as moderate Republicans deserted the obstinate, uncompromising Johnson. The Democrats' turn toward the Court reflected a desperate, last-ditch response to the Republican juggernaut. They were, however, grasping only at a will-o'-the-wisp.

Given the disparity of their political backgrounds, the Republicans cannot be pinned down to any consistent historical tradition regarding the Supreme Court. There were, for example, former Whigs who had placed a high premium on the value of judicial power. Charles Sumner, the protege and disciple of Joseph Story, is an obvious case in point. Some former Democrats, such as John P. Hale of New Hampshire, on the other hand, long had been committed to an essentially hostile point of view. In any event, it would be foolish to suggest that the Republican party considered the "annihilation" of the Supreme Court as necessary or desirable. It is difficult indeed to avoid the conclusion that the party's periodic hostility toward, and suspicion of, the Court involved anything more than occasional, pragmatic reactions.

Although no longer fashionable, historians have regarded congressional aggressiveness toward the executive branch as part of a concerted, preconceived Republican party drive during the Reconstruction period. But much the same idea has been advanced for the Republicans' attitude toward the Supreme Court. Just as they would restrain and, if necessary, destroy Andrew Johnson, the "Radicals" intended to subvert the Court if it interfered with their plans. Recent writings on the period have emphasized the fluid character of Republican party alignments and goals. Though some party members advocated legislative supremacy, it is clear that most of the party turned against Andrew Johnson only when convinced that he would not support a minimal program of southern reconstruction. Similarly the party's fears of the Court, whether real or imagined, followed much the same path.

It is true that Dred Scott occasionally colored Republican thinking. Naturally, the bitter memories of "judicial usurpation" could not be erased entirely. But following the war, the Republicans hardly could avoid the feeling that the judiciary now was *theirs*. After all, the 1862 reorganization and Lincoln's subsequent appointments had been designed for that purpose. "We believe in that Court," said

Greeley's *New York Tribune* in 1868, "and uphold it in the exercise of its rightful powers. But when it attempts to set its foot on the necks of Four Millions of our Countrymen—as it did in the Dred Scott case—we affectionately advise it not to do so again." Confidently, the *Tribune* concluded: "And we guess it will not."[20]

Despite the Supreme Court's decision in the *Milligan* case and the majority's seemingly aggressive dicta, the Republicans had restrained themselves from reprisal. While the Democrats had grasped at the majority opinion to build their constitutional roadblocks against Republican policies, the latter had ignored any such possible implications in the decision. True, Thaddeus Stevens had labeled Milligan as more odius than Dred Scott, and some congressmen had sought legislative redress; yet the party as a whole had refused to read any dangerous and threatening signals in the Court's action.

In short, the Republican party did not spend its waking hours scheming of ways to destroy the Court. What is more, the Republicans consciously and regularly relied on judicial doctrine to safeguard congressional control of reconstruction against judicial intervention. And, ironically enough, they primarily exploited an idea of their *bête noire*, Roger B. Taney. Time and again, Republican spokesmen fondly quoted his opinion in *Luther* v. *Borden* justifying congressional determination of political questions.[21]

Luther v. *Borden* had involved the constitutional provision guaranteeing each state a "republican form of government." The case grew out of the Dorr Rebellion in Rhode Island in which rival factions had contended for control of the state government. Although the main issue centered on an action of trespass, the case also raised the question of which group represented the properly constituted government of the state.

Taney, writing for the majority, neatly sidestepped this problem, dismissing it as a "political question" and consequently, not proper

[20]*New York Tribune*, January 22, 1868. Also see Representative William D. Kelley's rather restrained attitude toward Dred Scott in 1866 (*Cong. Globe*, 39 Cong., 1 sess., p. 197 [January 11, 1866]).

[21]7 Howard (48 U.S.) 1 (1849). "The United States shall guarantee to every State in this Union a Republican Form of Government. . . ." (*U.S. Constitution*, Art. IV, Sec. 4). The Jeffersonian-Jacksonian litany of concurrent review accompanied the Republicans' use of *Luther* v. *Borden*. See, for example, *Cong. Globe*, 39 Cong., 2 sess., p. 477 (January 15, 1867), and, in particular, remarks by Charles Sumner, *The Works of Charles Sumner*, 15 vols. (Boston: Lee & Shepard, 1872–83), 8:236–37, 239.

for judicial determination. Political problems, he said, had to be resolved by the legislative department: "It rests with Congress to decide what government is the established one in a State. For as the United States guarantee to each State a republican government, Congress must necessarily decide what government is established in the State before it can determine whether it is republican or not . . . . And its decision is binding on every other department of the government, and could not be questioned in a judicial tribunal."[22] How ironic that the Republicans chose a constitutional exegesis by the despised Taney as their most sacred text.

Taney's opinion in *Luther v. Borden* is the chief prop for his reputation as an advocate of "judicial self-restraint." The Republicans in the Reconstruction era regularly cited Taney's doctrine both as justification for their own policies and for a prediction of how the Supreme Court would treat their legislation. For example, Representative Samuel Shellabarger of Ohio, in an important speech on January 8, 1866, laid down the outline for what ultimately became the chief Republican theory and policy toward the South. Shellabarger constitutionally staked his ideas on the "guaranty" clause and, at the very end, approvingly cited the *Luther v. Borden* doctrine as authority for congressional control.[23]

Shellabarger's use of Taney's remarks constituted the most consistent thread in the Republicans' attitude toward the Court. For over two years, party spokesmen, in and out of Congress, followed suit and confidently expected the Supreme Court to abide by its own precedent. The *Chicago Tribune,* which rarely had respect for anything associated with Taney, referred to his opinion as "an elaborate assertion of the powers of Congress as exercised in the late Reconstruction acts." It contended that the determination of a proper state government was a "political question" and one which had to be decided exclusively by Congress. The Reconstruction Acts, the journal concluded, were "nothing but an affirmance or repetition of the decision of the Supreme Court in the Rhode Island cases."[24] Yet such application of *Luther v. Borden* may have been inappropriate. That case had involved the possibility of the federal judiciary adjudicating rival claims for control of a state government;

[22]*Luther v. Borden,* 7 Howard (48 U.S.), 1, 42.

[23]*Cong. Globe,* 39 Cong., 1 sess., p. 145 (January 8, 1866). Also see, for example, Representative J. L. Thomas, Jr., *ibid.,* p. 2091 (April 21, 1866).

[24]January 22, 24, 1868. The other prominent Republican newspapers followed the same line of reasoning.

the affair was wholly internal. The Reconstruction Acts, however, concerned national policy and national questions. In short, it is by no means clear that *Luther* v. *Borden* inherently precluded judicial intervention in such cases.

Despite the comfort found in *Luther* v. *Borden,* the Republicans had become increasingly uneasy and apprehensive about the judiciary. The Democrats' insistence that the Court would find the Republicans' reconstruction policies unconstitutional, and their regularly voiced idea that the Court had a right to review congressional policy, irked Republicans no end and compounded the latter's suspicions of the Court.

A letter-writer to the *Nation,* who described himself as "a wanderer back into the Republican fold," and who signed himself as "Conservative," raised a number of questions which probably summed up a widespread common attitude (then and now) concerning judicial power. He queried whether it was not within the Court's jurisdiction to decide which branch of government could initiate reconstruction; whether the Court should enlighten Congress as to the latter's powers and duties; and whether Congress had a right to legislate without such advice. "Is it not for the decision of such questions as these," he asked, "that the Supreme Court was instituted?" While the *Nation* had grown disenchanted with many Republican policies, it still maintained that reconstruction was a political question and its resolution lay with Congress. The journal again mentioned *Luther* v. *Borden,* but struck hardest at the popular misconception that it was the Court's duty to advise Congress of its powers in advance. In a sense, the *Nation* contended, the Court had tried to do this in Dred Scott, but with disastrous results. The *Nation* certainly was not hostile to judicial power; it simply believed that the Court lacked the authority to decide political questions. If it attempted to do so, the result might well be fatal: to have the Court predetermine the scope of congressional power would convert it "into a branch of the legislature, and bring it so throughly into the arena of party politics that we might look forward to seeing it abolished as a nuisance before ten years were over."[25]

Lyman Trumbull exploded when, in January, 1868, a fellow senator suggested that five of the eight Supreme Court justices had determined already that the Reconstruction Acts were unconstitutional. Senator James R. Doolittle of Wisconsin, who had deserted

[25]Vol. 4 (April 25, 1867):340.

the Republican party in all but name, implied that a majority of the Court was so inclined, and he taunted the majority for proposing the measure which would have required a two-thirds vote of the Court to invalidate congressional legislation. "I have heard enough of this on the streets," Trumbull countered, indicating the popular currency of the rumor regarding possible judicial action. Judges who expressed their opinions in advance, he said, were "infamous"; and if the reports were untrue, then those who circulated them deserved to be called "liars." The whole tenor of Trumbull's remarks illustrated the Republican predicament. He insisted that his party had no intention to "degrade or subjugate" the Supreme Court; yet the talk of what the Court would do certainly had put Trumbull and his colleagues on edge.[26]

During the early months of 1868, there were a number of attempts to prevent unfavorable judicial action against the Reconstruction Acts. It should be emphasized, however, that with but one exception, these measures failed to secure substantive support throughout the Republican party.

For example, despite the popular belief that a majority of the Court was hostile to Reconstruction, the Senate Republicans significantly failed to pass the two-thirds proposal. The *Nation,* which seemed to mirror the dominant, and perhaps responsible, opinion in the Senate, best summed up the thinking of this group. It steadfastly had opposed the idea that the Court had the right to invalidate the Reconstruction Acts, while maintaining that judicial review had a proper place in the scheme of American government. But the two-thirds idea was no solution: it merely granted an appearance of security, but one gained by conceding the "most important principle" that the Supreme Court *could* prevent Congress from legislating in this sphere. Moreover, it would be only a "flimsy" attempt to secure a decision which no one would respect. Finally, the *Nation* seemed to recognize a political danger in attacking the Court: to break down its authority, thereby making it "contemptible," the majority not only would alienate "thousands on thousands of voters, . . . but [would secure] for itself something which not enriches it, and makes the nation poor indeed."[27]

[26]*Cong. Globe,* 40 Cong., 2 sess., pp. 710–11 (January 23, 1868); *Chicago Tribune,* January 28, 1868. For a typically "inside" report on what the Court would do, see the *New York Herald,* January 9, 1868.

[27]Vol. 6 (January 30, 1868):86.

Even those newspapers supporting the two-thirds idea regularly acknowledged their respect for the Court and its power. The *Chicago Tribune,* in numerous editorials supporting the bill, conceded the validity of judicial review. It insisted, of course, that such an important power should not be used by a narrow majority or an evenly divided tribunal. The *Boston Daily Advertizer* lamented that the Court unfortunately had become a political institution, and the Republican measure was necessary "to save the court from itself, –to protect it from such a dangerous exercise of its own power as must inevitably subject it to a strain in the next few years, from which it cannot hope to save its authority."[28]

The Republican party, however, simply refused to act until confronted with what it believed was irrefutable evidence of the Court's hostility. This came after the Supreme Court accepted jurisdiction in *Ex parte McCardle* in February, 1868. The fact that the Court had announced it would hear arguments in *McCardle* did not mean *ipso facto* that it was prepared to void the Reconstruction Acts. But that is beside the point: Democratic spokesmen chortled that the Court would save the Constitution and the nation, and the Republicans, although disavowing such a value to judicial action, believed now that the Court would move against the laws. Accordingly, in March, 1868, Congress repealed the statute under which the Court had assumed jurisdiction, leading ultimately to the dismissal of McCardle's plea by the Court.[29]

Representatives James F. Wilson of Iowa and Robert Schenck of Ohio led the repeal movement in the House. Both men flayed the Democrats for spreading rumors that the Court intended to overturn the Reconstruction Acts, though the two admitted that they now had no choice but to accept the veracity of the reports. Schenck spoke of the need for Congress to "clip the wings of the Court" because the justices apparently were prepared to depart from their own principles, as applied and expressed in *Luther* v. *Borden.* The justices, he said, "arrogating to themselves the pretension to settle not merely judicial but political questions, and trampling upon the principle of [*Luther* v. *Borden*] . . ., are, the majority of them, pro-

[28]*Chicago Tribune,* January 11, 18, 20, 21, 1868; *Boston Daily Advertizer,* January 15, 1868.
[29]14 Stat. 885 (Habeas Corpus Act of February 5, 1867); 15 Stat. 44 (1868 repeal).

ceeding step by step to the usurpation of jurisdiction which does not belong to them."[30]

The Republicans actually moved against the Supreme Court only when confronted by what a majority of the party believed to be an overt threat from it. The reality of that threat is another story;[31] the point here is that the Republicans did not act from any preconceived plan for the annihilation or emasculation of the Court. Their response was wholly pragmatic, and it was predicated on the reasonable assumption that the Court would depart from *its* principles and traditions. *Luther* v. *Borden,* however imperfectly understood by the Republicans, formed the cornerstone of their constitutional rationale for congressional control; in this matter, at least, they simply could not allow the Court to reverse itself.

The Republicans' efforts were not wasted: a year later, on the same day that the Court dismissed the *McCardle* case, the justices upheld the party's basic position. In *Texas* v. *White,* Chief Justice Chase approvingly cited *Luther* v. *Borden* and held that only Congress could decide which was the established government within a state.[32] The Supreme Court undoubtedly had certain doubts regarding the mechanics of Republican policy. Yet, in the final analysis, the Court and the party stood together on the principles, if not the particular means, of congressional policy.

---

[30]*Cong. Globe,* 40 Cong., 2 sess., p. 1883 (March 14, 1868).
[31]See chaps. 5 and 6, *below.*
[32]7 Wallace (74 U.S.) 700, 730 (1869).

4

Congress and the Supreme Court: The Game of Numbers and Circuits

The congressional act of July, 1866, reducing the Supreme Court from ten to seven members usually is regarded as a typically cynical and sordid example of the Radical Republicans' accumulated misdeeds. Moreover, it is treated as symptomatic of the Radicals' violent hostility toward the Supreme Court and, consequently, as a distinct threat to the independence and integrity of the judiciary.

Charles Warren, a leading student of Court-Congress relations, set the tone for the standard interpretation of the law. "The Senate," he wrote, "was determined to curb the President in every move; and fearing that he might have the opportunity to make further appointments to the Bench, it passed [the] . . . bill." James G. Randall discussed the measure under a general heading of attacks on the Court and Republican proposals for its annihilation. Specifically, he found that the act was passed "in order to take from President Johnson the power to make [judicial] appointments." Johnson's biographers have viewed the subject in much the same way: "Congress . . . reduced the court from nine [*sic*] to seven to prevent Conservatives from being added to it by the President"; moreover, the step was part of the congressional attack upon the "foundations" of the Supreme Court. Writers of constitutional history have seen the act as "the first radical move against the Court" and have said it "became law over Johnson's veto."[1]

[1]Charles Warren, *The Supreme Court in United States History*, 3 vols. (Boston: Little, Brown & Co., 1922), 3:144–45; James G. Randall, *The Civil War and Reconstruction*, (Boston: D. C. Heath, 1937), p. 804; James G. Randall and David Donald, *The Civil War and Reconstruction* (Boston: D. C. Heath, 1961), p. 645; Robert W. Winston, *Andrew Johnson: Plebeian and Patriot* (New York: Henry Holt, 1928), p. 384; Milton Lomask, *Andrew Johnson: President on Trial* (New York: Farrar, Strauss, 1960),

Persistent though they are, such views are questionable. They conflict with basic facts and ignore the rich variety of causal factors. Congress did, indeed, pass a law reducing the size of the Supreme Court, but President Johnson signed it—he did not veto it. Strange it is to read vindictive motives against Andrew Johnson in the passage of a bill that he himself accepted. Strange it also is to find vindictive motives against the Supreme Court at a time, in July, 1866, when the Radicals had not yet been given sufficient reason for attempting to bridle or punish the justices. Finally, it is strange to attribute vindictive motives against the Court when its members may well have desired the legislation or, at least, seemed unperturbed by its passage.

Representative James F. Wilson, chairman of the House Judiciary Committee, reported a bill to reduce the membership of the Supreme Court on March 8, 1866. The intent of his bill, as Wilson explained it, was to return the Court to its previous number of nine, and again constitute a court of an odd number. When a tenth circuit and justice were added in 1863, there were complaints that such a number was unwieldy and detrimental to the Court's business. Wilson claimed to have private information that some of the justices themselves thought the number too large. On that basis, he hoped for a number less than nine. But his bill reduced the Court only to nine and it passed the House without a roll call.[2]

pp. 239–40; Alfred H. Kelly and Winfred Harbison, *The American Constitution*, 3d ed. (New York: W. W. Norton, 1963), pp. 477–78; C. Herman Pritchett, *The American Constitution* (New York: McGraw-Hill, 1959), p. 104; Carl B. Swisher, *American Constitutional Development*, 2d ed, (Boston: Houghton Mifflin Co., 1954), p. 495. See also the various judicial biographies for the period: Charles Fairman, *Mr. Justice Miller and the Supreme Court, 1862–1890* (Cambridge, Mass.: Harvard University Press, 1939), 338; Carl B. Swisher, *Stephen J. Field: Craftsman of the Law* (Washington: The Brookings Institution, 1930), p. 155; and, Willard L. King, *Lincoln's Manager: David Davis* (Cambridge, Mass.: Harvard University Press, 1960), p. 260. The last two quotes are from Winston, *Andrew Johnson*, and Kelly and Harbison, *The American Constitution*.

[2]*Cong. Globe*, 39 Cong., 1 sess., p. 1259. William A. Dunning, surely not disposed to look kindly upon Republicans or their measures, labeled Wilson as a "moderate" and "of conservative cast," in *Reconstruction, Political and Economic: 1865–1877*, Torchbook ed. (New York: Harper & Row, 1962), pp. 88, 103. Kenneth Stampp, however, designated Wilson as a "radical," in *Era of Reconstruction, 1865–1877* (New York: Alfred A. Knopf, 1965), p. 84. In this instance, Dunning's evaluation seems more valid—particularly in the light of Wilson's well-known reluctance to commit himself to impeachment. Most definitely, Wilson commanded the respect of all Republican factions and the opposition.

In the Senate, however, Lyman Trumbull, on instructions from his Judiciary Committee, successfully proposed a further reduction to seven. Although Senator John Sherman and several others expressed some misgivings about the mechanics of an accompanying reorganization of the circuits, there was no quarrel concerning the number of judges. The amended bill passed the Senate without a roll call.[3] A mild fracas erupted in the House when Wilson, without the usual routing through the Judiciary Committee, called for House concurrence in Trumbull's amendment. Some Democrats, led by Samuel J. Randall of Pennsylvania, vainly objected to the procedure. When the roll was called, the proposal won handily, 78–41. During the final debate in the House, Wilson explained that the proposed reduction would apply to Johnson's recent nomination of Henry Stanbery to replace Justice John Catron, who had died in 1865. Wilson did not speak critically of the President, however, and reiterated his knowledge that the Court itself favored the proposal.[4]

Wilson indeed admitted that the bill would cancel Johnson's new appointment but emphasized that the original bill, providing for a reduction of one, had passed before Johnson's nomination of Stanbery. At no time did Wilson or even the House Democrats contend that the bill's purpose was to nullify the appointment. The same was true in the Senate. The Republicans obviously did not disapprove personally of Stanbery for they soon confirmed his appointment as attorney general—a much more sensitive and influential position.[5]

If it be insisted that a vote for the reduction bill should be interpreted as an anti-Johnson gesture, and vice-versa, a comparison of roll calls on other substantive issues casts some doubt on the conten-

[3]*Cong. Globe,* 39 Cong., 1 sess., pp. 3697–98 (July 10, 1866). Sherman was unhappy because Ohio was placed with Michigan, Kentucky, and Tennessee.

[4]*Cong. Globe,* 39 Cong., 1 sess., p. 3909 (July 18, 1866).

[5]*Ibid.,* pp. 3909, 3697–99 (July 18, 10, 1866). Charles Warren, without a direct quotation, claimed Wilson stated that the "effect as well as purpose" of the act was to nullify Johnson's appointment (*Supreme Court in United States History,* 3:145). As noted above, there is no such comment by Wilson. The original proposal passed the House on March 8; Stanbery's nomination came on April 16. The latter event obviously could not, then, precipitate the issue as Warren claimed (p. 144). Warren further weakened his case that Stanbery's nomination forced congressional action when he cited the favorable Republican newspaper reaction to Johnson's choice. It is difficult to imagine that Congress had any misgivings about Stanbery in 1866. He was a Republican and recently had presented a forceful argument for the government in the *Milligan* case.

tion. Of the forty-one "nay" votes—what some might call a "pro-Johnson" stand—twenty-one were Republicans. Who were these Republicans, and what was their degree of loyalty to the Radical cause? Radical stalwarts such as George S. Boutwell, Henry L. Dawes, Rufus P. Spalding, and Frederick E. Woodbridge are easily recognizable. Yet, joining them were some well-known moderates such as Thomas A. Jenckes and John A. Kasson, and Johnson's most prominent supporter in the House, Henry J. Raymond.

The most useful House roll calls for comparative purposes seem to be the votes on the Civil Rights Bill (March 13, 1866), the motion to override the President's veto of that bill (April 9, 1866), the second Freedmen's Bureau Bill (July 3, 1866), and the motion to override Johnson's veto of the latter (July 16, 1866). On both bills, fifteen of the twenty-one Republicans voted "aye," essentially an "anti-Johnson" position. On overriding the veto, sixteen voted "aye," positively an "anti-Johnson" stance. Only one Republican voted "nay" on the Civil Rights Bill, three to sustain the veto; none opposed the Freedmen's Bureau Bill, while three supported the presidential veto. The Republicans who opposed the Court reduction decidedly opposed the President on crucial Reconstruction matters; over 71 per cent of these Republicans cast no "pro-Johnson" votes on any of the roll calls (some did not vote on all four), and 74-per cent of the total Republican votes were "anti-Johnson." The seventy-eight Republicans who supported Court reduction meanwhile scored nearly 86 per cent in "anti-Johnson" votes on the four roll calls. The differential of approximately 12 per cent between the Republican reductionists and their intraparty opponents is not very significant for comparative purposes.

The fairest conclusion, it seems, is that there is little correlation between "supporting" the President on Court reduction and general support for him in opposition to congressional policies. More specifically, such evidence indicates little reason to cast this issue into a simple "pro" and "anti" Johnson dichotomy.

The evidence of Johnson's attitude toward the bill must weaken the argument that it was directed primarily against him. The bill was enrolled by both houses on July 19, 1866, and Johnson signed it four days later. Approval of the bill could not have been a mere case of Johnson's bowing to the inevitable will of Congress because such was not his nature. If he were really opposed to the bill, he could have resorted to the simple expedient of a pocket veto, for

Congress adjourned on July 28. But viewed in the light of Johnson's lifetime attitude toward the judiciary, his action, or inaction, in 1866 is not surprising.[6] Furthermore, the fact that he signed the reduction act must shake any interpretation of congressional reprisal against him.

An interpretation of the reduction proposal as an assault or check against the Supreme Court must be made cautiously. While memories of Dred Scott were not entirely dimmed, the Supreme Court still commanded a good deal of respect and esteem at the war's end. The 1862 reorganization, deaths, resignations, and subsequent appointments to the high bench indeed had wrought great changes in that body since 1857. When the reduction measure came up in 1866, there were only three survivors from the Dred Scott decision, Robert C. Grier, Samuel Nelson, and James M. Wayne. Nathan Clifford, a conservative northern Democrat, had been appointed in 1858. Lincoln's five appointees, Salmon P. Chase, David Davis, Stephen J. Field, Samuel F. Miller, and Noah H. Swayne, were all recognized as vigorous opponents of slavery and its expansion. In what fashion, then, had the current justices sinned so as to bring forth congressional reprisal?

Despite Chief Justice Taney's solo performance in *Ex parte Merryman*,[7] the Court had demonstrated solid support for presidential and legislative wartime policies, as in the *Prize Cases*[8] and *Ex parte Vallandigham*.[9] Moreover, when the reduction bill passed Congress in July, 1866, the Court had yet to offer any indication of truculence or resistance to congressional authority. It is true that in April, 1866, the Court had announced its intention to declare against the jurisdiction of certain military commissions. But Justice Davis did not write the majority opinion in *Ex parte Milligan* until the end of the summer, and he did not read it until December. Only then did the Radicals and the country learn that five of the nine justices rejected all congressional authority to utilize military tribunals while the civil courts were open and functioning.[10] During the

[6] *Cong. Globe*, 39 Cong., 1 sess., pp. 3922, 3933 (July 19, 1866); 14 Stat. 209. See chap. 3, for Johnson's judicial attitudes.
[7] 17 Fed. Cases 144 (1861).
[8] 2 Black (66 U.S.) 635 (1863).
[9] 1 Wallace (68 U.S.) 243 (1864).
[10] The Court's first announcement is in 3 Wallace (70 U.S.) 776; the opinions are in 4 Wallace (71 U.S.) 2. Orville H. Browning's diary entry of March 25, 1866, relates that Justice Robert Grier already had informed Browning of the Court's

summer of 1866 there also were various rumors that the Court would rule against test oaths; again, however, there was no certainty until the opinions in *Cummings* v. *Missouri* and *Ex parte Garland* were announced in January, 1867.[11] There was no congressional reaction to these decisions until early 1867.

The dominant elements in the Thirty-ninth Congress had their share of faults and misconceptions. They were not, however, in the habit of setting up "straw men." A good deal of the later congressional program of reconstruction was in response to presidential (and, on one occasion, judicial) resistance to what the Republicans believed to be the proper course. But as of July, 1866, the Court simply had not yet acted so as to arouse a congressional response.

There is some supporting evidence for Representative Wilson's contention that the justices had no objection to a reduction in the Court's membership. Chief Justice Chase, in fact, at the same time had prepared a proposal for a decrease by the same number.

Chase was no stranger to the notion of reduction. As a senator in 1855 he had proposed that the Court be decreased to six members. The Senate then had been considering a bill to relieve the Supreme Court justices of circuit duties. Chase personally favored the idea but argued that there no longer would be a need for so large a court in Washington. He correctly reminded his colleagues in 1855 that the Court had been increased to nine members in 1837 so as to apportion more equitably the onerous burdens of circuit travels. Although Chase's reduction plan failed in 1855, he managed

plans. Browning did not indicate whether this information was widespread (Theodore C. Pease and James G. Randall, eds., *The Diary of Orville Hickman Browning*, 2 vols. [Springfield: Illinois State Historical Library, 1933], 2:67). "The decision in the Milligan case had occasioned no great outcry when it was first announced in April" (King, *Lincoln's Manager: David Davis*, p. 255). Davis's correspondence with his colleagues reveals that he was still writing his opinion during the summer of 1866. See, for example, Davis to Clifford, July 2, 1866, Clifford Papers, Maine Historical Society. Also see correspondence cited in note 15, *below*.

[11]4 Wallace (71 U.S.) 277, 333 (1867). In late June, there were rumors that the Court had decided against the test oaths. Reverdy Johnson seems to have been the source of the reports and Justice Stephen J. Field allegedly supplied Johnson with the information. In a long letter to Chief Justice Chase, Field stoutly disclaimed any such impropriety. Moreover, he acknowledged that the final decision of the Court still seemed to be in doubt (Field to Chase, June 30. 1866, Chase Papers, Library of Congress). Earlier, Field had informed Orville Browning that Justice Miller had succeeded in gaining Grier's acquiescence in postponing a decision until the next term much to Grier's later regret (Pease and Randall, eds., *Diary of Orville Hickman Browning*, 2:67, 69–70; also see Chase to Miller, July 3, 1866, Chase Papers, Historical Society of Pennsylvania.)

to attract an interesting variety of supporters. Many northern and southern Democrats, Whigs, and Free-Soilers either voted for Chase's amendment or declared their support in principle. While Chase, and those who spoke in behalf of his motion, talked about a lessened need for nine justices, there was a less apparent, but more subtle and significant, motivating factor. The Supreme Court of 1855 had a preponderance of southerners: five of the nine were from slave states. In many quarters, there was increasing concern that the Court did not properly reflect the national interest or, at the least, equally reflect the interests of the various sections. Chase argued that reducing the Court to six men would lead to greater sectional harmony. With six justices, no judgment of a lower court could be reversed, or no great constitutional principle promulgated, unless four justices concurred. He trusted that the four would represent separate sections. Chase claimed his amendment could only encourage greater stability and public confidence in the Court's decisions. Those rulings, he concluded, "will be most likely to command the respect of the bar, of the State courts, and of the people."[12]

Chase's motivation and inspiration are open to speculation. Certainly he may have felt an altruistic concern for the Court's image and prestige. But it is more likely that his proposal reflected the political drives of antislavery elements to alter the South's disproportionate share of power in national political institutions. Whatever the cause, the "Radical" legislation of 1866 had a rather respectable paternity.

The proposal that Chase apparently offered privately to Republican congressmen in 1866 provided for a substantial increase in judicial salaries and new arrangements for the Court's marshal.[13] For Chase, it was "very important" to reduce the size of the Court "if it [was] . . . important that adequate salaries should be paid" to the justices. In short, Chase had a most obvious and simple reason for supporting the bill. It would be easy to accuse him of obsequious-

[12]Chase's draft is in the legal file of his papers in the Historical Society of Pennsylvania. For his activity in 1855, see *Cong. Globe*, 33 Cong., 2 sess., pp. 216–17, 240, 275, 296–300 (January 9, 11, 16, 17, 1855). Also see speech by James A. Bayard in *ibid.*, Appendix, p. 85 (January 10, 1855).

[13]Chase's comments in favor of the reduction are in Chase to Miller, June 15, 1866, Chase Papers, Historical Society of Pennsylvania. Supreme Court salaries were not raised until 1873 (17 Stat. 486). The delay seemed to result from attempts to increase all federal judicial salaries. Congress enacted Chase's recommendations for the Court's marshal in March, 1867 (14 Stat. 443).

ness toward Congress or of attempting to salvage something out of a bad situation, but this would ignore his long-standing concern with judicial salaries and the size of the Court.

In the summer of 1866 Chase and Justice Miller exchanged views on various legislative schemes affecting the judiciary. Along with the reduction bill, Congress had been considering the so-called Harris bill, which involved certain circuit court reforms, including the creation of intermediate courts of appeal. As in 1855, there was a more than coincidental juxtaposition of proposals for Supreme Court reduction and circuit reforms. While Miller seemed particularly concerned with the pending Harris bill, both men, freely and without animus, discussed the reduction action. Miller, acting upon Chase's prompting, reported that he had urged Wilson, his Iowa neighbor, to support the salary increase. Imagine the audacity of Miller's request if Wilson, as is alleged, were a participant in a plot to destroy the Court! Chase and Miller, incidentally, were vigorous advocates of reducing the judicial burden, particularly by creating intermediate courts of appeal. The Harris bill of 1866 still required circuit duties of the justices, but they were to be reduced while the new courts ostensibly would lighten the appeals load on the high court in Washington. Chase's and Miller's implied support for the reduction bill might be explained as a tactical gesture in exchange for congressional passage of the circuit court bill. Considering Chase's 1855 bill, however, his support probably was more than merely tactical.

Miller noted that only Justice Clifford expressed dissatisfaction with the pending circuit court legislation; apparently he had no knowledge of Clifford's attitude toward the reduction proposal. Neither Chase nor Miller indicated awareness of any judicial opposition to it.[14] Justice Davis, however, feared the reduction was tied to the circuit court bill and would lead to an abolition of circuit duties for the justices. Davis enjoyed trial court work and the opportunity to work in his home territory, and he hinted he might resign if such a bill were passed. Davis admitted to his brother-in-law

---

[14]Chase to Miller, June 9, 1866, June 15, 1866, and July 3, 1866, Chase Papers, Historical Society of Pennsylvania; Miller to Chase, June 27, 1866, Chase Papers, Library of Congress. While the Senate approved the Harris bill, the House took no action. In all probability, the idea was too drastic a change for Congress to accept in 1866 (see Felix Frankfurter and James M. Landis, *The Business of the Supreme Court: A Study in the Federal Judicial System* [New York: Macmillan, 1928], pp. 71–73; *Cong. Globe*, 39 Cong., 1 sess., pp. 1712–14, and *passim*).

that he was "puzzled" by the reduction bill, but speculated that it had been designed to prevent any Johnson appointments. It is interesting that in numerous exchanges with his colleagues on issues affecting the Supreme Court, however, Davis offered no comment on the reduction proposal.[15]

Aside from Davis's concern for his circuit court work, there is no evidence indicating judicial hostility or resentment toward the congressional action. Quite significantly, Justice Stephen J. Field, in his outspoken, if not pretentious *Personal Reminiscences,* made no mention of the reduction incident in a chapter wholly devoted to postwar hostility against the Supreme Court.[16] The active lobbying of Chase and Miller, coupled with the lack of judicial protest, thus lends some credence to Representative Wilson's original assertion regarding judicial desires and attitudes.

The fact that Congress in 1869 increased the size of the Court to nine members is usually regarded as the critical point in the attempt to prove Republican contempt and vindictiveness toward the Court or the President.[17] But the usefulness of such "proof" is questionable. Quite simply, the increase proposal passed Congress *before* Johnson left office, and the President pocket vetoed the measure! Lyman Trumbull had proposed the increase on January 18, 1869, but he and his Republican colleagues also had plans for genuine and needed judicial reform. The bill provided for the creation of a new circuit judge in each of the existing circuits, who would have the same powers and jurisdiction as the assigned Supreme Court justice. The latter was still required to attend at least one term of his circuit court during each two-year period. Trumbull maintained that both parts of his bill served the same end: to relieve the Su-

[15]Davis to Julius Rockwell, March 11, 1866; Davis to William W. Orme, July 28, 1866; Davis to Rockwell, August 9, 1866; Miller to Davis, August 22, 1866; Davis to Clifford, August 22, 1866; Justice Samuel Nelson to Davis, September 3, 1866; Chase to Davis, October 4, 1866; Davis to Chase, October 22, 1866, Davis Papers, Chicago Historical Society. For Davis's *nisi prius* preference, see King, *Lincoln's Manager: David Davis,* p. 191. Miller's June 27 letter to Chase specifically noted that only Clifford opposed the circuit bill. Apparently Davis had not yet revealed his dissatisfaction. Incidentally, while Davis was a politically knowledgeable man, his private correspondence indicates that he was not fully attuned to Republican policies.

[16]Stephen J. Field, *Personal Reminiscences of Early Days in California* (Washington: privately printed, 1893), pp. 186–217.

[17]See, for example, Kelly and Harbison, *The American Constitution,* 3d ed., p. 481; Warren, *Supreme Court in United States History,* 3:169, 223; Henry J. Abraham, *The Judicial Process* (New York: Oxford University Press, 1962), p. 304.

preme Court's crowded docket, which was then two to three years in arrears, and thereby improve the administration of justice. Trumbull cited convincing statistics illustrating the rapid growth of judicial business within the previous three years.[18]

The increase of one Supreme Court member provoked absolutely no controversy, Republicans and Democrats alike conceding the need. The bill's progress, however, bogged down in the Senate over the circuit court reform. The recurrent issue of separate circuit judges had been bitterly contested ever since the Jeffersonian Republicans abolished similar positions created by their Federalist predecessors. The partisan descendants of Jefferson continued a policy of judicial hostility, specifically against the idea of separate circuit judges, well into the late nineteenth century. Briefly, their position rested on the assumption that it was desirable for members of the Supreme Court to deal with people and law on the local level. Quite often, however, the opposition seemed to be a reflex reaction to a long-taught tradition. Democratic opposition stirred again in 1869, but with a curious mixture of Republican allies.

Senator Charles R. Buckalew of Pennsylvania, one of the Democratic leaders, appropriately summed up his party's opposition to Trumbull's bill. He acknowledged the necessity for an increase in the Supreme Court, but countered that the bill's other features allowed for "too great" an increase in judicial power. Buckalew, perhaps reflecting his party's constant preoccupation with a fear of expanding federal power, believed that a total increase of ten federal jurists was an unreasonable demand. With some prominent Republican conservatives and radicals, Buckalew resorted to the argument that the new positions ultimately would separate Supreme Court members from circuit functions. The Court, he complained, then would be only a court of highest appeal, completely detached from "the people." The justices would not, he concluded, "be brought into contact with the great mass of the community, as they now are by traveling into different sections of the country, and becoming to some extent acquainted with local facts, the character of our people, and the various interests in different parts of the country."[19]

Some Republican senators, led by George Edmunds of Vermont

[18]*Cong. Globe,* 40 Cong., 3 sess., pp. 414, 1366, 1895 (January 18, February 19, March 3, 1869), and *passim.*
[19]*Ibid.,* pp. 1487, 1366–67 (February 23, 19, 1869).

and Charles Drake of Missouri, similarly motivated by a reluctance to have the justices removed from their circuit duties, proposed increasing the high court to fifteen men. The Court would then divide itself, with the chief justice and seven associate justices, chosen by annual lot, remaining in Washington while the others held court in their various circuits. There was only a sprinkling of Republican support for the idea and, with the prominent exception of Edmunds, it came from the Radical camp. Trumbull argued persuasively against the Drake amendment with constitutional and practical objections. He contended that dividing the Court for particular cases might be a violation of the constitutional requirement that the judicial power be vested in *one* Supreme Court. Whenever there was a Supreme Court duty to perform, Trumbull said, each justice had a right to participate. More effectively, he warned that the inconsistent character of such a Supreme Court inevitably would result in the unsettling of rules and precedents. A bipartisan coalition easily overwhelmed the attempt to raise the Court to fifteen, the proponents mustering only six votes. Trumbull's original bill, providing for an increase of one Supreme Court member and nine circuit judges, then passed with ease on February 23. The House concurred without debate on March 3.[20]

The bill passed one day before the expiration of the Fortieth Congress and of Andrew Johnson's administration. For perhaps any or all of a variety of reasons—a recurrence of his antijudiciary attitude, spite for Congress, or pressures of the last day in office—Johnson did not sign the bill. The provision for new circuit judges may have been the key to his inaction. True to the Jeffersonian-Jacksonian faith, Johnson probably regarded the innovation with great distaste. Then, too, few outgoing presidents would cheerfully acquiesce in handing a despised successor such a rich patronage plum.

Trumbull reintroduced the bill in the first days of the next Congress and, once again, there was no difficulty on the Supreme Court increase provision. Many senators recognized the need to raise the Court to an odd number. In 1869 there were eight men on the bench; judicial defiance of the mortality tables prevented fulfillment of the 1866 desire for the more decisive number of seven. As before, the circuit judgeships provoked opposition. Some

[20]*Ibid.*, pp. 1487–89, 1895 (February 23, March 3, 1869).

Republicans and Democrats renewed their efforts to secure a greatly enlarged Supreme Court, dividing itself for duties in Washington and in the circuits. A few Republicans, led by Roscoe Conkling, opposed the bill as utterly inadequate and preferred a more complete and autonomous circuit court system. There also was some delay over a newly introduced provision for retirement of Supreme Court members. Despite widespread dissatisfaction and an awareness of the bill's shortcomings, the demand for some reform seemed irrresistible, and the bill became law in April, 1869.[21]

The legislation of 1869 hardly reflects cynicism or even contempt toward the Supreme Court. Andrew Johnson's impending departure may have stimulated some support for an increase in the high court, but the dominant Republicans were far more concerned with the realities of judicial needs. The provisions for an additional justice, and the new circuit judgeships, more profitably can be seen as an accommodation to the Supreme Court, and as a limited attempt to improve the administration of justice. The 1869 judicial reform marked a significant step on the path to a fully developed system of intermediate courts of appeal; it was, in short, a bridge between the Federalists' abortive scheme of 1801 and the climactic Republican Act of March 3, 1891.[22]

Most writers on Reconstruction have relied on Charles Warren's account of the reduction proposal. It is instructive to trace Warren's sources. His only citation is to Ransom H. Gillet's *Democracy in the United States,* published in 1868.[23] Despite its title, the book is hardly a theoretical discussion of democracy in the United States. Gillet, a former Democratic member of the House of Representatives, penned an *apologia* and campaign document for the Democratic party and a defense of Andrew Johnson against alleged Radical Republican excesses. Moreover, he wrote of the reduction measure at a time when a small faction of the Republican party had launched an abortive assault against the independence and integrity of the

[21]*Ibid.,* 41 Cong., 1 sess., pp. 29, 62, 192, 207–15, 218, 336–45, 574, 464–650, 682 (March 8, 15 April 8, 9, 1869). See Frankfurter and Landis, *Business of the Supreme Court,* p. 76, for the law's failure to relieve the circuit work load. Charles Fairman has written that Justices Miller and Field prepared the bill's section on circuit judges (*Mr. Justice Miller,* p. 402). Justice Grier's physical and mental incompetency prompted the movement for a retirement provision.

[22]See Frankfurter and Landis, *Business of the Supreme Court,* pp. 4–102, *passim,* for a general outline of the drive for circuit court reform in the nineteenth century.

[23]New York: D. Appleton, 1868, pp. 344–48.

Supreme Court. Gillet thus neatly fitted the reduction legislation into that category. While Warren primarily advanced an interpretation of political reprisal and vindictiveness, he acknowledged a contrary contemporary appraisal. The *American Law Review* noted that there had been no serious opposition to the reduction bill and that it "was in no sense a political measure, however much political feelings may have aided its passage."[24]

It is quite probable that *some* congressmen viewed the 1866 reduction as a useful device to strike at Johnson and the Supreme Court. The congressional failure to provide for a future decrease of the circuits simultaneously with reductions in the Supreme Court is perhaps the best evidence, indirect though it is, of the Republican reluctance to allow a Johnson appointment. But unless one accepts Johnson as a masochist, the fact remains that he willfully acquiesced in the change. Given his prewar and final public views on the judiciary, this position becomes perfectly plausible. And again, the Supreme Court at that time had given Congress little cause for disenchantment or alienation. This notion that a reduction of membership would punish the Court incidentally begs the question of how this would prevent hostile opinions. An increase in the number of reliable justices would seem to be a rather more effective guarantee for Congress. It is quite likely that Wilson's remarks concerning judicial desires for a more manageable number actually reflected their wishes. In any event, the justices apparently never informed the opposition otherwise, and Wilson's statements went unchallenged. Surely the Democrats would have welcomed an opportunity to criticize the Republican measure if any valid basis could have been discovered. During Reconstruction, the Democracy always stood united in defense of the Court, if only for selfish reasons. Finally, the whole of the 1869 increase act must be read as an accommodation to the Court.

It would be entirely naïve to suggest that the reduction measure passed Congress in a political void. But ascribing political motivation to the Republican action has little to do with personalities, presidential or judicial. There is an apparent link between the reduction of the Court and the old matter of sectional representation in the judicial circuits. The alteration of the Court in 1866

[24]Quoted in Warren, *Supreme Court in United States History*, 3:145n. See *American Law Review*, 1 (October 1866):206-7. Warren's use of this quotation indicated some reservation on his part. This is not true of the writers who have followed him.

included a reshuffling of the circuits. These changes marked the culmination of a shift which began with the reorganization of July, 1862. Then, it will be recalled, with the South out of the Union, the dominant Republicans reconstructed the judicial system at the expense of the seceded states. In brief, they took the five judicial

TABLE 2

Circuit	1860 [a]	1862 [b]	1866 [c]
1st	Rhode Island, Maine, Massachusetts, New Hampshire 2,360,038	Rhode Island, Maine, Massachusetts, New Hampshire 2,360,038	Rhode Island, Maine, Massachusetts, New Hampshire 2,619,919
2d	New York, Vermont, Connecticut 4,655,890	New York, Vermont, Connecticut 4,655,980	New York, Vermont, Connecticut 5,250,764
3d	Pennsylvania, New Jersey 3,578,250	Pennsylvania, New Jersey 3,578,250	Pennsylvania, New Jersey, Delaware 4,553,062
4th	Maryland, Delaware, Virginia 2,395,583	Maryland, Delaware, Virginia, North Carolina 3,388,205	Maryland, Virginia, West Virginia, North Carolina, South Carolina 4,225,038
5th	Alabama, Louisiana 1,672,203	Alabama, Georgia, Florida, South Carolina, Mississippi 3,656,924	Alabama, Georgia, Florida, Mississippi, Louisiana, Texas 4,742,265
6th	North Carolina, Georgia, South Carolina 2,753,616	Louisiana, Arkansas, Texas, Kentucky, Tennessee 4,013,152	Ohio, Michigan, Kentucky, Tennessee 6,428,850
7th	Ohio, Indiana, Illinois, Michigan 6,151,003	Ohio, Indiana 3,689,939	Indiana, Illinois, Wisconsin 5,275,198
8th	Kentucky, Tennessee, Missouri 3,447,497	Michigan, Wisconsin, Illinois 3,236,945	Missouri, Iowa, Kansas, Minnesota, Arkansas 4,203,891
9th	Mississippi, Arkansas 1,226,755	Missouri, Iowa, Kansas, Minnesota 2,136,154	California, Oregon, Nevada 693,661

[a] Circuits according to Judiciary Act of 1837, with 1860 population census.
[b] Circuits according to Judiciary Act of 1862, with 1860 population census.
The Judiciary Act of 1863 temporarily created a Tenth Circuit for California and Oregon.
[c] Circuits according to Judiciary Act of 1866, with 1870 population census.

circuits (of nine) that consisted entirely of slave states and telescoped them into three. In 1863 Congress added a tenth circuit for the Far West. Then with nine men on the Court in 1866, the Republicans reduced the circuits to nine and left only the Fifth composed exclusively of former slave states. The remaining slave states were appended to free ones. Significantly, they combined the late Justice Catron's assignment of Kentucky and Tennessee with Justice Swayne's new circuit of Ohio and Michigan. Obviously this change and others lessened the demand and need for southern representation on the Supreme Court. In a sense, the act of 1866 was a variation on the underlying theme of Chase's reduction proposal in 1855.

The circuit reorganization and reduction in 1866 fit into the general Republican pattern to reduce what they believed had been undue and disproportionate southern influence in the national government —which was indisputable with regard to the judiciary. The 1862 reorganization relieved Lincoln of any obligation to appoint southerners. Even the usually obtuse Andrew Johnson apparently understood the determination and intentions of the Republican party. When he attempted to make an appointment to the Supreme Court, he nominated Stanbery, an Ohioan, to replace Catron, a Tennessean. Thus, without benefit of the 1866 changes Johnson proved a willing ally for the Republican cause. Stanbery's circuit, under the 1862 law, would have been composed of Louisiana, Texas, Arkansas, Kentucky, and Tennessee. The nomination of an outsider was a bold departure; even Lincoln waited until Congress redrew the circuit boundaries before he acted. After the reduction and realignment of 1866, only one southerner, Justice Wayne, remained to handle the exclusively southern Fifth Circuit. When he died in 1867, his Supreme Court seat remained vacant, while Justice Swayne did double duty in the Fifth and his own Sixth Circuit. When Congress increased the Court again in 1869, the new justice, Joseph P. Bradley of New Jersey, fell heir to the vacant circuit—the all-southern Fifth.

The Republican-ruled Congress thus tailored the judicial system of the United States to suit better the demands and needs of the dominant section and, of course, the dominant party. The reduction of the Court was another means to this end. All this was done with acquiescent presidents, and in no way did it signify an assault upon the *idea* or the *institution* of the judiciary. Viewed in this light,

Edward Bates's reaction to the reduction proposal becomes more meaningful: "The *Supreme Court*," he wrote, "is to be a mere party machine; to be manipulated, built up and pulled down as party exigencies require."[25] Bates significantly avoided any suggestion that the Republicans primarily sought to prevent a Johnson appointment. Although Henry Stanbery, Johnson's nominee for the vacancy in 1866, appeared to be a tolerable choice of the time, the reduction and realignment of the circuits constituted a surer guarantee to make the judiciary safe for the North—and Republicans.

There remains much to say concerning the standard accounts of a weak, pliant, frightened, and intimidated Supreme Court during the era of Reconstruction. Such a story necessarily must consider the real intentions and fulfillment of Republican attitudes and policies vis-à-vis the Supreme Court. Despite their critics, the Republicans were neither reckless nor always vindictive. Careless assumptions, preconceptions, and incorrect conclusions regarding the judicial legislation of 1866 and 1869 point up the necessity and usefulness of re-examining other aspects of the relationship between Congress and the Supreme Court in the postwar period.

---

[25]Howard K. Beale, ed., *The Diary of Edward Bates, 1859–1866* (Washington: American Historical Association, 1933), p. 553. Not until Grover Cleveland appointed Lucius Q. C. Lamar in 1888 did a southern Democrat again serve on the Court.

5

Congress and the Supreme Court:
The "Abortive Revolution"

However erroneous the analysis of Republican motives, their reduction of the Supreme Court in 1866 is often viewed as the first portent for the time of troubles that afflicted the judiciary during the most turbulent days of Reconstruction. The Republicans, once they had settled upon southern policy, were supposedly determined to brook no interference from either the executive or the judiciary. Thus, according to Professor Randall, the Supreme Court, like Andrew Johnson, did not escape "the menace of congressional intimidation entirely without injury." Congress, for example, did not hesitate to deprive the Court of some jurisdiction when it sensed a threat to the Reconstruction Acts, and the abrupt loss of power contributed to a general decline of dignity. That the Court did not suffer more, Randall wrote, "was due chiefly to its acquiescence in the main body of reconstruction legislation. This was largely an acquiescence of silence, that is, avoiding a review of the reconstruction acts on their merits." Professor Brock, in his recent analysis of the Thirty-ninth Congress, found the Supreme Court, along with the President, to be on the end of a two-pronged drive for legislative supremacy. Only the Court's "timely retreat" in cases such as *Mississippi* v. *Johnson*, *Georgia* v. *Stanton*, and *Texas* v. *White* "put an end to plans for altering the powers of the Court, and this abortive revolution was the prelude to an era of judicial veto and judicial legislation."[1]

Brock is absolutely correct when he writes of an "abortive revolution"; but the notion of the Court's "timely retreat" is another

[1]James G. Randall, *The Civil War and Reconstruction*, (Boston: D. C. Heath, 1937), p. 802; W.R. Brock, *An American Crisis: Congress and Reconstruction, 1865–1867* (New York: St. Martin's Press, 1963), p. 264.

matter altogether. Indeed, there were certain elements in Congress which frankly sought to suppress judicial independence and power in the name of legislative supremacy or, more crudely, to protect their pet legislative schemes from judicial interference. That drive, however, fell short; and the failure owed more to an inability to secure a party consensus in favor of such a goal than to any action, or inaction, by the Supreme Court. Quite to the contrary, for example, the Court persisted in asserting its prerogatives over the writ of habeas corpus even *after* Congress partly deprived it of jurisdiction in the McCardle affair. And as the Court continued to provoke its congressional enemies, the latter attempted further assaults upon judicial power, but to no avail. When it was all over, the Court stood stronger than ever, and at the threshold of its own heyday of power and glory.

Chronology is a crucial point in this whole relationship between Congress and the Supreme Court. Careful attention must be paid to it in order to determine first, whether legislative attacks upon the Court represented a drive by the advocates of congressional supremacy; or whether they simply marked a Republican reaction toward alleged judicial threats against the Reconstruction program. The timing of various Supreme Court moves then must be scrutinized to determine the extent to which congressional activity influenced its decisions, if at all. Here we can concentrate on the events in Congress and reserve until later a detailed analysis of the Court's work.

While the Republicans lacked any real cause to criticize and attack the Court when they reduced its membership, two subsequent decisions provided more solid ground for congressional hostility. The Court's formal opinions in *Ex parte Milligan* found the justices unanimously opposed to the operation of military tribunals in areas where the civil courts were open and functioning. The particular case involved only the legality of a military commission instituted by presidential order, but five members of the Court went beyond the question at issue and denied the power to Congress. The Court struck against both state and federal test oaths a few weeks later. In *Cummings* v. *Missouri* it voided a state act, and in *Ex parte Garland*, it held invalid a requirement that attorneys practicing in the federal courts take the oath.[2] It must have been

[2]*Ex parte Milligan*, 4 Wallace (71 U.S.) 2 (1866); *Cummings* v. *Missouri*, 4 Wallace (71 U.S.) 277 (1867); *Ex parte Garland*, 4 Wallace (71 U.S.) 333 (1867).

particularly galling to the Republicans to have the Democrats remind them that David Davis, who wrote the majority opinion in the *Milligan* case, and Stephen J. Field, who spoke for the Court in the Test Oath Cases, were both Lincoln appointees.

When Congress re-assembled for the second session of the Thirty-ninth Congress in January, 1867, Thaddeus Stevens used the *Milligan* decision as a wedge to push his pet reconstruction schemes. The Court's ruling, he claimed, made immediate action by Congress "absolutely indispensable." Playing on lingering enmity toward the Court, he warned of *Milligan's* dire consequences: "That decision, although in terms perhaps not as infamous as the Dred Scott decision, is yet far more dangerous in its operation upon the lives and liberties of the loyal man, black or white, who resides [in the South] . . . . If the doctrine enunciated in that decision be true, never were the people of any country anywhere, or at any time, in such terrible peril as are our loyal brethren at the South." Stevens also used the occasion to push his notions of legislative supremacy. Sovereignty, he argued, rested with the people and could be exercised only by their representatives. "The legislative power," he said, "is the sole guardian of that sovereignty." The grant of authority was indivisible, and the other branches of government could do nothing without the direction of legislative power. Stevens pointedly implied that Congress could do as it pleased, without interference by the executive or judiciary. His Radical ally, James M. Ashley of Ohio, made it quite clear that Congress need not allow any court decision to impair or abridge its authority. Ashley reminded his audience that if the Court again issued a "political decision," Congress could take advantage of the constitutional mode of getting rid of the Court, as well as the President. That Congress could do so, he concluded, indicated that the Constitution intended the legislative branch to be "master of the situation."[3]

[3]*Cong. Globe,* 39 Cong., 2 sess., pp. 251–52, 255 (January 3, 1867). Stevens's latest biographer splendidly captured the implications of his performance. "At no other time in his life did he show more dramatically the destructive flexibility of a truly revolutionary leader. Caught in the meshes of the check-and-balance system of the American constitutional government, he now showed not the slightest hesitation in tossing the whole thing overboard. He would redefine the power relationships in the government in his own terms; and these terms were: first, that Congress was to be sole sovereign power, and second, that none of this power was to be shared with the President or the Court" (Fawn M. Brodie, *Thaddeus Stevens: Scourge of the South* [New York: W. W. Norton & Co., 1959], p. 292.

The Democrats, sensing the value of *Milligan* for their arguments against a vigorous Republican reconstruction program, staunchly defended the Court. Senator Reverdy Johnson, still intimate with some of the justices, said that the decision was "not to be surpassed," and he applauded the Court's restriction of the prevailing latitudinarian conceptions of the war power. Representative Charles A. Eldridge of Wisconsin, who usually adhered to his old-line Democratic antecedents in opposing the expansion of judicial power, nevertheless rejoiced that the decision "may save us from just such usurpation as this Congress . . . would inflict upon us." The Democrats indeed had come a long way from Thomas Jefferson and Andrew Jackson as Eldridge solemnly proclaimed that the Supreme Court's "voice of authority" had settled "the question finally and fully as to what laws are to be executed . . . in the government of the United States."[4]

The *Milligan* decision is central to contemporary and historical interpretations of how the Supreme Court really felt about the Republican program. The Reconstruction laws of 1867 were enforced by both the bayonet and the military commissions. Relying upon the *Milligan* doctrine, the Democrats had no doubts that the Court would invalidate the legislation. Some Republicans— radicals, moderates, and conservatives, differing in motivation —recognized the same implications. Most historical accounts rest upon this presumption. Simply stated, the overwhelming consensus is that the Reconstruction Acts were "palpably unconstitutional under the *Milligan* doctrine." It is worth a brief pause here to note that Justice Davis, author of the majority opinion in *Milligan*, did *not* share these views. Writing in February, 1867, Davis seemed bewildered by the Republicans' denunciation of his effort and by their fears of what it might do to their program. But, he noted, there was "not a word said in the opinion about reconstruction, & the power is conceded in insurrectionary States."[5]

When the Republicans did react to the *Milligan* decision in late 1866, they as yet had no clearly defined, cohesive southern policy. Therefore how could the decision inhibit a nonexistent program?

[4]*Cong. Globe*, 39 Cong., 2 sess., pp. 562–63 (January 18, 1867).

[5]Robert G. McCloskey, *The American Supreme Court* (Chicago: University of Chicago Press, 1960), p. 111; Davis to Julius Rockwell, February 24, 1867, Davis Papers, Chicago Historical Society. The relationship of the *Milligan* case to the constitutionality of the Reconstruction Acts will be discussed at length in the next chapter.

Perhaps Stevens could visualize the threat to *his* plans. The outraged protests of Stevens and Ashley notwithstanding, the Republican legislative response to *Milligan* actually was quite limited, indirect, and, ultimately, fruitless. On December 10, 1866, John Bingham presented a bill to approve and declare valid all presidential proclamations relating to the suppression of rebellion between March 4, 1861, and December 1, 1865. To strengthen the legality and power of the military commissions, Bingham's bill further provided that no civil courts could have jurisdiction of, or reverse any proceedings resulting from, such proclamations. Finally, no person could be made to answer in civil courts for acts committed in pursuance of such orders and proclamations. Representative James F. Wilson of Iowa, chairman of the Judiciary Committee, guided the bill through the House during January and February of 1867. The bill, he explained, provided a complete indemnity for persons who acted in behalf of the United States under color of presidential acts, orders or proclamations. He also admitted that the proposal brought "the legislative department of the Government in conflict with the views of [the Supreme Court] . . . as expressed by the majority."[6]

While Wilson candidly conceded that the bill challenged Justice Davis's opinion, he did not exactly advocate that Congress ride roughshod over the views of the Court. He called the majority opinion "a piece of judicial impertinence" which Congress had no obligation to respect because the issue of congressional power was not at stake in the *Milligan* case. He correctly noted that the case in no way provided an excuse for the examination of legislative power. When the Court found that Congress simply had not authorized the Milligan commission, this, Wilson believed, "should have closed the door against the voluntary wanderings of the court into the fields of congressional power." In advocating the indemnity bill the Iowan seemed anxious to test the Court again, for at one point he stated that *"if Congress possesses the constitutional power to pass it* [the indemnity act] we should place it among the statutes of the nation without unreasonable delay."[7] The more moderate Republicans clearly dominated the House debate; to be sure, Wilson's arguments in behalf of the bill were rather calm and dispassionate.

[6]*Cong. Globe,* 39 Cong., 2 sess., p. 47 (December 10, 1866); *ibid.,* pp. 645–46 (January 22, 1867).
[7]*Ibid.,* pp. 1484–87 (February 22, 1867). Emphasis added.

Primarily, he spoke of the need to provide security for those who acted as agents of the government in its time of peril, as many of them had already been made defendants in civil and criminal actions because of their service. He contended that the Court had been unrealistic and had avoided a recognition of the true state of affairs which existed in Indiana, where Milligan and his cohorts had conspired against the government. Wilson resorted to previous judicial statements in cases such as *Houston* v. *Moore, Martin* v. *Mott,* and the recent wartime decisions in *The Prize Cases* and *Ex parte Vallandigham* for justification of a broad exercise of the war power.

The bill passed the House on February 23, 1867, by a wide margin, 96–27, although 67 representatives did not vote.[8] The Democratic opposition really could offer little constitutional or political objection against an attempt to provide protection for government officials. They did, however, express concern that there was no remedy for those citizens punished by military tribunals. But they never directly raised the issue of habeas corpus and thereby lost an important opportunity to nail down the Republican position on the Great Writ.

The Senate accepted the House bill a week later after a brief and restrained debate. Some of the Democrats, led by Reverdy Johnson, raised the whole issue of appeals to the civil courts from military commissions or tribunals. Trumbull, however, countered that no civil court ever had authority to revise court-martial proceedings, and that he considered military commissions just as legal and in the same category. Most significantly here, Trumbull offered a clue to Republican theorizing that *Milligan* was no bar to the system of military commissions provided for in the Reconstruction Acts then pending: "There has been no decision that you cannot try a person by military commission. The decision was that a particular military commission in a certain State, under the peculiar circumstances of that case, was not authorized to try the party, *but military commissions in the disloyal States have never been pronounced to be illegal.*" Perhaps Trumbull was aware of Justice Davis's similar thoughts; more simply perhaps, the Senator had carefully read the *Milligan* opinion. Trumbull did not believe that the indemnity bill really would prevent a civil court from acting if it believed the bill

[8]*Ibid.,* pp. 1535 (February 23, 1867). The mentioned decisions are in, respectively: 5 Wheaton (18 U.S.) 1 (1820); 12 Wheaton (25 U.S.) 19 (1827); 2 Black (67 U.S.) 635 (1863); 1 Wallace (68 U.S.) 243 (1864).

to be unconstitutional; he did think, however, that the bill rightfully would prevent such a court from "going behind" the particular conviction. Like Wilson in the House, Trumbull appeared eager to test whether the Court would allow Congress a blanket authority for indemnity. Senator Daniel S. Norton, a Republican from Minnesota, who usually sided with the Democrats, ultimately voted against the bill but conceded there was no question of its constitutionality, and thought that the courts would act accordingly.[9]

The Senate passed the bill on March 2 by an overwhelming 31–6 margin. While the opposition was exclusively Democratic, there was an important break in the ranks of the minority party. Two Democrats, James Dixon of Connecticut and David T. Patterson of Tennessee (Andrew Johnson's son-in-law) joined the Republican majority on this issue. Senators James R. Doolittle of Wisconsin and Peter G. Van Winkle of West Virginia, nominal Republicans who usually opposed their party on reconstruction issues, also voted for the indemnity bill. The break in the usual party-line voting on reconstruction measures would indicate that these five men saw a different issue at stake. Quite likely, they supported it as a war measure which protected acts done in behalf of the war effort. It is most unlikely that they viewed the measure as a means of punishing the Supreme Court for the *Milligan* decision.

For some unexplainable reason, the bill never became law. Passed in the waning days of the Thirty-ninth Congress, the measure went to the President with a welter of other legislation. Johnson never signed it. At this time, the President was preoccupied with more substantial legislation such as the Reconstruction Act of March 2, 1867, and the Tenure of Office Act, both of which he vetoed. The rush of events, the pile of bills, or a genuine opposition to the indemnity bill are all possible explanations for Johnson's inaction. Similarly unexplainable is the fact that despite the bill's overwhelming support, the congressional leaders did not push the measure again when the next congress assembled.

The *Milligan* decision, however, remained basic for the long-run determination of legislative and partisan attitudes and behavior toward the Court. The Republicans' reaction was mixed. Many conceded the Court's soundness on the real issues, particularly on the preference of civil courts to military commissions. Yet, the fact that Justice Davis and four of his colleagues chose to wander beyond

[9]*Cong. Globe,* 39 Cong., 2 sess., pp. 1959–64 (March 2, 1867). Emphasis added.

the basic questions did, as the *Nation* warned it would, "arouse a suspicion that the court is anxious to express its views upon these great questions before they are legitimately presented to it."[10] The Democrats, of course, found the majority opinion convenient and fundamental as a touchstone for their opposition to the later program of military reconstruction. The majority opinion thus created a vicious circle: the Democrats built a mountain of rumors and predictions upon it; and as the Democrats exploited it, they further activated the Republicans' suspicions and latent hostility toward the Court. The irony is that the expectations and fears of both sides were unwarranted.

The Republicans reacted to the test oath decisions as promptly as they did to *Milligan.* In *Cummings* v. *Missouri* and *Ex parte Garland,* the Court had struck down, respectively, a state loyalty oath for teachers and others and a federal requirement that attorneys practicing in the federal courts subscribe to the ironclad oath. Justice Field, speaking for a narrow majority, found both rules to be in violation of the constitutional prohibition against ex post facto laws and bills of attainder. A week after the Court's pronouncement, Representative George S. Boutwell of Massachusetts offered a bill excluding any attorney who had been guilty of treason, bribery, murder, or any other felony, or who had participated in the rebellion, from practicing in the federal courts. Boutwell had no hesitation in having Congress declare what laws and rules were necessary for the administration of the executive or judicial branches of the government. Congress, he said, had to protect the Court from itself: "If there be five judges upon the bench . . . who have not that respect for themselves to enact rules and to enforce proper regulations by which they will protect themselves from the foul contamination of conspirators and traitors against the Government of this country, then the time has already arrived when the legislative department . . . should exercise its power to declare who shall be officers of the Government in the administration of the law in the courts of the Union."[11]

The House Republicans smothered the Democratic opposition

[10]*Nation,* 4 (January 10, 1867):30.

[11]*Cong. Globe,* 39 Cong., 2 sess., pp. 646–47 (January 22, 1867). For the Test Oath Cases, see the excellent discussions in Charles Fairman, *Mr. Justice Miller and the Supreme Court, 1862–1890* (Cambridge, Mass: Harvard University Press, 1939), pp. 129–36, and Harold Hyman, *To Try Men's Souls: Loyalty Tests in American History* (Berkeley and Los Angeles: University of California Press, 1959); Hyman,

which once again invoked its interpretation of constitutional matters in vain. The Democrats charged that the majority encroached upon the just powers of an independent and co-equal branch of the government, and berated the bill as "an attack on constitutional liberty itself." The Republicans allowed the Democrats to fulminate only briefly, and one day after Boutwell introduced the bill, it passed by better than a two-to-one margin.[12]

The House's haste and decisiveness were not matched in the Senate. The bill went to the Judiciary Committee which delayed putting an amended version of the proposal on the calendar until March 2.[13] Two days later, the Thirty-ninth Congress expired with no further action taken. The last weeks of the session may well have marked the peak period of Radical influence and power in many matters. Eric McKitrick has related the complicated legislative process of the Reconstruction Act of March 2, 1867, in which the Radicals exploited a party-wide determination to have some program, although their views were not shared by most of the party.[14] The failure to come forth with a legislative response to the test oath decisions seems to indicate that there was no party-wide determination to rectify the Court's "error." The House immediately let its indignation be known; but the Senate, under somewhat more moderate influence, particularly in its Judiciary Committee, effectively stalled off a precipitate response. That many Republicans deplored the decisions of December, 1866, and January, 1867, is not at all surprising; that their response was so limited, if not ineffectual, is perhaps indicative of the limited influence of the extreme opponents of judicial power and the party's willingness to tolerate some adverse judicial decisions.

While the House responded vigorously to the Test Oath Cases, its action of precisely one year earlier affords an interesting contrast.

Era of the Oath: Northern Loyalty Tests during the Civil War and Reconstruction (Philadelphia: University of Pennsylvania Press, 1954).

[12]*Cong. Globe*, 39 Cong., 2 sess., pp. 671–72, 685 (January 23, 1867).

[13]*Ibid.*, p. 1992 (March 2, 1867). The *Globe* reported that the bill was placed on the Senate's calendar. Justice Field, in his memoirs, added that Senator William M. Stewart of Nevada, chairman of the relevant subcommittee of the Judiciary Committee, secured a recommendation for indefinite postponement (*Personal Reminiscences of Early Days in California* [Washington: privately printed, 1893], p. 205n.)

[14]Eric L. McKitrick, *Andrew Johnson and Reconstruction* (Chicago: University of Chicago Press, 1960), chap.14. *Harper's Weekly*, 11 (March 31, 1867): 130, for example, opposed Boutwell's bill.

Thaddeus Stevens—of all people—then offered a resolution instructing the Judiciary Committee to inquire into the expediency of amending the test oath act so as to allow attorneys to practice their profession without taking the oath. Stevens was the only one to speak on his measure, and his logic laid the pattern for what Justice Field was to say in his Supreme Court opinions the following January. Stevens asserted that the oath was proper enough during wartime, but he pointed out that there was no need to prohibit a man from pursuing a calling and making a living once the war ended. He also expressed a belief that the oath unduly discriminated against lawyers as no oath was required of other professions. Stevens's resolution squeaked through the House by a margin of five votes. Old Thad's support came from a curious mixture of Democrats and Republicans, some usually linked with the Radical camp, others often identified with the more moderate wing of the party. No Democrats opposed the resolution.[15] One of the dissenters, however, was Wilson, chairman of the Judiciary Committee. In all probability, he used his position to bury the resolution, for no report ever was made.

We can only speculate on Stevens's motives. Edward Bates claimed to have information that the repeal was a "mere trick" to avoid a decision by the Supreme Court for fear that the justices would declare the test oath unconstitutional.[16] If so—and it may well be—then it would indicate that Stevens and others regarded the Court with a certain wariness and, perhaps, some fear. There is another, less subtle suggestion to make: Stevens's critical remarks on the unreasonableness of singling out the legal profession just might be taken at face value. Motivation notwithstanding, Stevens's sponsorship of the resolution, and the support he commanded, casts a questionable light upon the usual simple dichotomy of the Radicals versus everyone else during the Reconstruction Congresses.

The Republican party's determination to protect its reconstruction legislation lay at the heart of Court-Congress relations during the late 1860's. The *Milligan* and Test Oath Cases sent a wave of alarm through the party, although there was no immediate, concrete reprisal. The boldness and vitality of judicial power certainly gave pause for thought; even more important, the Democratic opposition persistently exploited *Milligan* to label the Reconstruction Acts unconstitutional. Whatever Republican differences existed during the debates on those measures, it is clear that for the next few years, the party stood united in a willingness to enforce and protect that program. It is in this context that some Republican congressmen sought insurance against an unfavorable verdict from the Supreme Court. But it was the proximity of danger which proved crucial to the fate of each proposal dealing with the Court. That is, as long as there seemed to be no real threat from the justices, such measures were easily thrust aside; when, however, a threat seemed imminent and substantial, as it did in February, 1868, almost all Republicans joined to withstand the ostensible judicial assault.

On December 4, 1867, the Senate passed Trumbull's bill, which simply provided for a Supreme Court quorum of five while it had eight members and for its continuing at five when the membership fell to seven as required by the 1866 reduction.[17]

The House committee, perhaps somewhat more inclined to radical measures, amended Trumbull's seemingly innocuous bill with a provision requiring the concurrence of two-thirds of the justices to void congressional legislation. But this was only one strain of thought. Thomas Williams of Pennsylvania went further and proposed an amendment requiring unanimity for such cases. Throughout the period, Williams had a close affinity for extremist measures and later was one of the House managers for Johnson's impeachment trial. Speaking to the House in January, 1868, Williams claimed that he long had been concerned with the awesome power of the judiciary and that he had been considering his proposal for over a year. He conceded nothing by way of the rightfulness of judicial power, arguing that the Court had claimed "the power of legislating by construction." Taking note of the traditional argument that the Court would only declare laws unconstitutional in cases free from any doubt, he argued that the presence of one dissenter indicated some uncertainty. Touching on arguments first offered by John Randolph in John Marshall's day, Williams believed that decisions of the two Houses of Congress, containing over one hundred and sixty lawyers, were not to be taken lightly by the judiciary. It was not, he said, "exacting a great deal to require unanimity."[18]

[17]*Cong. Globe*, 40 Cong., 2 sess., p. 19 (December 4, 1867).
[18]*Ibid.*, pp. 478–80 (January 13, 1868).

The Democrats, quite naturally, greeted Williams's amendment with a chorus of denunciation and outrage. Samuel Marshall of Illinois called it "one of the very worst" of all the Republicans' revolutionary measures: "A more monstrous proposition . . . has never been brought before any deliberative body . . . . This proposition . . . amounts to a plea of guilty on the part of the majority . . . to the charge so often preferred against them. It is a confession of guilt, a committal of suicide, an admission that they dare not allow acts passed by them to be brought before the supreme judiciary of the country."[19] In heaping scorn on the Republicans, Marshall and other Democrats incidentally revealed their own strategy of reliance upon the Court to undo the various works of Reconstruction.

While the Democrats ranted against Williams's amendment, the main body of Republicans concentrated on the Judiciary Committee's two-thirds proposal. The opposition again charged that the purpose was to protect the Reconstruction Acts, and that it was "an attempt to dictate to the judicial department as to the manner in which they shall exercise their judicial power."[20] Suddenly, the descendants of Thomas Jefferson conveniently resorted to common law principles to defend the majority vote principle. It was John Bingham and his fellow Republicans who now put on the Jeffersonian cloak, countering that common law could be changed by statute.

Bingham also seized the opportunity to strike at the constitutional position of the Democrats. They had no right, he said, "to assume that . . . [Republicans] trample the Constitution under foot. I hold myself the peer of . . . any . . . man who volunteers to become my accuser in the discharge of my duties on this floor." Bingham challenged the Democrats' unstinted praise of the Supreme Court as he conjured up the horrible specter of Dred Scott once again. In that decision the Court had "disgraced our common humanity when it mouthed . . . the horrid blasphemy that there were human beings . . . who had no rights which white men were bound to respect." Yet, despite his opinions of the Dred Scott case, Bingham made it abundantly clear that he approved of judicial review when he referred to the "sound decision" in *Marbury* v. *Madison*, as written by the "peerless" John Marshall.[21]

[19]*Ibid.*, pp. 479–80.
[20]*Ibid.*, pp. 483–87, 481–83.
[21]*Ibid.*, p. 483.

Bingham attempted to justify the two-thirds proposal on a variety of grounds. First, he drew a rather weak analogy from the Judiciary Act of 1789, which required four of the six members of the Court for a quorum. But it is not entirely clear that the First Congress consciously strove for the two-thirds principle. Bingham also pointed out that no one denied congressional power to set the size of the Court; if, then, it were set at three, two-thirds definitely would be necessary for a decision! Bingham therefore insisted that Congress could rightfully determine the requisite number of votes for a decision, as well as the number of men who sat on the court.[22]

Representative James F. Wilson, in tones anticipating twentieth-century attacks upon the Court, belabored the dangers of a "one-man power." The Iowan, who managed the two-thirds proposal as it came from his Judiciary Committee, cleverly praised Williams's unanimity amendment in order to improve the chances of his own modest proposal. Arguing from the premise that the Court should void congressional acts only in cases free from doubt, he maintained that a divided court *ipso facto* proved that the question before it was in some doubt. Therefore, he suggested, "we would not be straining the power conferred on us by the Constitution by requiring" a unanimous vote of the Court. Yet, Wilson insisted that the committee's two-thirds proposal was a "conservative measure." Laughter erupted when a Radical colleague reminded Wilson that that was ample reason for opposition! Wilson's ploy worked quite well as the House scuttled the unanimity idea by a vote of 124–25, and overwhelmingly accepted the more moderate two-thirds amendment.[23]

The amended bill returned to the Senate on January 14, 1868. Before referral to Trumbull's Judiciary Committee, Charles Sumner attempted to rouse support for a more thoroughgoing reform. The idea that a bare majority could void acts of Congress, he said, was "contrary to reason, almost contrary to common sense." He went on to advocate the requirement of a three-fourths or possibly a unanimous vote by the Court. There was no response, either on the

[22]*Ibid.*, pp. 483–84.

[23]*Ibid.*, p. 488. An observation of the debate and the roll call makes it difficult to believe that any significant part of the Republican party was enthusiastic about Williams's proposal. Yet James Ford Rhodes could write: "While . . . [the bill] was not taken up for consideration [*sic*] it is an evidence of the bitter feeling in the legislative halls toward the majority of the Supreme judges" (Rhodes, *History of the United States from the Compromise of 1850,* 7 vols. [New York: Macmillan, 1893–1907], 6:12). The gap between reality and interpretation is often great indeed.

Senate floor or, more significantly, in the Judiciary Committee. Trumbull and his colleagues made no further report, and the bill lay buried in the committee graveyard.[24]

The Republicans were unable, however, to agree on any legislation to prevent an unfavorable court decision. They could arrive at no consensus on judicial reform so long as they felt no need to react against an obvious transgression on the part of the judiciary. They had a basic respect for judicial power and particularly for the judicial review of congressional acts. There was, in any event, an ambiguous and unreal quality to the two-thirds proposal, for it amounted to saying that six justices might do what five could not.

Considering the actual behavior of the Supreme Court, the advocates of restrictive devices on judicial power truly seemed to be making much ado about nothing. Through the first half of February, 1868, the dominant elements in Congress could comfortably reflect that their moderate course had been proper and successful. The Court on two occasions had admitted an unwillingness, or more properly, a lack of power to interfere with the congressional program. In *Mississippi* v. *Johnson*, on April 15, 1867, the tribunal refused to enjoin presidential execution of the Reconstruction Acts and, on February 10, 1868, in *Georgia* v. *Stanton*, the Court similarly declined to interfere against subordinate officers.[25] Whether the justices had been prompted by the latent hostility of Congress or by a genuine determination that no jurisdiction existed is an intriguing question that can be raised in a fuller discussion of the cases. For the present purpose, it is only relevant that a direct confrontation with Congress was avoided until that point.

Those who thought the Court quiescent, compliant, or even cowardly must have received a rude shock when, a week after the Georgia case, the tribunal announced it would take jurisdiction in

---

[24]*Cong. Globe*, 40 Cong., 2 sess., p. 504 (January 14, 1868). The House Judiciary Committee was discharged from further consideration of the bill on January 21, 1868, following a motion of its chairman, James F. Wilson (*ibid.*, p. 668). The *New York Herald* typified the despair of the anti-Radical forces with regard to proposals for curbing the Court. After the House passed the two-thirds bill, the Herald believed that it would "doubtless" become law because the radicals controlled two-thirds of each house of Congress. The Senate's lack of action, however, again indicates that fears for the Court's safety were quite exaggerated. The *Herald* (January 14, 1868), interestingly enough, readily conceded the constitutionality of the contemplated legislation.

[25]*Mississippi* v. *Johnson*, 4 Wallace (71 U.S.) 475 (1867); *Georgia* v. *Stanton*, 6 Wallace (73 U.S.) 50 (1868).

Ex parte McCardle.[26] William McCardle, a Mississippi editor, had been held for trial by a military commission for publishing articles critical of the military government. He thereupon sought a writ of habeas corpus in the lower federal court, challenging the military authority under the Milligan doctrine. After the circuit court denied his plea, McCardle appealed to the Supreme Court on the basis of the Habeas Corpus Act of February 5, 1867.

The congressional response to the Court's action began slowly and inconspicuously. On March 11, Senator George Williams of Oregon introduced a bill to amend the Judiciary Act of 1789 so as to provide that judgments against or for any act committed by a revenue officer in the performance of his duties could be re-examined and reversed or reaffirmed by the Supreme Court upon writ of error. The Secretary of the Treasury urged passage so that the highest court could pass upon any great principle that might be involved in a particular case. There was no debate, and the bill passed the same day.[27] The measure went the next day to the House, where Robert Schenck of Ohio brought it up. Just before the final reading, however, Schenck allowed James F. Wilson to present an amendment. Wilson unobtrusively proposed a repeal of as much of the Habeas Corpus Act of February 5, 1867 as authorized appeals from the judgment of a circuit court to the Supreme Court, "or the exercise of any such jurisdiction by said Supreme Court on appeals *which have been* or may hereafter be taken." The amendment and the bill passed without debate or division.[28]

In the Senate on the day following the House's action, some Democrats seemed bewildered by the new amendment and requested a one-day postponement. This was denied, and the Senate promptly accepted the amendment by an overwhelming majority. Six Democrats, admittedly ignorant of the meaning of the bill, nonetheless followed their natural instincts to oppose any Republican measure.[29]

Two days later, the House Democrats suddenly divined the Republicans' strategy. Representative Benjamin M. Boyer of Pennsylvania objected to the amendment as not germane to the original bill and accused Schenck and Wilson of devious methods. He recognized that the purpose was to protect the Reconstruction Acts

[26]*Ex parte McCardle,* 6 Wallace (73 U.S.) 318 (1868).
[27]*Cong. Globe,* 40 Cong., 2 sess., pp. 1807–8 (March 11, 1868).
[28]*Ibid.,* pp. 1859–60 (March 12, 1868). Emphasis added.
[29]*Ibid.,* p. 1847.

from the apprehended danger that the Court would declare them unconstitutional. Boyer expressed shock and surprise that Wilson, who, he claimed, enjoyed "the respect of this House as well of the minority as the majority," should have acted in such bad faith.[30]

Schenck soon returned to the floor, although James G. Blaine had already undertaken his defense. At first, Schenck was amused that the Democrats—the "vigilant watch-dogs on the walls of liberty," as he sarcastically characterized them—had been so inattentive a few days earlier as to fail to rush to the Court's defense. Schenck averred that he had never seen Wilson's amendment before it was introduced; nevertheless he frankly admitted that he welcomed it and that it was designed to thwart the judiciary. "I have lost confidence in the majority of the Supreme Court . . .," he snapped. "I believe that they usurp power whenever they dare to undertake to settle questions purely political, in regard to the status of the States, and the manner in which those States are to be held subject to the law-making power." He had no hesitation, he continued, in resorting to repeal when the Court abused its "proper powers" by operating under a statute that happened to be on the record. He insisted that it was his right and duty as a representative "to clip the wings of that court wherever I can, in any attempt to take such flights."[31]

Wilson returned to the subject a week later to defend himself against Democratic charges that he had conspired to sneak through the measure. He denied any collusion with Schenck and claimed that no discussion occurred because no one called for it. But Wilson had no hesitation in admitting the real purpose of the amendment, namely, to withdraw jurisdiction in the cases affected by his amendment. Wilson reflected ironically on the Democrats' concern for the rights of McCardle, an editor who had exhorted his fellow Mississippians to shoot down agents of the federal government, to "shoot them down like dogs, as they are." The Iowan brushed aside protesting Democrats by stigmatizing them as rebel supporters; yet, on a higher plane, Wilson clearly had the better of the debate as to the legality of the Republican action. Woodward of Pennsylvania, for example, charged that Congress had no "right" to withdraw previously granted jurisdiction once a cause was pending. Wilson retorted that Congress could rightfully take away what it had

[30]*Ibid.*, pp. 1881–86 (March 14, 1868).
[31]*Ibid.*, pp. 1883–84.

granted and, following Supreme Court doctrine, he claimed that jurisdiction could be withdrawn anytime prior to judgment. Wilson properly accused his opponents of confusion over the meaning of "right" as opposed to "power." Apparently Woodward found his bearings, for he could only counter that the bill was "indecent" and "a misuse and an abuse" of legislative power.[32]

Wilson incidentally offered an interesting revelation of Republican motivation. He noted the flood of press reports insisting that McCardle's case was to be a vehicle for the Court's majority to declare the Reconstruction Acts unconstitutional. Had the reports only stated that the Court would pass upon the return of the writ and simply decide that McCardle could or could not be lawfully detained by the military authorities, Wilson claimed there would have been no cause for apprehension. But, he complained, "when we were told day by day that the majority of the court had practically made up its judgment, not only to pass upon the sufficiency of the return to the writ, which involves the only question properly before them in the *McCardle* case, but also to do as the court did once before in the Dred Scott case, go outside of the record properly involving the questions really presented for its determination, undertaking to infringe upon the political power of Congress, and declare the laws . . . unconstitutional, it was our duty to intervene by a repeal of the jurisdiction and prevent the threatened calamity falling upon the country."[33] In short, the Republican leader in the repeal drive confessed that his party acted entirely on the basis of talk circulating in the community, talk that had been inspired largely by Democratic politicians and newspapers. The Democrats certainly could thank themselves for the precipitate Republican move. Although the Republicans lacked direct evidence that the Court intended to void the Reconstruction Acts, they acted within

[32]*Ibid.*, pp. 2059–65 (March 21, 1868).

[33]*Ibid.*, p. 2062. McKitrick, *Andrew Johnson and Reconstruction*, pp. 465–66, notes how southern newspapers staked their hopes on the Court as early as 1866. Also see chap. 3, *above*. In late 1867 the idea snowballed, and after the Court assumed jurisdiction in *McCardle*, the hopes became firm convictions. When a newspaper reported the "fact" that at a private gathering, one of the justices (Field) asserted that the Court would void the Reconstruction Acts, Wilson's committee promptly launched an investigation. Aside from the comical overtones (it was a case of mistaken identity), the incident casts light on the Republicans' apprehensiveness. (*Cong. Globe*, 40 Cong., 2 sess., pp. 862–65 [January 30, 1868]; House Judiciary Committee Files, 40A–F13.3, National Archives; Field, *Personal Reminiscences*, pp. 186–217).

a climate of opinion which only accentuated their determination to protect their southern policy. The three weeks' hiatus between the Court's acceptance of jurisdiction in the *McCardle* case and Wilson's amendment, seems to support further a conclusion that rumors, gathering momentum, had prompted Republican fears.

The repeal measure was enrolled on March 13. The full constitutional allotment of ten days, Sundays excepted, passed before Andrew Johnson vetoed the bill. The President's dilatoriness hardly justified the unctuous defense of the Court offered in his veto message of March 25.[34] Justice David Davis, along with other members of the Court, expected Johnson to sign the bill. Apparently Johnson even took his Democratic supporters by surprise. They later admitted no knowledge or forewarning of his intention, and surely the President's known antipathy to judicial power fully warranted the surprise. But Johnson's political posture and need for consistency regarding congressional policy made a veto imperative. Orville Browning, who claimed to have drafted the veto message, nevertheless disparaged the final product as "very much diluted and toned down."[35]

For once, Andrew Johnson's constitutional interpretation did not vary much from the Republican party's. By his silence, he conceded the constitutional question, preferring to twit the Republicans on their reluctance to allow a judicial ruling on the Reconstruction Acts. The withdrawal of jurisdiction, the President taunted, "will be justly held by a large portion of the people as an admission of the unconstitutionality of the act on which its judgment may be forbidden or forestalled." It was in this message that Andrew Johnson, for perhaps the first and only time, discovered the value and desirability of judicial power over congressional legislation. The Republican assault, he warned, "cannot fail to affect most injuriously the

[34]*Cong. Globe,* 40 Cong., 2 sess., p. 2094 (March 25, 1868).

[35]David Davis to Julius Rockwell, April 22, 1868, Davis Papers, Chicago Historical Society. For indications that Johnson's veto surprised the Democrats, see *Cong. Globe,* 40 Cong., 2 sess., p. 2095. Theodore C. Pease and James G. Randall eds., *The Diary of Orville Hickman Browning* (2 vols. Springfield: Illinois State Historical Library, 1933), 2:188–89. Apparently Thomas Ewing had a great deal to do with Johnson's veto. After Ewing learned of the repeal, he urged his close friend, Browning (who was then in the Cabinet), to press for a veto. Ewing also prepared a draft veto message which was used in part *(ibid.)*; Thomas Ewing to Browning, March 18, 1868, cited in Ralph J. Roske, "The Post Civil War Career of Lyman Trumbull" (Ph.D. dissertation, University of Illinois, 1949), p. 88; Maurice G. Baxter, *Orville H. Browning, Lincoln's Friend and Critic* (Bloomington: Indiana University Press, 1957), p. 208.

just equipoise of our system of Government; for it establishes a precedent which, if followed, may eventually sweep away every check on arbitrary and unconstitutional legislation." Then came Johnson's new-found recognition of the status and role of the Court in American government: that institution, he contended, had thus far "been viewed by the people as the true expounder of their Constitution, and in the most violent party conflicts its judgments and decrees have always been sought and deferred to with confidence and respect. In public estimation it combines judicial wisdom and impartiality in a greater degree than any other authority . . .; and any act which may be construed into or mistaken for an attempt to prevent or evade its decisions on a question which affects the liberty of the citizens and agitates the country cannot fail to be attended with unpropitious consequences."[36]

If Browning wrote this message, then he conveniently forgot his own criticism of the Dred Scott decision. It also was no mean feat for him to impose these ideas—that "the people" regarded the Court as the "true expounder" of the Constitution and needed its judgments in the most violent party controversies—on a man who always had contended that "the people" regarded the Court with distrust and suspicion and had sought to restrict the judiciary's most important safeguard, lifetime tenure.

Congress wasted little time in overriding the veto. The Democrats, complaining that they had been unaware of the President's intention, asked for a postponement in order to marshal their arguments. When the Democrats refused to specify a certain date for a vote, they must have aroused Republican suspicions of a delaying strategy in the hope that the Court would decide the issue. Senator Thomas A. Hendricks of Indiana, one of the Democratic leaders, claimed information that the Court would not act until Congress had settled the matter (which was quite true), but this did not make much of an impression on the Republican majority as they agreed to only a one-day postponement.[37] Accustomed to overriding Johnson's vetoes with ease, they seemed anxious to get to the inevitable.

In the Senate, Lyman Trumbull offered the most significant defense of the repeal. He maintained that the Democrats were unduly concerned about the Habeas Corpus Act of February 5, 1867, as the nation had survived quite well since 1789 without any

[36]*Cong. Globe*, 40 Cong., 2 sess., p. 2094 (March 25, 1868).
[37]*Ibid.*, p. 2095.

statute authorizing appeals from the circuit court to the Supreme Court in habeas corpus cases. The original Judiciary Act of 1789, he continued, *authorized the issuing of all such writs to persons deprived of their liberty under authority of the United States.*[38] This explanation is crucial to understanding precisely what did happen to the Court in the McCardle affair, and what it did later. Trumbull concluded that the repealed measure originally had been intended to protect federal officers and other citizens from spurious state prosecutions under laws which operated to subject the freedmen to new forms of bondage, such as the Maryland apprentice system. The Court, Trumbull believed, had misconstrued the proper meaning of the 1867 law and thus had made repeal necessary.

When the debate resumed the next day, the Democratic senators heatedly objected to the procedure and substance of the affair. Senator Hendricks again charged that the Republicans feared a court test on their reconstruction policy, and he also indulged in the hyperbole that over one-half of the American people believed the policy unconstitutional. At the core of Hendricks's efforts, however, was the insistence that there was a proper judicial role to be fulfilled. "Who is prepared to say that the Supreme Court ought not to pass upon the constitutionality of your legislation? It is impossible that it should be otherwise," he challenged. "If it be a court at all, and the case come before it, the Supreme Court must decide what is the law in that case."[39] In short, the Court was the proper constitutional arbiter, and the reconstruction legislation was a proper sphere for judicial activity. Once again, the Democrats indicated that they had traveled a long way from their political heritage.

Senator William M. Stewart of Nevada took exception to the Democratic taunts. Every time the Democrats exalted judicial power for their own ulterior purposes, they raised an automatic Republican response which insisted on narrow limits for the power, again as a matter of immediate interest. Stewart insisted that the Court had no power to interfere with reconstruction or to determine the status of the rebel states. The Court, he argued, had only power to decide cases, but it had "no will, no policy; it must," he insisted, "follow the law-making power of the Government."[40]

The Republicans allowed the opposition to spout its theories of

[38]*Ibid.,* pp. 2096–97.
[39]*Ibid.,* p. 2117 (March 26, 1868).
[40]*Ibid.,* p. 2118.

judicial power and views on constitutional matters as the affair moved to its inevitable conclusion. On March 26, the Senate overrode Johnson's veto by a comfortable margin of 33–9, and the question went to the House on the next day. Here the debate proceeded along the same lines as in the Senate. Representative Wilson, however, more frankly admitted that the repeal would bar the Court from further consideration of the *McCardle* case and cited one of Chase's recent opinions to that effect. Again, the Republicans easily secured the requisite two-thirds majority to overcome the veto.[41]

As the debate concluded, Wilson mentioned that higher considerations than hostility toward the Court motivated the Republican action. If McCardle's case were abandoned, he claimed, the nation would have escaped the danger of another political decision which, in the long run, could only be as harmful to the Court as the Dred Scott case had been. Wilson further maintained that the repeal served the cause of justice besides saving the Court from itself and its alleged friends. The repeal would relieve some of the Court's docket and advance the causes of waiting suitors, causes that had been delayed "by the persistent efforts . . . made to induce the court to enter upon political questions involved in the reconstruction legislation of Congress."[42] Wilson's statements, while they exaggerated the altruism in the Republicans' motives, nevertheless contained a germ of truth and wisdom.

With Chase detained by the impeachment proceedings, the Court did not re-hear the *McCardle* case until the December 1868 term. A year later, in April, 1869, Chase delivered the Court's final decision in *Ex parte McCardle*. The Chief Justice conceded congressional power to alter the Court's appellate jurisdiction; in this case, he admitted, "it is hardly possible to imagine a plainer instance of positive exception." Furthermore, he acknowledged that the repeal exhausted McCardle's case. Like Representative Wilson, Chase cited his own recent opinion in *Ritchie* v. *Insurance Company,* which held that no judgment could be rendered in a suit after repeal of the act under which it was prosecuted.[43]

After the dismissal of *McCardle,* contemporaries such as Orville H. Browning, Gideon Welles, and ex-Justice Benjamin R. Curtis

[41]*Ibid.,* pp. 2119–28.
[42]*Ibid.,* pp. 2165–70 (March 27, 1868).
[43]*Ex parte McCardle,* 7 Wallace (74 U.S.) 506, 514–15 (1869).

lamented that the justices had "caved in" and that Congress had "subdued" the Supreme Court.[44] It is interesting to note, however, that Congress returned with further assaults upon the Court in late 1869 and early 1870. For in those months, there were attempts to withdraw habeas corpus jurisdiction in *all* cases stemming from the Reconstruction Acts, to restrict the Court from deciding "political questions," and finally, to abolish judicial review of congressional acts altogether. What prompted all this? Was not the Court effectively "subdued" to the Republicans' satisfaction after the McCardle affair? Or truly were there no limits to their insatiable determination to crush the Supreme Court?

Chase's concluding remarks in *McCardle,* together with the decision in a similar case of six months later, form the backdrop for the events of 1869–70. Near the end of his *McCardle* opinion, the Chief Justice offered some interesting and significant remarks on the repeal and judicial power: "Counsel [for McCardle] seems to have supposed," he wrote, "if effect be given to the repealing act . . . that the whole appellate power of the court in cases in *habeas corpus* is denied. But this is an error."[45] Chase's words become more meaningful in the light of that other decision, *Ex parte Yerger.*

The essentials of this case are as follows: Edward M. Yerger had been held for trial by a military commission in Mississippi for killing an army officer. Before Congress denied jurisdiction in *McCardle,* the Court could handle habeas corpus pleas either on appeal as a result of a denial in the lower courts or on direct petition for the writ. The congressional act of March, 1868, abrogated only the former on appeals arising under the Reconstruction Acts but left intact the other procedure. Operating along the direct route, the Court accepted jurisdiction of Yerger's petition in October, 1869.[46]

The Court now made it quite clear that it would not allow a total denial of its power over the writ of habeas corpus, and thus leave citizens without possibility of a remedy. There was still plenty of fight left in this supposedly moribund court. In many respects,

---

[44]Pease and Randall, eds., *Diary of Orville Hickman Browning,* 2:91–92. Howard K. Beale, ed., *The Diary of Gideon Welles,* 3 vols. (New York: W. W. Norton, 1960), 3:320. Benjamin R. Curtis, *A Memoir of Benjamin Robbins Curtis,* 2 vols. (Boston: Little, Brown & Co., 1879), 1:421.

[45]*Ex parte McCardle,* 7 Wallace (74 U.S.) 506, 515 (1869).

[46]*Ex parte Yerger,* 8 Wallace (75 U.S.) 85 (1869). Bernard Schwartz, *A Commentary on the Constitution of the United States,* 2 vols. (New York: Macmillan, 1963), 1:380.

Ex parte Yerger represented the Court's most significant challenge to Congress.

Considering that Congress acted so vigorously at the time of the McCardle hearing, one might have expected Republicans to pursue further restrictions with the same degree of intensity and success. But this time only isolated congressmen offered menacing proposals, and these were to prove fruitless. Charles Sumner, Chase's good friend, ally and ardent booster for the chief justiceship, proposed abolishing the Court's appellate jurisdiction in causes commenced by the writ of habeas corpus. Sumner's bill directly challenged Chase's position. Trumbull's Judiciary Committee favorably reported the bill two weeks later, but with an amendment denying the Court any power to act in cases involving "political questions." Trumbull clearly specified that his amendment covered the Reconstruction Acts. On the same day that Sumner submitted his bill, Senator Charles D. Drake of Missouri, a prominent Radical, proposed the outright abolition of judicial review of congressional acts.[47] Thus, in a three-pronged attack, some elements within the Republican party again tried to secure the southern policy from possible judicial destruction. But all of the 1869–70 proposals failed; and it is significant that the failure occurred against the backdrop of a direct challenge by the Supreme Court.

Apparently most senators were satisfied that the Court had no intention of abandoning its basic position on "political questions" as expressed in the Mississippi and Georgia cases. In *Ex parte Yerger*, moreover, Congress was presented with a *fait accompli* such as it had not faced at the time of the *McCardle* appeal. Some senators admitted that there was now no pressing need for any legislation. The Court was about to adjourn, and as military reconstruction was being abandoned, even in Mississippi, there were few challenges to the Reconstruction Acts. Accordingly, the Senate moved in December, 1869, to postpone action, and six months later buried Sumner's original bill along with Trumbull's amendment.[48]

Senator Drake's bill to abolish judicial review received even more brusque treatment. Unlike most of his party colleagues, whose fears concerning the Court centered on the Reconstruction Acts, Drake seemed disturbed by the possible fate of other important congres-

[47]*Cong. Globe,* 41 Cong., 2 sess., p. 3 (December 6, 1869); *ibid.,* p. 45 (December 9, 1869); *ibid.,* p. 2 (December 6, 1869).
[48]*Ibid.,* p. 169 (December 16, 1869).

sional measures, such as the legal tender acts, the cotton tax, and the state bank note tax. For probably the first time since Hale's leveling assault in 1861, Drake came down to the very basics of judicial power. His assault upon the "hoary error" of judicial review followed traditional lines: the power existed only by implication; the Constitution established legislative supremacy; and Congress had to assert the right of final judgment of its own acts or accept a status subordinate to the courts.[49]

Congress chose not to assert its "rights," and the bill never came out of Trumbull's committee. Before it was sent to committee, however, some of Drake's fellow senators passionately defended the Court. The outstanding rebuttal came from a Republican, George F. Edmunds of Vermont. He admitted that the Court sometimes unfortunately tended to interfere in political questions, but Drake's proposal was another matter. Borrowing his text from his Whig predecessors, and perhaps unwittingly from the Democrats of the Reconstruction period, Edmunds confidently declared that history demonstrated the "greatest safeguard of liberty and of private rights, . . . is found, not in the legislative branch of a government, not in the executive branch of a government, but in its fundamental law that secures those private rights, administered by an independent and fearless judiciary. There is the security of liberty; there is the security of progress in society; there is the anchor that holds together the wishes of all good men." Edmunds's defense of judicial review here was a fitting overture to many of his later appearances before the Supreme Court, most notably in the income tax case of 1894 when he invited the Court to submit its wisdom for the judgment of Congress. A Democratic colleague, Saulsbury of Delaware, argued from virtually the same premise—that congressional powers were enumerated, limited, and not absolute—and concluded: "I should have supposed that it was too late in the day . . . to attempt to overturn the settled judgment of the American people and of the legal profession."[50]

The conjunction of the Supreme Court's defense by Edmunds and by Saulsbury—the one a respected and prominent Republican and

[49]*Ibid.*, pp. 86–96 (December 13, 1869).
[50]*Ibid.*, pp. 94–95. For Edmunds's fully developed views on judicial power, see Gerald G. Eggert, "Richard Olney and the Income Tax Cases," *Mississippi Valley Historical Review*, 48 (June, 1961): 33–34. Incidentally, Congress restored the revoked appellate jurisdiction in 1885 (23 Stat. 437). There was no debate in either house at the time.

the other a leader of the states'-rights, conservative Democratic bloc—symbolically prefigured the bipartisan consensus that was to regard judicial power benignly throughout the rest of the century and beyond. As Reconstruction drew to a close, neither of the two major parties again took an antijudiciary posture. Whatever the danger had been to the Court's security, the threat had failed to materialize. Thaddeus Stevens indeed had *his* notions of legislative supremacy. As a recent biographer states, the Court "would have been made truly impotent as far as the legislation on Reconstruction was concerned" had Stevens had his way.[51] But there is the rub: Stevens and his like-minded compatriots found few who shared their preconceptions. This suggests the true picture of the Court-Congress relationship during the period. In the late nineteenth and the early twentieth century, the Supreme Court unquestionably exercised power and commanded prestige as it never had before; yet this development did not mark a sharp break in judicial history. Examination of the Court's whole range of activities and its status during the Reconstruction era demonstrates only a relative and quantitative difference from the activities and status of the later period.

[51]Brodie, *Thaddeus Stevens: Scourge of the South*, p. 323.

6

The Supreme Court and Reconstruction: Judicial Impotence?

Contemporary judgments regarding the Supreme Court in the Reconstruction era illogically both bemoaned Congress' aggressiveness and belittled the Court's courage. Historical interpretations, once again, have differed very little from these century-old notions. Yet, if Congress failed to mount much of a sustained and effective threat against the Supreme Court's independence and power, then what is to be made of the charges of judicial "impotence" and "cowardice?" These, too, it seems, must be discarded in view of what the Court actually did in the "Reconstruction" cases.

The justices who decided such cases as *Ex parte Milligan, Mississippi* v. *Johnson, Georgia* v. *Stanton, Ex parte McCardle, Ex parte Yerger,* and *Texas* v. *White,* were a varied lot. Eight men participated constantly throughout the period: Chief Justice Salmon P. Chase and Associate Justices Samuel Nelson, Robert C. Grier, Nathan Clifford, Noah H. Swayne, Samuel F. Miller, David Davis, and Stephen J. Field.[1] While the last four plus Chase were appointed by Lincoln, the eight as a whole were evenly divided in political affiliation. It was a comparatively youthful group, averaging fifty-nine years when the war ended. Lincoln decidedly favored younger men: Miller, Davis, and Field were under fifty when nominated. Lincoln also gave the Court a new geographical character; all five of his appointees were western-

---

[1]This composite of the Chase Court includes only those who sat in all the relevant cases. Justice James M. Wayne of Georgia died in the summer of 1867. Interestingly enough, he supported the minority position in *Ex parte Milligan,* which conceded congressional power to establish military commissions. Justices William J. Strong of Pennsylvania and Joseph P. Bradley of New Jersey, both Republicans, were appointed by Grant in 1869. The only "Reconstruction" case in which they sat was *Slaughter-House,* and then they were on opposite sides. That decision is discussed below in a different context (see chap. 7).

ers, with two, Miller and Field, coming from the trans-Mississippi country which never before had been represented on the Court. The prewar holdovers, Nelson, Grier, and Clifford, were all from the eastern seaboard. The South, which had dominated the Court for over three decades, was left without representation after Justice James M. Wayne's death in 1867. By 1865, the eight justices had an average tenure of seven years, and only Nelson and Grier remained from the relatively recent Dred Scott fiasco. While five of the eight had previous judicial experience, they ranged from Field's service as Chief Justice of the California Supreme Court to Miller's brief tenure as a justice of the peace and judge of a county court. Most important, Lincoln's appointees had played significant roles in antislavery politics and had loyally supported the war.

Certainly in the sense of supporting the various avowed purposes of the war—the preservation of the union, emancipation, and the protection of liberty—the Supreme Court had to be considered "safe" on all counts. The *Chicago Tribune* seemingly could well afford its smug confidence of the outcome when this court would "sit in the final earthly judgment upon the rebellion and its authors and upon the Government and its upholders."[2]

The Court's decision in *Ex parte Milligan* dispelled some of that Republican confidence while it buoyed Democratic hopes; yet it signified little as far as the Court's future attitude toward the Reconstruction Acts which were still to be enacted. Nevertheless, the sweep of the dicta in Justice Davis's majority opinion partly justified both attitudes. But the majority opinion did not *ipso facto* mean that the Reconstruction Acts were unconstitutional and that the Court would have so ruled.

Like so many others who have lent their names to great efforts in behalf of civil liberty, Lambdin P. Milligan was a dubious character. A major general in one of the Copperhead organizations in Indiana, Milligan was arrested in 1864, then tried, convicted, and sentenced to hang by a military commission for conspiring to overthrow the government, fomenting insurrection, and giving aid and comfort to rebels. In January, 1865, after the military proceedings, a federal grand jury in Indianapolis met and refused to present any bill of indictment against Milligan and his alleged co-conspirators. Milligan thereupon petitioned the federal courts

[2]October 15, 1864.

for a writ of habeas corpus (under authority of the Habeas Corpus Act of 1863), contending that the military commission had no jurisdiction because the civil courts were open and that he improperly had been deprived of his constitutional rights of trial by jury. The Circuit Court, which included Justice Davis, divided on the questions and certified them to the Supreme Court for decision in May, 1865.

During March, 1866, the Court heard arguments from a brilliant array of legal counsel. Major General and Congressman James A. Garfield, former Attorney General Jeremiah S. Black, Joseph E. McDonald, and David Dudley Field, brother of the Justice, appeared for Milligan and contended that the use of military commissions in peaceful areas was a "gross and monstrous usurpation of proper historical practices and constitutional purposes." Attorney General James Speed presented the Government's case, along with Benjamin F. Butler and Henry Stanbery, who appeared at the request of the War Department and the President, respectively. They maintained that Indiana was a war zone, bristling with traitors and that the military commissions were justified under the Constitution's war powers. Stanbery also argued that the Court lacked jurisdiction to grant a writ of habeas corpus.[3] The plaintiff's pleas seemed better prepared, organized, and presented; at any rate, they certainly impressed the Court.

On April 3, 1866, Chief Justice Chase announced that the writ had been granted and that the military commission lacked jurisdiction. Formal opinions, he concluded, would be delivered in December at which time some members of the Court would "state the grounds of their dissent." Until those opinions were read in December, the nation was unaware of how far the Court would go. Even Justice Davis, although selected as the majority's spokesman, was not certain of his complete views until early autumn.[4]

A recent, and wholly favorable, treatment of the majority opinion in *Milligan* acknowledges that the Court's April announcement "occasioned no great outcry."[5] The hostility between President Johnson and Congress was still in an embryonic state and the battle over Reconstruction had not been fully joined; more important,

[3]*Ex parte Milligan*, 4 Wallace (71 U.S.) 2, 9–21, 22–84 (1866).
[4]3 Wallace (70 U.S.) 776 (1866). Also see chap. 4, note 15, *above*.
[5]Willard L. King, *Lincoln's Manager: David Davis* (Cambridge, Mass.: Harvard University Press, 1960), p. 255.

the mere statement that there was no military jurisdiction surely touched sympathetic and responsive chords in the political and legal communities.

During the war, there had been widespread discontent with the government's policy. Congressional antipathy to military arrests and trials, for example, was evident in various provisions of the Habeas Corpus Act of 1863. While the act superficially weakened civil judicial powers by authorizing blanket suspension of habeas corpus, there were safeguards to insure civilian superintendence of military arrests. For example, Section 2 required the Secretaries of State and War to submit lists of detained persons to the federal courts. These persons were to be discharged if a grand jury failed to return an indictment. Furthermore, the act also granted new powers to the federal judges as part of a general Republican policy to extend federal judicial power.[6]

Henry Winter Davis, cousin of Justice Davis, a leading radical spokesman in the Thirty-eighth Congress and co-author of the Wade-Davis Bill, repeatedly had spoken out against military trials of civilians in non-Confederate states. In March, 1865, he secured House passage of a rider to an appropriations bill prohibiting the use of such military commissions. A joint House-Senate conference committee, however, deleted the amendment, although there is evidence that the upper house approved the idea in principle. At any rate, there certainly was not any decided congressional consensus *in favor of* courts martial for civilians in northern states. After the Court delivered its opinions, the leading law journal exulted that the unanimous verdict against presidentially created military commissions had re-established "the ancient liberties of the people."[7]

Justice Davis, who probably had been closer to Lincoln than any man on the Court, had been deeply disturbed by military trials of civilians in non-combat areas throughout the war. He always insisted that only the apparent necessities of war overcame Lincoln's own misgivings over the policy. Davis therefore regarded his opinion as a determined effort to re-affirm traditional values over an expedient wartime policy which he regarded at best as an aberration. With the war over, Davis believed that the relevant questions could be decided "without passion or the admixture of any element not

[6]12 Stat. 755. Also see chap. 8 for the expansion of federal jurisdiction.
[7]*Cong. Globe*, 38 Cong., 2 sess., pp. 1323–29, 1421–22 (March 3, 1865). *American Law Review*, 1 (April 1867): 572–75.

required to form a legal judgment." His opinion and his private correspondence clearly indicate his belief that the time had come for a re-statement and a re-invigoration of traditional constitutional values.[8]

Speaking also for Justices Nelson, Grier, Clifford, and Field, Davis found that the Habeas Corpus Act of 1863 amply covered Milligan's plea for the writ. But the Justice rested most of his argument on English and American constitutional guarantees and traditions, particularly those regarding jury trials and the permissibility of courts martial to try civilians. Milligan's trial by a military commission deprived him, Davis said, of his constitutional right to a trial by a constitutionally endowed court. He admitted that there were occasions when martial law could be properly applied; specifically, during civil war or foreign invasion when the civil courts were closed, it might, Davis admitted, be necessary to substitute military power for civilian authority. But, he added, "martial rule can never exist where the courts are open, and in the proper and unobstructed exercise of their jurisdiction. It is also confined to the locality of actual war." The Indiana courts were open and functioning, and Indiana was not a scene of actual war; therefore, Milligan had been tried illegally and was entitled to be discharged from custody.[9]

Chief Justice Chase, with Wayne, Swayne, and Miller, submitted a "dissenting" opinion which, however, actually concurred in the result. Chase, perhaps more emphatically, insisted that Milligan's plea came under the Act of 1863 and that the military had no right to try him after the civil authorities had refused to hand down an indictment. A totally unnecessary bit of dicta by Davis, however, caused division within the Court—and the later controversy over the decision. Davis contended that Milligan had been unlawfully tried because the military commission was not a court created by Congress as the Constitution dictated, but then, almost gratuitously, he added that Congress lacked the power to establish such courts.[10]

[8]*Ex parte Milligan,* 4 Wallace (71 U.S.) 2, 109; King, *Lincoln's Manager: David Davis,* chap. 20, *passim.*

[9]4 Wallace (71 U.S.) 2, 115–23.

[10]*Ibid.,* 121–22. Davis had no trouble in justifying the dicta. In a letter to his brother-in-law, he said: "The opinion wᵈ have been worth nothing for future time if we had cowardly toadied to the prevalent idea that the legislative Dept[.] of the Govt[.] can override everything. Cowardice of all sorts is mean, but judicial cowardice is the meanest of all" (Davis to Julius Rockwell, February 24, 1867, Davis Papers, Chicago Historical Society). Davis also believed that Chase "wrote for an object."

Chase bluntly rejected this idea: "we think that Congress had power, though not exercised, to authorize the military commission." Chase primarily relied on the concept of war powers and held that they were no more likely to be abused than any other legislative power. The majority dicta, he feared, seemed "calculated, though not intended, to cripple the constitutional powers of the Government, and to augment the public dangers in times of invasion and rebellion."[11]

The *Milligan* decision presents a myriad of technical problems on jurisdiction, the laws of war, the nature of habeas corpus, and military commissions. Later critical opinion has been divided on the merits and reality of the majority position.[12] But the important question here centers on the relevance of *Milligan* to the future course of Reconstruction.

When the opinions were announced in December, 1866, as Congress assembled, there was, as yet, no definite, agreed-upon Republican program for reconstruction and certainly no general intention to institute military commissions and control in the South. Thaddeus Stevens, to be sure, recognized the danger of *Milligan* to such a program; but in January, 1867, it was by no means certain that Stevens would gain party-wide support for his military plans. The break between Johnson and Congress was not yet clear-cut, and there was nothing inevitable about military reconstruction. It is worthwhile to point out that the immediate congressional response to the decision concerned attempts to secure indemnification for military officers who had engaged in such trials and largely neglected the constitutional and legislative issues raised by Davis. Chase, in his opinion, had expressed similar concern regarding the liability of military officers.

Were the majority justices themselves writing with an eye to such a possible program? Davis's grandiloquent phrases on civil liberty suggest that he might have been hinting toward the unconstitutionality of such legislation. But just as easily they can be interpreted as being intended to apply only to the case's subject: courts martial in northern states which were not in the locale of

[11]4 Wallace (71 U.S.) 2, 142. The *American Law Review* criticized the majority dicta but also berated the minority's determination to reply. The journal feared that this tended to weaken the impact of the unanimous ruling on presidential commissions—and it probably did. (1 [April, 1867]:572–75).

[12]See, for example, Charles Fairman, *The Law of Martial Rule* (Chicago: Callaghan & Co., 1930), pp. 106 ff., and King, *Lincoln's Manager: David Davis*, p. 258.

hostilities. Davis had contended that the "laws and usages of war" could never be applied to citizens where the courts were open, but he qualified this by specifying only those "states which have upheld the authority of the government." Moreover, at one point, Davis said that "if there was law to justify this military trial, it is not our province to interfere; if there was not, it is our duty to declare the nullity of the whole proceedings."[13] By "law" he obviously meant constitutional authorization and congressional enactment. Did he therefore mean to suggest that if a specific law, for example, the later Reconstruction Acts, authorized military trials and the imposition of martial law, the courts would not interfere?

Davis's opinion is opaque concerning Reconstruction; both sides could find some comfort in it. Of course there were no Reconstruction Acts when Davis wrote. But a few months later, as the Republican program became defined more clearly, Davis himself offered an interpretation of the relationship—and found none. "Not a word said in the opinion about reconstruction, *& the power is conceded in insurrectionary States.*"[14] The crucial question, then, was whether there was "peace" in the South. Congress, in the Reconstruction Acts, quite simply said "no."

In any event, Davis' statement should weaken the idea that the *Milligan* decision necessarily implied the unconstitutionality of the Reconstruction Acts. Certainly others on the Court viewed the matter differently, but Davis is a key figure. In what may have been the most important test—a supplementary motion following the decision in *Georgia* v. *Stanton*—Davis aligned himself with his fellow Republicans, Chase, Swayne, and Miller. Had his vote gone the other way, the Court probably would have found the laws invalid as a deprivation of property rights. But more of this later.

The first legal challenge to the Reconstruction Acts of March 2 and 25, 1867, came less than a month after passage. In *Mississippi* v. *Johnson*, and then in *Georgia* v. *Stanton*, the Court is alleged to have "evaded" and "dodged" its responsibilities and "retreated behind technicalities" to avoid a direct decision on the constitutionality of the Republican program. Some interpretations have been more charitable, allowing that the Court engaged in a "timely retreat" in the face of a hostile Congress, or acted with great "prudence."

---

[13]4 Wallace (71 U.S.) 2, 121, 119.
[14]Davis to Julius Rockwell, February 24, 1867, Davis Papers, Chicago Historical Society. Emphasis added.

Both interpretations, however, ignore the probability that the Court's decisions may have been entirely proper and, indeed, the only course available.

On April 5, Robert J. Walker, A. H. Garland, and William L. Sharkey, on behalf of Mississippi, sought the Court's permission to file a bill seeking a permanent injunction against Andrew Johnson and General E. O. C. Ord, the district military commander, from executing and enforcing the Reconstruction Acts. A week later, Attorney General Henry Stanbery, who believed that the laws were unconstitutional, urged the justices to deny the request. Stanbery appeared, as he said, with the "approbation, advice and instruction" of the President. Attacking the bill as "scandalous," the Attorney General cautioned the plaintiffs and the Court not to misunderstand the President's role: after Congress had passed the legislation over his veto, "there was but one duty in his estimation, resting upon him, and that was faithfully to carry out and execute these laws." The Court, he insisted, should refuse the bill because it made the President a defendant and sought to restrain his proper duties as chief executive, namely, to execute the laws of Congress. It was this issue alone—and hardly a technicality at that—which the Court examined.[15] Chase's opinion for a unanimous court accepted Stanbery's position almost verbatim. It was at once an important statement on separation of powers, executive duties, and, in particular, the relationship of the Court to the other branches of government. Chase's remarks were not "evasive"; moreover, if a respect for proper jurisdiction means anything at all, then the Court did not "retreat behind technicalities."

The only question to consider, the Chief Justice said, was whether the Court could restrain the President from executing an act "alleged" to be unconstitutional. Chase first broached the problem in elliptical fashion by distinguishing between "ministerial" and "executive" duties. The former were ones in which the officer had no discretion and arose in consequence of a condition imposed by law. Such, for example, was the situation in *Marbury* v. *Madison*, which the Court could have enforced by a writ of mandamus had it had proper jurisdiction in the case. "Executive" duties, however, such as those specified in the Reconstruction Acts, Chase maintained, involved "political" discretion and were not enjoinable.[16]

[15] *The State of Mississippi* v. *Johnson, President*, 4 Wallace (71 U.S.) 475, 478–97 (1867).
[16] *Ibid.*, 498–99.

Chase correctly contended that Mississippi had asked the Court to take a wholly unprecedented action, one which in the words of John Marshall would be "an absurd and excessive extravagance." In addition, he postulated the probable consequences of such an interference. If the injunction were allowed, and the President refused to heed it, the Court had no power to enforce its will. And if he complied, then would this not precipitate a collision between the executive and legislative departments, with a possible result of impeachment? Then what? Would the Court then issue an injunction restraining the Senate from sitting as a court of impeachment? The dialectical synthesis was all too apparent; as Chase stated it: "These questions answer themselves."[17]

Mississippi v. *Johnson* is an absurd case upon which to judge the character and courage of the Court. The petition for such an injunction met opposition from every corner. Justices Field, Grier, Nelson, Clifford, and Wayne, whose objections to the Reconstruction Acts soon became clear, refused to exploit this opportunity. Stanbery's appearance and argument point even more clearly to the weakness of the case. Whatever his opinion of the Reconstruction Acts, he was not in the least prepared to condone an assault upon the independence, integrity, and obligations of his President in order to secure a desirable end. And this, of course, reflects most interestingly upon Andrew Johnson, who certainly had fixed ideas on executive power and independence—ideas which indeed transcended his views of the Reconstruction Acts.

The Court really "dodged" nothing. The bill for an injunction was misconceived and misguided. A positive answer would have been dangerous and suicidal for judicial security; but more than that, it simply would have been destructive of basic ideas and respect for the political workings of the American governmental system.

Almost simultaneously with the Mississippi action, the state of Georgia instituted proceedings to enjoin the operation of the Reconstruction Acts, but this time the suit was filed against Secretary of War Edwin M. Stanton, General of the Army U. S. Grant, and General John Pope, commander of the Third Military District. On the same day that the Court denied the Mississippi bill, it accepted the one for *Georgia* v. *Stanton*. Attorney General Stanbery offered no objection to the policy of the bill. The Mississippi and Georgia

[17] *Ibid.*, 499–501.

cases often are linked together, the contention being that only a technical difference in title allowed the Court to hear the latter. Furthermore, both are considered similar in that the Court supposedly relied on technicalities to avoid a decision on the constitutionality of the Reconstruction Acts. There were, however, significant differences between the two cases.

Once again, in the Georgia case, Johnson had his attorney general oppose the suit. Stanbery insisted that it involved political questions which, following the Court's precedent in *Luther* v. *Borden*, were best left for legislative determination. The Georgia lawyers maintained that Congress had no right to annihilate a state and its government and to deprive its citizens of their political and legal rights.[18]

At the outset of his opinion for the Court, Justice Nelson clearly indicated agreement with Stanbery's arguments distinguishing judicial and political power. Briefly citing American and English precedents, among them *The Cherokee Nation* v. *Georgia* and *Rhode Island* v. *Massachusetts,* Nelson contended that a question submitted to judicial determination "must be . . . appropriate for the exercise of judicial power; the rights in danger . . . must be rights of persons or property, not merely political rights, which do not belong to the jurisdiction of a court, either in law or equity."[19] The real question, then, centered on whether the Court could take judicial cognizance of the issues presented in Georgia's bill. Nelson found it obvious that the state's petition called for a judgment of political questions and rights. Georgia had asked for judicial protection of its rights of sovereignty, political jurisdiction, and corporate existence as a state. "No case of private rights or private property infringed, or in danger of actual or threatened infringement," Nelson said, "is presented by the bill, in a judicial form, for the judgment of the court."[20]

In short, Georgia had asked for protection of political, and not property, rights, a subject unfit for judicial cognizance. The state had averred in the bill that destruction of the state government would deprive Georgia of its title to state property. But Nelson

[18]*State of Georgia* v. *Edwin M. Stanton, Ulysses S. Grant and John Pope,* 6 Wallace (73 U.S.) 50, 53–71 (1868). After the Court dismissed *Mississippi* v. *Johnson,* it allowed Mississippi to alter its bill so as to bring proceedings against Stanton *et al.* See *Mississippi* v. *Stanton, ibid.*
[19]*Ibid.,* 76.
[20]*Ibid.,* 77.

pointed out that the state had failed to request the protection of property as a specific ground of relief. The bill's reference to state property only showed a grievance resulting from the potential destruction of the state. Nelson's conclusion, however, clearly hinted that if Georgia were to present a bill based primarily on the property issue, the Court would consider the substantive issues of the Reconstruction Acts.[21]

The Court seemed to be in nearly unanimous agreement. Chief Justice Chase concurred in dismissing the case for want of jurisdiction, but briefly noted his disagreement with the reasoning.[22] The only possible grounds for the difference lay with the property rights argument. Did this mean that eight of the nine justices were prepared to entertain a new bill and scrutinize the constitutionality of the Reconstruction Acts? Not quite.

Georgia v. *Stanton* and a similar suit presented by Mississippi had been argued in late April and early May of 1867. Nelson's full opinion was not presented until February of the next year. But one week after the final arguments—on May 13, 1867—the Court announced its decision to dismiss both suits. The Mississippi attorneys immediately moved to amend their bill to emphasize the property interest. Here was the crucial moment. An equally divided Court, however, rejected the motion.[23] While the Court's minutes did not record individual votes, it is obvious that Justices Swayne, Miller, and Davis joined Chase, the original dissenter. Nelson and his fellow Democrats, Wayne, Clifford, and Field undoubtedly favored the motion. This division is significant and probably truly indicative of the Court's position on the Reconstruction Acts. Equally important at this time was the absence of Justice Grier. A Pennsylvania Democrat, Grier, along with Field, became the Court's most outspoken opponent of congressional policy. His remarks in the *McCardle* case and his dissent in *Texas* v. *White* leave no doubt about his position. If he had been present at the time of Mississippi's motion, the Court would undoubtedly have had a new case on its hands. But if there were to be a 5–4 decision invalidating the laws, it would have had to come quite soon, for Justice Wayne died the following July. In all

---

[21]*Ibid.*

[22]*Ibid.*, 77–78.

[23]*The Minutes of the Supreme Court,* May 16, 1867; *Docket,* 1866, December Term, National Archives. Also see *Washington Evening Star,* May 17, 1867. Warren, *Supreme Court in United States History,* 3 vols. (Boston: Little, Brown & Co., 1922), 3:186, suggests a similar judicial division.

probability, the Court was divided equally on the constitutional question after the summer of 1867; and this division, perhaps more than any other fact, made the Court unwilling to rule on the issue. Southern lawyers, however, persisted in their efforts to secure a judicial ruling on the Reconstruction Acts. The next attempt, in *Ex parte McCardle*, turned out to be the most sensational and resulted in the most famous clash of legislative and judicial power. It also became, as one commentator has written, "a case more celebrated than understood."[24]

Ex parte McCardle is one of those rare Supreme Court cases, like *Marbury v. Madison* or Dred Scott's, which has had profound political implications in its contemporary setting and persistent relevance to the nature of judicial power in the American system of government. The *McCardle* decision has often been used to clinch the common interpretation that during the Reconstruction era the Court was utterly impotent against the will and excesses of an allegedly Radical-dominated Congress. For longer-range institutional purposes the case has been taken as a key example of the absolute and potentially dangerous power of Congress to limit the exercise of judicial authority.

The familiar rendition of the McCardle affair is simple and blunt. After the Supreme Court accepted jurisdiction in the case in 1868, the so-called radical element in Congress, fearing that the justices would invalidate the Reconstruction Acts, repealed the particular jurisdictional authority. A year later, the Court "ignominiously" abandoned its earlier doctrines and "meekly submitted" to what was "an abominable subterfuge on the part of Congress and a shameful abuse of its powers."[25] The Reconstruction period aside, the incident has been used to demonstrate that Congress' authority

[24]Bernard Schwartz, *A Commentary on the Constitution of the United States*, 2 vols. (New York: Macmillan, 1963), 1:376.

[25]See, for example, the traditional accounts by authors cited in the Bibliographical Essay and elsewhere, such as Dunning, Burgess, Randall, and Coulter. Sever L. Eubank, "The McCardle Case," *Journal of Mississippi History*, 18 (April, 1956):111–27, is standard. The newest account of Reconstruction implies the same idea: Kenneth M. Stampp, *The Era of Reconstruction, 1865–1877* (New York: 1965), p. 146 n. A recent study of Chief Justice Chase is more thorough in its treatment of the Court's Reconstruction activities but, for the most part, accepts the traditional views of judicial quiescence vis-à-vis Congress (David F. Hughes, "Salmon P. Chase: Chief Justice" [Ph.D. dissertation, Princeton University, 1963], pp. 251–60, 331). Warren, *Supreme Court in United States History*, 3:195–219, concentrates on congressional chicanery. The standard constitutional history texts and the Andrew Johnson biographies blend their criticisms of Congress and the Court.

to provide exceptions to appellate jurisdiction is the Court's "Achilles' heel," and that this power constitutes a threat to individual liberties. A doomsday quality permeates the interpretation: "The right of a mere majority of the Congress to put the Supreme Court out of business in habeas corpus cases [as in *Ex parte McCardle*] changes the character of this Government from one of separation of powers to something else. Knock out the Supreme Court and the President and a mere transient majority in the Congress are free to violate the constitutional rights of all of us."[26]

But both the historical and contemporary uses of *McCardle* are quite removed from reality. The actual circumstances and limited nature of the repeal, Chief Justice Chase's opinion for the Court, and ensuing judicial and congressional developments indicate an altogether different picture. A reconsideration of the whole affair challenges the traditional idea of an impotent and quiescent judiciary and suggests, instead, a thrust toward the boldness and vitality which characterized the Court in later years.

McCardle, a Vicksburg, Mississippi, editor, had been arrested and held for trial before a military commission under authority of the Reconstruction Acts for publishing inflammatory and insurrectionary articles. He petitioned the United States Circuit Court

[26]The "Achilles' heel" remark was used by the late Justice Harold H. Burton in "Two Significant Decisions: *Ex parte Milligan* and *Ex parte McCardle*," *American Bar Association Journal*, 41 (February, 1955):176. See also James M. Beck, "The Supreme Court—Today and Tomorrow?" Boston *Bar Bulletin* (May, 1936); and Owen J. Roberts, "Now Is the Time: Fortifying the Supreme Court's Independence," *American Bar Association Journal*, 35 (January, 1949):1–4. The other quotation is taken from Arthur John Keeffe's column, "Practicing Lawyer's Guide to the Current LAW MAGAZINES" .in the *American Bar Association Journal*, 50 (1964):1095. Keeffe has other comments on the case (*ibid.*, pp. 500, 596, 787), and his interest in *McCardle* reflects the A.B.A.'s long-standing desire for a constitutional amendment which would abolish Congress' power to make exceptions or regulations of appellate jurisdiction. See *American Bar Association Journal*,34 (November, 1948): 1072–73; S. J. Resolution 44, 83rd Congress (1954). There have been some notable attempts to restrict appellate jurisdiction in the last number of years, such as the Jenner-Butler Bill in 1957–58, which would have withdrawn jurisdiction in cases involving state subversive legislation and congressional investigatory powers among others. To counter the Jenner-Butler bill, Senator Jacob K. Javits, and others, sponsored a bill to secure the Court's appellate jurisdiction over constitutional issues against legislative interference (S. J. Resolution 57, 86 Cong., 1 sess. [1959]). More recently in the 88th Congress, Representative William M. Tuck proposed abolishing jurisdiction in reapportionment cases (H. R. 11625, 88 Cong., 2 sess. [1964]). In general, see Leonard G. Ratner, "Congressional Power over the Appellate Jurisdiction of the Supreme Court," *University of Pennsylvania Law Review*, 109 (December, 1960):157–202, for a thorough statutory analysis.

for a writ of habeas corpus, contending that according to the *Milligan* doctrine he had been charged and held illegally. The Circuit Court denied McCardle's plea and remanded him to military custody. McCardle appealed the judgment to the Supreme Court under authorization of the Habeas Corpus Act of February 5, 1867.

Ironically, the Republicans had sponsored this act in furtherance of their southern policy. Passed as an amendment to the Judiciary Act of 1789, the law of 1867 provided, "in addition to the authority already conferred," that all federal courts and judges could grant a writ of habeas corpus to any person restrained of liberty in violation of the Constitution or laws of the United States. The law also provided for specific appellate procedure: appeals were allowed to the Circuit Court from *any* inferior court, and from the judgment of the Circuit Court to the Supreme Court. As pointed out by the bill's sponsor, Representative William Lawrence of Ohio, and by Lyman Trumbull in the Senate and before the Court in McCardle's case, this act had been designed primarily to protect freedmen who were being reduced to new forms of slavery because of state vagrancy and apprentice laws; the statute's original purpose was directed at state laws, actions and courts. Trumbull appeared in behalf of the War Department and unsuccessfully urged the Court to dismiss McCardle's plea because the Act of 1867 "expressly" exempted appeals from persons in military custody charged with a military crime.[27]

Early in March, 1868, the Court heard four days of arguments on the merits of McCardle's plea. By the time the justices had assembled for their consultations, Congress had abrogated the relevant sections

[27]14 Stat. 885. For the congressional debates, see *Cong. Globe,* 39 Cong., 1 sess., pp. 4150–51 (July 25, 1866), 4228–30 (July 27, 1866); *ibid.,* 2 sess., pp. 730 (January 25, 1867), 790–91 (January 28, 1867), 899 (January 31, 1867), 935, 945 (February 1, 1867). Trumbull served as special counsel for the government in *McCardle* and his argument denying jurisdiction is summarized in 6 Wallace (73 U.S.) 318, 321–23 (1868); *File Copies of Briefs,* 1868, 6: 28–29, United States Supreme Court Library. The War Department hired Trumbull and Senator Matthew H. Carpenter of Wisconsin as counsel when Attorney-General Stanbery refused to appear. Recent Supreme Court decisions expanding federal courts' power to issue writs of habeas corpus have relied on the 1867 statute. In turn, there have been a number of scholarly criticisms of the Court's historical interpretation. See Lewis Mayers, "The Habeas Corpus Act of 1867: The Supreme Court as Legal Historian," *The University of Chicago Law Review,* 33 (Autumn, 1965): 31–59. For a complete, provocative discussion of habeas corpus legislation and the Reconstruction period, emphasizing the effects of such laws on federalism and national power, see William M. Wiecek, "The Reconstruction of Federal Judicial Power, 1863–1875" (M.A. thesis, University of Wisconsin, 1966), chap. 3.

of the 1867 Habeas Corpus Act, but the President had not yet signed the repeal bill. Despite bitter objections from Justices Grier and Field, the Court decided to stay its hand; it was, as Justice Davis said, "unjudicial to run a race with Congress, and especially as the bill might be signed at any moment by the President." After Johnson's veto was overridden, the Court announced a postponement until the next term and called for new arguments on the jurisdictional question.[28]

Finally, in April, 1869, on the same day that the Court decided *Texas* v. *White*,[29] Chase announced the Court's final opinion in *McCardle*. The Chief Justice conceded Congress' right to make exceptions and regulations to the Court's appellate power; in this case, he admitted, "it is hardly possible to imagine a plainer instance of positive exception." He refused to analyze legislative motivation and seemingly left little doubt as to the effect of the repeal: "Without jurisdiction the Court cannot proceed at all in any cause. Jurisdiction is power to declare the law, and when it ceases to exist, the only function remaining to the court is that of . . . dismissing the cause." Appropriately, Chase cited one of his recent opinions to the effect that no judgment could be rendered in a suit after repeal of the act under which it was prosecuted. With a final bow to legislative power—but not as a close to his opinion—Chase concluded that "judicial duty is not less fitly performed by declining ungranted jurisdiction than in exercising firmly that which the Constitution and the law confer."[30]

Shortly after the withdrawal of jurisdiction by Congress, Orville H. Browning (who helped draft Johnson's veto message on the repeal) learned that Justices Field and Grier had been eager to

[28]Davis to Julius Rockwell, April 22, 1868, Davis Papers, Chicago Historical Society. Chase expressed an idea similar to Davis's: "It would not become the Supreme Court to *hasten* their decision of an appeal for the purpose of getting ahead of the legislation of Congress" (Chase to John D. Van Buren, April 5, 1868, Chase Papers, Historical Society of Pennsylvania). (Stephen J. Field, *Personal Reminiscences of Early Days in California* [Washington: privately printed, 1893], pp. 208–11.) Grier bitterly dissented in open court when the justices decided to postpone the case. Field concurred in Grier's remarks.

[29]7 Wallace (74 U.S.) 700 (1869).

[30]*Ibid.*, 506, 514–15 (1869). See Chase's earlier opinion on repealed jurisdiction: *Insurance Company* v. *Ritchie,* 5 Wallace (72 U.S.) 541, 544–45 (1867). When the *McCardle* case was postponed in 1868, Chase privately expressed some doubt as to whether Congress could oust an appeal already taken and perfected (Chase to John D. Van Buren, April 5, 1868, Chase Papers, Historical Society of Pennsylvania).

proceed in the case before Congress acted but had been overruled by the other justices who "did not wish to run a race with Congress" —precisely the same idea that Chase and Davis were expressing in private letters. Browning went on to write in his diary that the "exhibition of cowardice on the part of the Court, and their readiness to surrender the inalienable rights of the citizens to the usurpation and tyranny of Congress is among the alarming symptoms of the times." Gideon Welles, in the "privacy" of his diary, mourned that "the Judges of the Supreme Court have caved in, fallen through, failed, in the McCardle case." And, finally, ex-Justice Benjamin R. Curtis, in an oft-quoted letter, resignedly noted "that the legislative power, . . . with the acquiescence of the country, conquered one President, and subdued the Supreme Court."[31]

Historians almost unanimously have followed the tenor of these criticisms. Most writers berate Congress for having resorted to such chicanery; then, ignoring the logical contradiction, they cite the above remarks to show the weakness and cowardice of the justices. But in view of subsequent events, such conclusions by contemporaries and historians alike might profitably be reconsidered.

To understand properly the whole story and meaning of the *McCardle* case, we must begin with Chase's closing remarks in his 1869 opinion and then turn to another Supreme Court decision announced some six months after the McCardle denouement. In a final, rarely quoted paragraph in *McCardle,* Chase directed a bit of advice toward McCardle's attorneys, and perhaps as well toward Congress: "Counsel seems to have supposed, if effect be given to the repealing act . . . that the whole appellate power of the court in cases in *habeas corpus* is denied. But this is an error." The repealing measure, he concluded, excepted only appeals emanating from the Act of February 5, 1867.[32] Chase's words assume more relevance when we again examine the decision in *Ex parte Yerger.*

Like the McCardle case, Yerger's case also arose under the Reconstruction Acts. A civilian, Edward M. Yerger petitioned for his freedom from an army prison in Mississippi under a writ of habeas corpus—and the Court accepted jurisdiction. It is remarkable that

[31]Theodore C. Pease and James G. Randall, eds., *The Diary of Orville Hickman Browning,* 2 vols. (Springfield: Illinois State Historical Library, 1933), 2:91–92; Howard K. Beale, ed., *The Diary of Gideon Welles,* 3 vols. (New York: W. W. Norton, 1960), 3:320; Benjamin R. Curtis, *A Memoir of Benjamin Robbins Curtis,* 2 vols. (Boston: Little, Brown & Co., 1879), 1:421.
[32]7 Wallace (74 U.S.) 506, 515 (1869).

so many accounts of Reconstruction and constitutional history ignore this case.[33] To be unmindful of it, of course, allows for a convenient exploitation of *Ex parte McCardle* as a focal point of conceptualization to "prove" how Congress intimidated the Court, and the latter submitted.

Yerger had been arrested and detained for trial by a military commission in Mississippi for killing an army officer. He thereupon applied to the United States Circuit Court for the Southern District of Mississippi for a writ of habeas corpus, charging that proceedings before a military commission were unlawful. The Circuit Court, however, declared Yerger's imprisonment to be lawful and dismissed the plea.[34] Yerger subsequently appealed to the Supreme Court for a writ of certiorari to review the Circuit Court proceedings and for a writ of habeas corpus.

Before the high court, Yerger's distinguished counsel, Philip Phillips and James M. Carlisle, and his brother, William Yerger, took their cue from Chase's hint in *McCardle*. They argued that, as an amendment to the original Judiciary Act of 1789, the Habeas Corpus Act of 1867 had been intended to augment the Court's powers to hear habeas corpus cases. When Congress repealed the latter a year later, it merely negated the increased jurisdiction

---

[33] 8 Wallace (75 U.S.) 85 (1869). The failure of Reconstruction historians to take note of the *Yerger* case is curious, particularly because Warren, *Supreme Court in United States History*, 3:213, mentions the case, albeit briefly. Warren's work, along with Dunning's, is a staple item for Reconstruction historians anxious to illustrate congressional aggressiveness or judicial weakness. Charles Fairman, *Mr. Justice Miller and the Supreme Court, 1862–1890* (Cambridge, Mass.: Harvard University Press, 1939), pp. 142–44, and Bernard Schwartz, *A Commentary on the Constitution*, 1:375–77, are rare exceptions in their treatment of *McCardle* and *Yerger*. E. Merton Coulter, *The South during Reconstruction* (Baton Rouge: Louisiana State University Press, 1947), p. 122, briefly mentions *Yerger* but incorrectly states that the "judges were relieved of the uncomfortable duty of making a decision." Sever Landon Eubank, "The Yerger Case: A Side Light of Reconstruction" (M.A. thesis, Colorado College, 1950), is useful only for the local background of the case.

[34] Judge Robert A. Hill's circuit court opinion is in *Transcript of Records,* December Term, 1868, 6:19–22, United States Supreme Court Library. A copy of the charges and specifications against Yerger are in the Chase Papers, Legal File, Historical Society of Pennsylvania. In a letter to his good friend, Judge Hill, Chase seemed to prefer that Hill deny Yerger's application so that an appeal could be taken to the Supreme Court. The Chief Justice apparently was anxious to test his own views on appellate jurisdiction under the Act of 1789 (Chase to Hill, June 22, 1869, Chase Papers, Historical Society of Pennsylvania). Chase made similar remarks to Justices Nelson and Clifford on the same day (Chase to Clifford, June 22, 1869, *ibid.*).

without disturbing the original grant of authority. More ingeniously, Phillips and Carlisle contended that if the 1867 law repealed the pertinent section of the 1789 act, while the 1868 law repealed that of 1867, then the 1789 act automatically was renewed because a repeal of a repealing act revived the original law.[35]

Speaking for a unanimous court, Chief Justice Chase eagerly accepted the plaintiff's argument and affirmed the Court's jurisdiction to issue the writ of habeas corpus. Aside from the verdict, which in itself testified strongly to the Court's determination and independent will, Chase's opinion made it emphatically clear that the Court would not tolerate any interference with its proper constitutional functions. "It would have been, indeed, a remarkable anomaly," Chase wrote, "if this court, ordained by the Constitution for the exercise, in the United States, of the most important powers in civil cases of all the highest courts of England, had been denied, under a constitution which absolutely prohibits the suspension of the writ, except under extraordinary exigencies, that power in cases of alleged unlawful restraint, which the Habeas Corpus Act of Charles II expressly declares those courts to possess."[36]

Chase then went on to balance delicately a liberal interpretation of the Court's habeas corpus powers with a narrow construction of the 1867 statute and its subsequent repeal. Basically, Chase believed that the constitutional provision on the writ of habeas corpus necessarily implied judicial action, and accordingly, Congress had implemented the constitutional sanction with positive legislation. Section 14 of the Judiciary Act of 1789 provided that federal courts had the power to issue "writs of *scire facias, habeas corpus,* and all other writs, not specially provided by statute, which may be necessary for the exercise of their respective jurisdictions, and agreeable

[35] 8 Wallace (75 U.S.) 85, 89–92, 94 (1869). *File Copies of Briefs,* December Term, 1869, 1:2 ff., United States Supreme Court Library. Copies of Chase's orders granting a hearing on the writ and the Court's jurisdiction are in the Chase Papers, Legal File, Historical Society of Pennsylvania.

[36] 8 Wallace (75 U.S.) 96, 102 (1869). Gideon Welles's *Diary,* upon which historians have been excessively reliant, might be cited again in order to demonstrate the origins of historical interpretation: "By trick, imposition, and breach of courtesy an act was slipped through both houses repealing the laws of 1867 and 1789, the effect of which is to take from the Supreme Court certain powers, and which is designed to prevent a decision in the McCardle case" (Beale, ed., *Diary of Gideon Welles,* 3:314). The repeal was neither a "trick" nor an "imposition." The Republicans had the votes and had no need for such tactics. Moreover, Welles must have had a news source in that 1868 version of the Ministry of Misinformation, for there was no repeal of the 1789 law.

to the principles and usages of law." Further provision was made that either Supreme Court justices or district court judges could have "the power to grant writs of *habeas corpus* for the purpose of an inquiry into the cause of commitment; provided that writs of *habeas corpus* shall in no case extend to prisoners in jail, unless they are in custody, under, or by color of the authority of the United States, or are committed for trial before some court of the same, or are necessary to be brought into court to testify." Incidentally, no review as of right to the Supreme Court was available, but in 1807, John Marshall's court construed the section to allow normal appellate jurisdiction.[37]

In *Yerger*, Chase believed that the constitutional and statutory intentions regarding habeas corpus were to guarantee that "every citizen may be protected by judicial action from unlawful imprisonment." Moreover, the "general spirit and genius" of American institutions had tended to widen and enlarge habeas corpus jurisdiction through the years. Indeed, Chase warned, the denial of jurisdiction in such cases would "greatly weaken the efficacy of the writ, deprive the citizen in many cases of its benefits, and seriously hinder the establishment of that uniformity in deciding upon questions of personal rights which can only be attained through appellate jurisidiction."

Turning to the repealing act of 1868, Chase noted the specific language which affected only appeals authorized by the Act of February 5, 1867. It did nothing, he said, to "touch the appellate jurisdiction conferred by the Constitution, or to except from it any cases not excepted by the act of 1789." He rejected a current argument that the 1867 statute by implication repealed the relevant section of the 1789 law. "Repeals by implication are not favored"; moreover, Chase tartly concluded, "addition is not substitution."[38]

The *McCardle* and *Yerger* opinions are filled with complicated jurisdictional and habeas corpus questions; to be sure, Chase may have overstated the constitutional basis of habeas corpus jurisdiction. In *Yerger*, too, subtle behind-the-scenes political maneuverings between the Grant Administration and Mississippi state authorities form a large part of the story.[39] But one important conclusion

[37]8 Wallace (75 U.S.) 85, 95–96; 1 Stat. 81 (1789); *Ex parte Bollman* and *Ex parte Swartout*, 4 Cranch (8 U.S.) 75, 100 (1807); Mayers, in *University of Chicago Law Review*, 33:41, n. 43.
[38]8 Wallace (75 U.S.) 85, 102–6 (1869).
[39]Fairman, *Mr. Justice Miller*, pp. 142–44.

stands out: the Court's full position in *McCardle,* and its later behavior in the *Yerger* case, are clearly inconsistent with the usual
charges of judicial impotence and cowardice. When the Court
postponed action in the *McCardle* case after the repeal measure,
Jeremiah S. Black, one of the plaintiff's attorneys, bitterly complained that "the court stood still to be ravished and did not even
hallo while the thing was being done." Former Justice Curtis
bitterly conplained that Congress had "subdued" the Court.[40] But
the Court did "hallo" and was anything but "subdued"; indeed, in
the light of prevailing political passions, the Court's counter-response
in the two cases indicates the quintessence of judicial independence
and courage, besides being a clever bit of judicial strategy. All this
should alter the general picture of a moribund and intimidated
Supreme Court during the Reconstruction era. And whatever merit
there may be to changing the exceptions and regulations clause
regarding appellate jurisdiction, the narrow use of *McCardle* as an
example and a prophecy simply does not fit the historical record.[41]

In *Texas* v. *White* the Court had one other opportunity to express
its views on Republican reconstruction policy.[42] Here a majority of
the Court affirmed the basic premises of the mainstream of Republican opinion: that the seceded states and their people were out of
their proper relation to the Union; that their reconstruction constituted a political question; and that it therefore had to be resolved
by the legislative, and not the judicial, branch of the national
government.

In an original suit, Texas filed a bill in equity in the Supreme
Court against citizens of other states, seeking to enjoin payment of
bonds originally issued by the national government to Texas as part
of a border dispute settlement. Part of this issue remained in the
state treasury when the Civil War erupted and the Confederate
state legislature thereupon authorized their disposition and sale to
defray costs of the war. The new state authorities then attempted
to recover the bonds following the war.

[40]Jeremiah S. Black to Howell Cobb, April, 1868, Ulrich B. Phillips, ed., *The
Correspondence of Robert Toombs, Alexander H. Stephens, and Howell Cobb,* American
Historical Association, *Annual Report, 1911,* 2 (Washington, 1913): 694; Curtis,
Memoir of Benjamin Robbins Curtis, 1:421.

[41]*United States* v. *Klein,* 13 Wallace (80 U.S.) 128 (1872) is worth noting as
another example of the Chase Court's determination to resist congressional abuses
of the power to make exceptions in appellate jurisdiction. It is discussed in chap.
7, *below.*

[42]7 Wallace (74 U.S.) 700 (1869).

Speaking for the majority, Chief Justice Chase devoted fifteen pages of a nineteen-page opinion to the jurisdictional question—that is, was Texas one of the United States and therefore entitled to bring suit in the federal courts? Chase first set forth various definitions of a "state" as used in the Constitution. Essentially, it was both a geographic entity and a "political community of free citizens, occupying a territory of defined boundaries, and organized under a government sanctioned and limited by a written constitution, and established by the consent of the governed." After reviewing the process of secession and the actions of the state Confederate government, Chase discussed the state's relation to the Union. The United States, he contended, was not an "artificial and arbitrary relation"; both the Articles of Confederation and the Constitution comprehended the idea of "an indestructible Union, composed of indestructible States." Texas' secession, and all acts committed under the Confederate government, including the sale of bonds, therefore were void and of no effect, and Texas continued to be a state of the Union. This conclusion, Chase argued, was "not in conflict with any act or declaration of any department of the national government, but entirely in accordance with the whole series of such acts and declarations [since 1861]."[43]

While Texas' obligations as a member of the Union continued, the relations of the state Confederate government to the Union obviously had changed. The Texas government and the state's citizens refused to recognize their obligations to the Union; therefore, Chase noted, during the war, "the rights of the State as a member and of her people as citizens of the Union, were suspended." And this, he continued, imposed new responsibilities upon the national government, namely, to re-establish the disrupted relations. He found clear constitutional authority for this duty in the national government's obligation to guarantee a republican form of government to each state.[44]

The Chief Justice then confirmed the underlying rationale of congressional reconstruction. Quoting Taney's *Luther* v. *Borden* opinion, Chase acknowledged that the "power to carry into effect the clause of guaranty is primarily a legislative power and resides in Congress." There was nothing in the present case which required the Court to pronounce judgment on the reconstruction laws; yet

[43]*Ibid.*, 720–21, 725–26.
[44]*Ibid.*, 727–30.

he found in them additional support for his contention that the state still existed, as the acts implied recognition of existing governments, albeit subject to military commanders and the paramount authority of Congress. Chase refused to discuss the constitutionality of the military program and congressional power; and properly so, for there was no such challenge in the case.[45]

Justice Grier dissented from every aspect of Chase's opinion. Texas, he argued, was not a state, this being a question not of theory but of "political fact." Eschewing "legal fiction," Grier contended that events of the previous eight years made it obvious that Texas was not a state. Secession, he said, was a sovereign act of a sovereign state and only trial "by battle" made this "illegal"; in the interim, however, Texas clearly was out of the Union. Basing his definition of a "state" primarily upon the fact of congressional representation, he cited this as further evidence that Texas was not a member of the Union following the war. Two Republican members of the Court, Swayne and Miller, joined the Democrat Grier, while agreeing with Chase that Texas was entitled to recover the sold bonds.[46]

Did Chase and the majority seek to appease Congress and the Republican party? Did they allow the reconstruction program to stand by default? Professor McKitrick has demonstrated that there was nothing new in Chase's thinking in *Texas* v. *White;* his opinion confirmed ideas he had advanced publicly following the war. Furthermore, his views on Texas' standing in the Union coincided with the moderate and dominant Republican view and not with the more extreme ideas of Thaddeus Stevens.[47] Perhaps it is significant to note the intramural division among the Court's Republicans. Miller and Swayne, who probably were most sympathetic to the party's program (Swayne indeed had close ties with the Radicals), disagreed with the Chief Justice. Incidentally, Democrats Nelson, Clifford, and Field, who in other cases clearly indicated a willingness to challenge Congress, joined in Chase's opinion.

Texas v. *White* is perfectly in accord with the ideas expressed in *Georgia* v. *Stanton* and with the Supreme Court's traditional view that it would not interfere in "political questions." Of course, this

[45]*Ibid.*, 730–32. A few years later, the Court said in dictum that congressional power to declare war carried with it the power to remedy the evils which had given rise to war (*Raymond* v. *Thomas*, 91 U.S. 712 [1876]).

[46]*Texas* v. *White,* 4 Wallace (74 U.S.) 700, 737–41.

[47]Eric L. McKitrick, *Andrew Johnson and Reconstruction* (Chicago: University of Chicago Press, 1960), pp. 115–17.

doctrine sometimes becomes a convenient rationalization for the Court to avoid judgment. But most often, it mirrors the Court's realistic recognition of the limitations of its powers and, perhaps, a genuine cognizance of majority rule and the way in which republican government should operate.[48] Furthermore, as McKitrick has well said, "Reconstruction was hardly one of those Gordian knots that could be cut by a clean judicial blade."

Did a majority of the Supreme Court justices believe the Reconstruction Acts unconstitutional, and were they prepared to rule against them? The usual assumption is that the Court opposed the congressional program and could have ended the whole sordid business if it had not been so wary of reprisal. *Post hoc ergo propter hoc:* the idea is tenuous, and the evidence points to a contrary conclusion.

The starting point still is *Ex parte Milligan*. Francis P. Blair, Jr., the Democrats' 1868 Vice-Presidential candidate claimed that *Milligan* negated the "vital principle" of the Reconstruction Acts. One historian has stated flatly that the *Milligan* doctrine made the Acts "palpably unconstitutional."[49] But *Milligan* involved the use of military commissions in northern states which were not scenes of military hostilities. Whatever implication can be drawn from Justice Davis's sweeping dicta in his opinion, he himself was bewildered by contemporary arguments that *Milligan* automatically nullified the Republican program. He noted that there was "not a word said in the opinion about reconstruction, & the power is conceded in insurrectionary States." Was the postwar South still in a state of insurrection? Congress, at least, thought so; and Justice Davis himself silently acquiesced in *Texas* v. *White*.

Davis certainly had his doubts about the merits of the congressional legislation and the basic ideas motivating the Republican party. But this is quite different from assuming that he believed, and was prepared to declare, the Reconstruction Acts unconstitutional. If he did, then he neglected a perfect opportunity to act in the aftermath of *Georgia* v. *Stanton*. Had he joined the Court's Democrats in

[48]Charles G. Post, Jr., *The Supreme Court and Political Questions* (Baltimore: Johns Hopkins University Press, 1936), *passim. Cf.* Justice Douglas's concurrence in *Baker* v. *Carr*, 369 U.S. 186, 245–46, n. 3 (1962).

[49]Charles H. Coleman, *The Election of 1868* (New York: Columbia University Press, 1933), p. 267; Robert G. McCloskey, *The American Supreme Court* (Chicago: University of Chicago Press, 1960), p. 111.

accepting a new bill based on an alleged deprivation of property rights, then it might be fair to state that the Court would have declared the acts invalid. But the point is that he did not. In this instance, physical and not intellectual or spiritual circumstances dictated the Court's action, or lack of it. Grier, an obvious opponent of the laws, was absent when the vote was taken, thus creating a four-to-four division. Shortly afterward, Justice Wayne died, apparently leaving the situation the same. The Court wisely chose not to act with an equally divided bench.

Nor does the evidence indicate that the justices were prepared to decide the constitutional issue in *Ex parte McCardle.* In the 1890's, William McCardle himself stated that six of the nine justices, including Chase, had decided to reverse his conviction.[50] McCardle may or may not have been a scoundrel; in any event, he could not count: there were only eight men on the Court at the time. In all probability, however, he was correct in his estimate of what the Court would have done in his case. Indeed, Chase admitted to the Circuit Court judge who first heard the plea that "had the merits of the McCardle case been decided the Court would probably have held that his imprisonment for trial before a military commission was illegal."[51] But in order to free McCardle, the Court did not have to void the Reconstruction Acts. It would have been perfectly plausible, and apparently acceptable to the Republican congressmen, for the justices to have granted the writ of habeas corpus under authority of the Act of 1867. Without that statute, they still could have freed McCardle had his attorney argued differently, as did Yerger's, and without invalidating the whole southern program.

The Supreme Court does three things with regard to legislative

[50]See Arthur John Keeffe's column in the *American Bar Association Journal,* 50 (November, 1964): 1093.

[51]Chase to Robert A. Hill, May 1, 1869, Chase Papers, Library of Congress. Chase's correspondence in 1868 is full of innuendos regarding the constitutionality of the congressional program, but he never flatly committed himself. It must be remembered that Chase was eager for the Democratic presidential nomination. In letters to leading party figures, he suggested that the laws were "unwise" or "unnecessary," but he refused to endorse a party declaration denouncing the program as unconstitutional. Furthermore, he carefully distinguished between the military commissions, on the one hand, and the state governments temporarily established by the Reconstruction Acts, on the other. These acts probably were "unwise" and "inconsistent with the true principles of civil liberty"; yet he refused to concede that the Court would find them illegal. See, for example, Chase to Richard C. Parsons, July 3, 1868, Chase Papers, Cincinnati Historical Society.

policy: it legitimates, it invalidates, or it does nothing.[52] The Reconstruction Court exercised all the options. To some extent, as in the Mississippi, Georgia, and Texas cases, it legitimated the congressional program by indirection. Later, in the *Slaughter-House* and various Negro rights cases, it invalidated and neutralized some aspects. But with regard to the basic constitutional issue surrounding the Reconstruction Acts, it did neither. And this was not for want of courage—*Ex parte Milligan,* the determination to accept a new bill in *Mississippi* v. *Stanton,* which failed only by a freak circumstance, and *Ex parte Yerger* offer ample testimony to the Court's flintiness. Probably an equally divided bench dictated the wisdom of refusing to resolve the constitutional question either way by default. This illustrates Justice Brandeis's aphorism that "the most important thing we do is not doing." For the Court to have voided *or* sustained the Reconstruction Acts by a tie division based on party affiliation would have accomplished little except to aggravate political tensions and weaken judicial authority.

For those who prefer the authoritative testimony of the contemporary "insider," there is one last item. Justice Field, of course, was not a disinterested or a dispassionate observer of events. Undoubtedly, he believed the Reconstruction Acts unconstitutional. He was a favorite target for Republican scorn and invective, being considered an ingrate to the party which had placed him in high position. His ambitions for a Democratic presidential nomination sharpened his disapproval of the Republican program. When he prepared his memoirs in later years, long after the passions of Reconstruction had subsided, and there were none of his Chase Court colleagues left to contradict or refute him, he included a lengthy account of those times. He recalled the attacks and threats made against the Court, but concluded that they had no basis in fact: "It came to be generally believed," Field wrote, "that it was the purpose of the Court, if an opportunity offered, to declare invalid most of the legislation relating to the Southern States which had been enacted during the war and immediately afterwards. Nothing could have been more unjust and unfounded."[53] Agreed.

[52]Alexander M. Bickel, *The Least Dangerous Branch: The Supreme Court at the Bar of Politics* (Indianapolis: Bobbs-Merrill, 1962), p. 69.

[53]Field, *Personal Reminiscences,* p. 191.

7

The Expansion of Power: Judicial Activism

The historical awareness of the Supreme Court's work at any time is dominated by the dramatic issues decided by the Court, ones that are politically controversial or important. And so, for the postwar decade, attention has focused on the so-called Reconstruction cases as representative of the Court's work and hence as symbolic of its lack of influence. Yet even the most cursory examination of the Court's more than fifteen volumes of reports in this period reveals the minuscule proportion of effort devoted to "Reconstruction" issues as compared to the usual broad range of judicial inquiries. The excessive concentration on problems of southern policy, of course, only tends to distort further the reality of the Supreme Court's status during the period.

Despite its willingness to tolerate congressional determination of the burning political issue of the day, the Court still functioned and, what is more, determined policy in a large number of public questions. For example, it is in this period that the Court increasingly employed its distinctive power to declare laws of Congress unconstitutional. On ten occasions the justices voided congressional acts—a statistic which takes on more meaning when compared with only two judicial vetoes in the previous seventy-six years.[1] Equally

[1] The relevant cases are *Gordon* v. *United States*, 2 Wallace (69 U.S.) 561 (1865); *Ex parte Garland*, 4 Wallace (71 U.S.) 333 (1867); *Reichart* v. *Felps*, 6 Wallace (73 U.S.) 160 (1868); *The "Alicia,"* 7 Wallace (74 U.S.) 571 (1869); *Hepburn* v. *Griswold*, 8 Wallace (75 U.S.) 603 (1870); *United States* v. *Dewitt*, 9 Wallace (76 U.S.) 41 (1870); *The Justices* v. *Murray*, 9 Wallace (76 U.S.) 274 (1870); *Collector* v. *Day*, 11 Wallace (78 U.S.) 113 (1871); *United States* v. *Klein*, 13 Wallace (30 U.S.) 128 (1872); *United States* v. *Railroad Company*, 17 Wallace (84 U.S.) 322 (1873). There is some difference of opinion whether all of these cases should be included in the category of judicial review. I have followed the compilation of the Law Division of the Library of Congress. See Wilfred C. Gilbert, *Provisions of Federal Law Held*

revealing of the judicial activity were the varied cases involving the Court's traditional function of adjudicating controversies involving the mechanics of the federal system and, in particular, national and state powers.[2] The historical preoccupation with the politics of Reconstruction has obscured the other interests and activities of the Chase Court. Yet its work and efforts, in large part, foreshadowed the well-known activism and interventionism of its successors.

Many of the Chase Court's decisions invalidating congressional laws involved prosaic, undramatic, and oftentimes relatively narrow issues. Yet, the very assertion of the power, and the accretive force of doctrine, hold great significance. In quantity and, on occasion, in substance, the justices of the postwar decade far surpassed their predecessors in the use of judicial review. But in addition, the Court here took a long step in asserting its crucial role in determining the legitimacy of policy.

Prior to 1865 the Supreme Court had voided only two federal statutes. First, in *Marbury* v. *Madison*, John Marshall and his colleagues held that Congress' grant of original jurisdiction to issue writs of mandamus violated the severe constitutional limitations of the Court's original jurisdiction. Five decades later the Taney Court ruled the Missouri Compromise unconstitutional in the Dred Scott case. Neither decision provided much of a showcase for the doctrine of judicial review. Marshall's statutory construction was somewhat dubious and strained, while Taney's opinion in 1857 invalidated a repealed law. Both decisions generated widespread opposition because of their obvious political cast and bold assumptions of judicial power. But however tenuously established, there was a general acknowledgment of the Court's unique function.

During the nine years in which Chase presided, the judicial review cases ranged from long-forgotten, narrow, and unspectacular jurisdictional issues to the emotion-laden question of legal tender. The rationale for the use of a judicial veto at times was perfunctory; but with legal tender, for example, the Court offered one of its historically most extreme and involved justifications for judicial intervention. The cases divide between those issues affecting the

Unconstitutional by the Supreme Court of the United States (Washington: Government Printing Office, 1935).

[2]John R. Schmidhauser, *The Supreme Court as Final Arbiter in Federal-State Relations, 1789–1957* (Chapel Hill: University of North Carolina Press, 1958), pp. 80–96, is a useful survey. I disagree, however, with the conclusions.

Court's own powers and those which restricted substantive congressional authority. The former, of course, had little effect on Congress' policy-making capacity. They nonetheless signified the Court's insistence on maintaining constitutional limitations on its own functional capacities, thereby preserving its independence.

In *Gordon* v. *United States,* the Supreme Court refused to accept jurisdiction in an appeal from a decision of the Court of Claims. The latter had rejected Gordon's petition for allowance of supplemental damages and interest on a claim that dated back to military operations against Florida Indians in 1813. Gordon tried to take his case to the Supreme Court under the 1863 Court of Claims Act, but the Court refused to hear the appeal.[3] Chief Justice Chase noted that Section 14 of the 1863 law permitted the Secretary of the Treasury to revise the judgment of the Court of Claims, and he argued that this destroyed its status as a constitutionally endowed court from which appeals could be taken. He reasoned that the judgment of a federal court must be final, binding, and not subject to revision by other departments if that court were to possess "the judicial power of the United States" as specified in Article III of the Constitution. Because the executive revisory power of Section 14 violated its concept of the separation of powers principle, the Supreme Court would not take appeals from the Court of Claims.

In retrospect, the *Gordon* case turned out to be a lever to enhance judicial power. A year afterward, Senator Trumbull successfully sponsored a repeal of the obnoxious section. Trumbull claimed that Congress in 1863 had intended the Court to hear such appeals. The clause dealing with executive review was a floor amendment which, Trumbull believed, did not affect the appellate provisions. He

[3] 2 Wallace (69 U.S.) 561 (1865). The 1863 act followed Lincoln's recommendation (December 3, 1861) that the Supreme Court be given appellate power in such cases (Roy P. Basler, ed., *The Collected Works of Abraham Lincoln,* 9 vols. (New Brunswick: Rutgers University Press, 1953–55), 5:44. Chase's opinion capsulized a lengthy opinion prepared by Taney but not published until 1886. See 117 U.S. 697. There also is a copy in Chase's Legal File. Chase's opinion was never printed in the official reports. The Reporter's synopsis in 2 Wallace is inaccurate. Cf. *United States* v. *Jones,* 119 U.S. 477 (1886). Chase's opinion, allegedly secured from the Clerk, does appear in the unofficial Lawyers' Edition Reports, 17 L. Ed. 921. The Gordon claim was finally determined on its merits in 1868 in an opinion remarkable for Justice Grier's sarcastic criticism of both the rapacity of the claimant and the complacence of the Attorney-General and the Secretary of the Treasury (7 Wallace [74 U.S.] 188 [1868]). Also see William M. Wiecek, "The Reconstruction of Federal Judicial Power: 1863–1875" (M.A. thesis, University of Wisconsin, 1966), chap. 5.

nevertheless expressed his willingness to satisfy the Court, with the understanding that it would hear appeals from the Court of Claims. He said he wished to remove the executive review section so as to make the judgment "what the law intended it to be, a final judgment." One step backward led to two forward: in 1872 the Court happily noted the repeal and asserted its right to a proper and full jurisdiction on appeals from the Court of Claims—and now without the encumbrance of executive review.[4]

The Supreme Court manifested further willingness to safeguard its jurisdictional authority in a series of rebel claims cases. In *United States* v. *Padelford*, early in 1870, the Court ruled that the loyalty oath taken under the amnesty proclamation of 1863 sufficiently absolved one as a rebel.[5] Shortly afterward, Congress responded with an appropriation act provision to the effect that no pardon or amnesty granted by the President would be admissible as evidence in support of a claim against the United States. Furthermore, any such pardon used in pending cases had to be accompanied by an oath disclaiming support of the Confederacy. Without this disclaimer, the proviso required the Court to dismiss the claim for want of jurisdiction.[6]

The Court unanimously held the statute unconstitutional two years later in *United States* v. *Klein*. In his opinion, Chase followed the *McCardle* reasoning and conceded congressional control over appellate matters. But this time he found the jurisdictional denial to be a means toward an unconstitutional end. The controlling purpose, he said, was to deny presidential pardons the effect they had been given in the *Padelford* case. Congress, in other words, had allowed jurisdiction to a given point; after that the Court's role ceased and it was required to dismiss the cause. "It seems to us," Chase commented, "that this is not an exercise of the acknowledged power of Congress to make exceptions . . . to the appellate power." With disarming deference, he concluded that Congress inadvertently had violated the limits of its power. Chase later repeated his notion of "inadvertence," and believed, quite rightly, that the proviso passed Congress with little consideration.[7]

---

[4]*Cong Globe*, 39 Cong., 1 sess., pp. 770–71 (February 9, 1866); *United States* v. *Klein*, 13 Wallace (80 U.S.) 128, 144 (1872). Also see *DeGroot* v. *United States*, 5 Wallace (72 U.S.) 419 (1867).

[5]9 Wallace (76 U.S.) 531 (1870).

[6]16 Stat. 235 (1870).

[7]*United States* v. *Klein*, 13 Wallace (80 U.S.) 128, 145–46, 143, 147–48 (1872). Justices Miller and Bradley dissented on other grounds but agreed that the proviso

But Chase's tactfulness merely masked a bold interpretation of the theory of separation of powers, for he argued that Congress had interfered with matters of judicial determination. He contended that Congress had gone beyond a simple denial of jurisdiction; instead, it had conferred judicial power in a class of cases, but then made exceptions when faced with an unwelcome and obnoxious decision. Chase also rebuked Congress for encroaching upon executive powers. In effect, he found, Congress had changed the force of a presidential pardon: "This certainly impairs the executive authority and directs the court to be instrumental to that end"—an end in which, of course, the justices refused to comply.[8]

The Supreme Court's restriction of substantive congressional powers in this period is of greater significance as a backdrop for its activism of the last quarter of the nineteenth century. During the Chase years, the Court limited such important congressional powers as control over interstate commerce, taxation, and regulation of the currency.

United States v. *Dewitt* revived the ante bellum judicial debate on federal commerce power versus state police powers. A section of the internal revenue act of 1867 prohibited the sale of naphtha for illuminating purposes if it were flammable at less than one hundred degrees Fahrenheit. The question certified to the high court was whether the federal government could prohibit trade within the limits of a state.[9]

Chase's opinion reverted to the narrow construction of the commerce clause maintained, for the most part, by the Taney Court Democrats. He found in the clause "a virtual denial" of federal power to interfere with the internal trade of a separate state. Although conceding the validity of regulation designed as a necessary and proper means for implementing an expressly granted power, Chase rejected the government's argument that the naphtha

was unconstitutional in its attempt to direct to the judiciary the effect of a presidential pardon (*ibid.*, 148).

[8]*Ibid.*, 147, 148. See *New York Times*, January 3, 1872. Ultimately, its resources exhausted, the Supreme Court bowed to the legislative will when it later admitted that Congress need not appropriate funds due pardoned persons (*Hart* v. *United States*, 118 U.S. 62 [1886]). In *Knote* v. *United States*, the Court declared that "money once in the treasury can only be drawn by an appropriation by law" (95 U.S. 149, 153–54 [1877]). The provision voided in *Klein* was omitted from the Revised Statutes.

[9]9 Wallace (76 U.S.) 41, 43 (1870).

prohibition was necessary to protect revenue officers from potential danger while carrying out their duty of collecting taxes.

The *Dewitt* decision marked the first judicial rejection of a law based on the commerce clause, and it illustrated the Court's willingness to examine legislative purpose. In his opinion Chase remarked that the regulation only remotely could be considered as a spur to revenue in that it might increase sales of other illuminating oils. Yet the Chief Justice noted that in 1868, Congress repealed taxes on all such oils, while retaining the prohibition on naphtha sales; thus the exclusion, he said, plainly was "a regulation of police," and therefore constitutionally invalid. Although the Court recognized an incipient federal police power in the *Veazie* case of 1869, sustaining confiscatory taxation of state bank notes, it proved unwilling to accept a similar implication under the commerce clause.[10] More significantly, perhaps, the Court refused to apply the *Veazie* principle that Congress could regulate channels of national business.

The decision in *Collector* v. *Day* circumscribed congressional tax powers and again marked a narrow view of federal authority while displaying concern for the "rights" of states.[11] Joseph M. Day, judge of a county probate court in Massachusetts, challenged the 1864 income tax as applied to his salary, contending that state officials should be exempt from federal taxation. Day primarily relied on the thirty-year-old precedent of *Dobbins* v. *The Commissioners of Erie County* in which the Supreme Court had granted federal officials immunity from state taxation.[12] Justice Nelson, speaking for the Court in 1871, accepted the *Dobbins* analogy and buttressed it with the Tenth Amendment to sustain the plea. The Civil War and the new amendments apparently changed little for Nelson; indeed, his opinion anticipated the traditionalist logic of the *Slaughter-House* decision of two years hence: "The General government, and the States, although both exist within the same territorial limits, are separate and distinct sovereignties, acting separately and independently of each other, within their respective spheres." Thus, if the instrumentalities of the federal government required tax

[10]9 Wallace (76 U.S.) 41, 43–45. The voided section was omitted from the Revised Statutes. *Veazie Bank* v. *Fenno*, 8 Wallace (75 U.S.) 533 (1869).

[11]11 Wallace (78 U.S.) 113 (1871). See *U.S.* v. *Railroad Company* in which the wartime income tax was further restricted in its scope (17 Wallace [84 U.S.] 322 [1873]).

[12]16 Peters (41 U.S.) 435 (1842). Also see *Weston* v. *Charleston*, 2 Peters (27 U.S.) 449 (1829), which exempted federal securities from state and local taxation.

immunity from the states for self-preservation, then those of the states deserved similar exemption. The two governments, Nelson drily concluded, "are upon an equality."[13]

Justice Bradley alone dissented and offered an opinion, "the force of which gathered rather than lost strength in time." He refused to accept the *Dobbins* analogy and its correlative immunities implication. Furthermore, he contended that the limitation on national taxation power was "founded on a fallacy" which would "lead to mischievous consequences." Nearly seventy years later, the Court heeded Bradley's warning and overruled the doctrine of the 1871 decision. It was ironic, however, that a more nationalist-minded Court should reverse *Collector* v. *Day* in a case sustaining the right of states to tax federal employees.[14]

In *Collector* v. *Day* the Court did not invalidate the income tax laws; its decision merely construed the act so as to negate its application in an exceptional area. But in this way, and with some tenuous constitutional metaphysics, the Court significantly restricted the scope of the federal tax power. Incidentally, there was little possibility of a congressional response since the wartime tax expired in 1871.

The Chase Court's boldest rationalization for judicial review came in the first legal tender case, *Hepburn* v. *Griswold*.[15] The background, facts, and decision of the case are familiar and need little retelling here, but the ambitious and far-reaching statements of judicial authority merit special emphasis. The Court's close division on the constitutionality of legal tender, moreover, was paralleled by a sharp cleavage over the nature of judicial power.

Chief Justice Chase, speaking for the narrow majority of four, disavowed his earlier views when he had supported the legal tender legislation as Lincoln's Secretary of the Treasury and found the law invalid. Chase relied on the obligation of contracts clause and the due process clause of the Fifth Amendment for constitutional authority. By demonstrating the difference between depreciated paper notes and gold, he found, first that the act arbitrarily altered

[13]11 Wallace (78 U.S.) 113, 124, 127.

[14]*Ibid.*, 128–29; *Graves* v. *New York ex rel. O'Keefe*, 306 U.S. 466 (1939). Aside from a brief partisan exchange between *The New York Tribune* and *The World*, there seems to have been little public reaction to *Collector* v. *Day*.

[15]8 Wallace (75 U.S.) 603 (1870). The decision was overturned a year later in *Knox* v. *Lee*, 12 Wallace (79 U.S.) 457 (1871). The best account of the judicial politics and doctrines of the legal tender cases is in Charles Fairman, *Mr. Justice Miller and the Supreme Court, 1862–1890* (Cambridge, Mass.: Harvard University Press, 1939), chap. 7.

pre-existing contracts, thus impairing their obligation; and second, that the requirement of legal tender payments deprived persons of property rights without due process of law. Chase, however, entered into what essentially was a legislative debate on the wisdom of legal tender. Near the end of his tenure in Lincoln's cabinet, Chase composed an epigram concerning the need and desirability for greenbacks:

> When public exigencies require
> Coin must become paper.
> When public exigencies allow
> Paper must become coin.[16]

Six years later, he used his judicial office as an extension of his own, earlier policy-making position in the Treasury Department. The result was one of the most dubious examples of judicial review in the Court's history.

Chase began gingerly enough, acknowledging the time-honored truism that acts of Congress are constitutional unless clearly shown otherwise. He then followed with the inevitable *argumentum per reductionem*: the Constitution is the fundamental law defining governmental powers, and no department has other than its delegated powers. The judiciary, of course, served as the medium for interpreting the occult, or for consulting the Constitution in search of expressly granted powers. If a judicial decision were to turn on a conflict between legislation and the Constitution, it was, Chase wrote, "the plain duty of the Court to compare the act with the Constitution, and if the former cannot, upon a fair construction, be reconciled with the latter, to give effect to the Constitution rather than the statute."[17]

Chase predicated his whole view of judicial power upon John Marshall's dicta in *McCulloch* v. *Maryland*.[18] Marshall's discursive commentary on implied powers and the "painful duty of this tribunal" with regard to laws inconsistent with the "letter and spirit of the Constitution" particularly entranced Chase. But the

[16]March 24, 1864, Chase Papers, Huntington Library.
[17]8 Wallace (75 U.S.) 603, 610, 611–12. Chase applied the same interpretation to executive and judicial powers: "All the same observation is equally true in its application to the executive and judicial powers granted respectively to the President and the courts. All these powers differ in kind, but not in source or in limitation. They all arise from the Constitution, and are limited by its terms" (*ibid.*, 611).
[18]4 Wheaton (17 U.S.) 316 (1819).

attempt to recreate constitutional doctrines in the image of Marshall seemed tenuous at best. Marshall's view of implied powers was designed for a liberal construction of congressional powers. Chase, on the other hand, interpreted the "necessary and proper" clause narrowly; moreover, he regarded the traditional notions of limited government as inhibiting whatever could be implied or deduced from granted powers.[19]

The "letter" of the Constitution was not Chase's prime prop for invalidating legal tenders; rather, the "spirit"—that hedge in Marshall's dramatic metaphor—proved more usable. Since the legal tender acts applied to payment in greenbacks for pre-existing debts, the obligation of contacts clause came into question. The "letter" of the Constitution, however, limited the clause only to impairment of contracts by *state* governments. For Chase, the "spirit" of the fundamental law nevertheless made the limitation similarly applicable against the federal government.[20] How paradoxical that the Chief Justice should construe the Constitution narrowly and adhere to its literal meaning only until he needed a constitutional limitation! In other words, Congress could not imply powers, but the Court could well imply *its* authority from nothing less than a constitutional cabala.

Justice Miller, dissenting along with Swayne and Davis, had no doubts about the law's constitutionality. He also had some decided thoughts on what John Marshall meant and so deduced quite the opposite view of implied powers and judicial authority. The majority's finding that the law violated the "spirit" of the Constitution was "too abstract and intangible" for Miller. Above all, he saw it as a "dangerous" doctrine because it permitted the judiciary the dubious luxury of substituting its theoretical ideas for matters of policy. While Chase eagerly opted for the judicial prerogative of constitutional determination, Miller insisted on the need for restraint. Specifically, he warned that principles of abstract justice did not necessarily control legislative policy. And if action were necessary to execute an acknowledged power, Miller suggested that "the degree of that necessity is for the legislature and not for the court to determine."[21]

[19]8 Wallace (75 U.S.) 603, 617–18.
[20]*Ibid.*, 623–24.
[21]*Ibid.*, 638–39. The constitutional convention of 1787 rejected a specific prohibition against federal impairment of contracts (Benjamin F. Wright, *The Contract Clause of the Constitution* [Cambridge, Mass.: Harvard University Press, 1938], p. 9).

When the legal tender decision was overturned a year later after two new members were added to the Court, it was significant that Justice Miller did not write the majority's opinion. Instead, William Strong of Pennsylvania, one of the new justices, was chosen to speak for the Court. Strong picked up much of Miller's reasoning on the validity of national power and the necessity for congressional control of currency policy. But Strong in no way repudiated Chase's methodology and ignored altogether Miller's insistence on the need for judicial self-restraint.[22] However ephemeral the results of Chase's opinion, his ideas of judicial power remained persuasive and apparently acceptable to most of his colleagues.

The most striking aspect of the Court's activity was the relative lack of critical response to the judicial dynamism. Nearly half of the judicial review decisions involved jurisdictional matters and, as had happened with John Marshall's decision in *Marbury* v. *Madison*, this may have taken some edge from potential criticism. Yet, with the obvious exceptions of the legal tender and test oath cases, judicial efforts in this area passed almost unnoticed.

The reaction to the legal tender cases perhaps is revealing of the Court's status in public and political opinion. Naturally, in both cases, the result was criticized according to partisan lights. Within the Court itself, the justices divided according to their political backgrounds. All the Republicans favored the constitutionality of the law, while the Democrats (and by that time Chase had returned ideologically to the party of his youth) voted to invalidate it. But in outside political circles, criticism generally was tepid as the importance of the issue waned. One of the more rabid Republican organs remarked after the first decision that it "is of much less consequence than it would have been if it had been rendered five years sooner."[23]

The particular concern for the outcome, one way or the other,

---

[22]*Knox* v. *Lee* and *Parker* v. *Davis*, 12 Wallace (79 U.S.) 457 (1871). Justice Strong had been a member of the Pennsylvania Supreme Court and there played a leading role in asserting the judicial veto over legislation. See Stanley I. Kutler, "John Bannister Gibson: Judicial Review and the 'Positive State,'" *Journal of Public Law*, 14 (Spring, 1965):196. There is a large body of literature on the alleged "court-packing" which brought about a reversal of the legal tender decision. See, for example, Charles Fairman, "Mr. Justice Bradley's Appointment to the Supreme Court and the Legal Tender Cases," *Harvard Law Review*, 54 (April–May, 1941): 977, 1129.

[23]*New York Independent*, February 10, 1870. See chap. 5, *above*, for the limited attack upon the test oath decisions.

seemed to preclude any interest in the manner and rationale of the Court's exercise of judicial power. The legal and popular publications were almost completely silent on the subject. The *Chicago Legal News,* for example, gave strong support to Chase's strictures on adhering to the "spirit of the Constitution." But two prominent, self-anointed constitutional oracles, *Harper's Weekly* and the *Nation,* were exceptional in their criticism. The former disapproved of the first decision and accused the Court of restricting a proper legislative function. The *Nation* seemed to be in a quandary: it approved the voiding of legal tenders, but in a qualified way it admitted the appropriateness of Justice Miller's criticism of the Court's assumption of legislative powers. Yet the *Nation* really had come quite a distance from its Dred Scott criticism of judicial usurpation: "If the interpretation of a written Constitution is not committed to Judges," it queried, "what use is it? If the majority can do whatever they choose . . . , what better is it than the revocable charters which absolute sovereigns in Europe amused themselves by granting, for some years after 1815?"[24]

Perhaps the most widespread criticism of the Court occurred as a result of its sudden reversal in the second case and the alleged "court-packing." There were various remarks, all attuned to the same theme: that the reopening of the case was improper and therefore weakened the force of judicial opinions and respect for judicial authority. With only a few exceptions, however, this type of commentary came from the "losers" and was quite predictable.[25] To be sure, the remarks about the Court's loss of "popular respect" had another curious twist: most of them came from Democratic sources which had naïvely expected judicial power to serve and save their cause during the heyday of Reconstruction.

While the Court's vetoes of congressional legislation passed almost

[24]*Chicago Legal News,* 2 (March 5, 1870):178; *Harper's Weekly,* 14 (March 19, 1870):178–79; *Nation,* 10 (February 10, 1870):81–82. Also see editorial note in the *American Law Review,* 4 (April, 1870):607; J. I. Clark Hare, "The Legal Tender Decisions," *American Law Register,* 10 (November, 1871):73; C. A. Kent, "The Power of the Judiciary To Declare a Law Unconstitutional," *ibid.,* 11 (October, 1872): 729.

[25]For a typical example, see the *Albany Law Journal,* 1 (March, 1870): 197. Chase apparently hoped that the reversal game could go on indefinitely. After the second decision, he wrote: "If a decision, made by five to three can be reviewed by five to four it may happen that, under a new President, the later decision may be itself reversed and the former one reinstated" (Chase to E. D. Mansfield, April 24, 1871, Chase Papers, Library of Congress). So much for the judicial view of constitutional stability.

unnoticed during the period, this does not detract from their historical significance. For one thing, the judicial activity both quantitatively and qualitatively again belies the notion of a Supreme Court at bay. Historians focusing almost exclusively on Negro and southern issues for this period have tended to treat what they see as judicial reticence in particular cases as representative of the Court's whole range of work. But questions of the propriety of national authority and separation of powers were important to the Court. The fact that the issues adjudicated were not always as dramatic as, for example, military reconstruction in Mississippi, does not lessen their importance to the continuing pattern of constitutional interpretation and development.

Perhaps the greatest relevance of the judicial review cases is as an adumbration of future developments. The role and record of the Supreme Court as a legislative censor in the late nineteenth century are clearly established. The activities of the post–Civil War decade, however, might be seen as a foundation for the Court's later behavior and character. The regular pattern of asserting the propriety of judicial review, the willingness to examine legislative purpose, and the perfection of vested rights characterized the Chase Court's decisions almost as much as those of later years. While the history of judicial review properly goes back to *Marbury* v. *Madison,* and beyond, the Court's performance from 1864 to 1873 marked a significant deviation. The sheer volume alone is different. But more important was the political and public acceptance of this judicial function as a standard for measuring the legitimacy of power.[26] *Marbury* v. *Madison* and Dred Scott occasioned bitter disagreements over the role of the judiciary. But while dissatisfaction occasionally existed with the *results* of the Chase Court's decisions, there were few who called into question the *idea* of exercising the judicial veto.

---

[26]I think this is a valid observation despite Chase's one-time retreat to an older view of judicial review in *Mississippi* v. *Johnson.* There, in words reminiscent of ante bellum attitudes regarding judicial power, Chase remarked that Congress was not bound by the Court's holding that a congressional law was unconstitutional. Oliver Wendell Holmes strongly criticized Chase's remarks as obfuscating the principle that "when the Supreme Court . . . had once declared an act unconstitutional, every department of government was bound to respect their position" (Mark DeWolfe Howe, *Justice Oliver Wendell Holmes: The Proving Years, 1870–1882* [Cambridge, Mass.: Harvard University Press, 1963], p. 33). Chase's dictum perhaps stemmed from his basic motive in that case, that is, to illustrate the folly of issuing an injunction against the President.

The problem of states' rights within the federal system proved as perplexing after the Civil War as before. The Supreme Court under Salmon P. Chase was even more active than its predecessors in adjudicating questions which arose from either a positive thrust of national power or from state legislation which allegedly intruded upon national concerns, such as the interstate market or instrumentalities of the national government.

There is always a temptation to paste a definitive label on a particular era of judicial activity. Thus "reactionary," "conservative," "liberal," "nationalist," and so forth, are standard descriptive tools for interpretation. On one of the few occasions that the Chase Court has escaped the usual tags of "impotent" or "intimidated," it has been described flatly as the "outstanding 'states'-rights' court in American judicial history."[27] It would be difficult to measure such a judgment quantitatively. Certainly the Chase Court denied numerous attempts to invoke dormant national power against state legislation. But with regard to state taxation of banks, corporations, and railroads, the justices regularly hinted that state statutes were valid only insofar as they did not conflict with a congressional statement of policy. In other words, the Court often operated without the benefit of asserted national policy.

The judicial responses do not fit into a neat doctrinal pattern. They were, instead, pragmatic in nature and attuned to the justices' conception of the economic and social needs within the federal system. Although they were favorably disposed toward state regulation, they also were alert to the possibility that such legislation could unduly burden the national market or the instrumentalities of the national government. The Court's reluctance to articulate an exclusivist interpretation of national control over interstate commerce, for example, might be explained in another way: as the nationalistic spirit of Reconstruction waned, it became increasingly unlikely that Congress would fill the void left by the invalidation of state regulation.[28]

In this period the states were quite active in their attempts to

[27]Schmidhauser, *The Supreme Court as Final Arbiter*, p. 96. Benjamin F. Wright, however, notes that the Court was "more vigorous in its condemnation of state legislation than at any time since Marshall's most active years" (*The Growth of American Constitutional Law*) [New York: Reynal & Hitchcock, 1942], p. 82. There were 46 judicial vetoes of state laws in this period.

[28]James Willard Hurst, *Law and the Conditions of Freedom in the Nineteenth Century* (Madison: University of Wisconsin Press, 1956), p. 51.

regulate the burgeoning power of banks and railroads, particularly by means of taxation. As both enterprises usually had some kind of involvement with the federal government, the legislation raised the persistent questions of intergovernmental immunities and the relationship of state power to matters of national concern. The resulting litigation, in turn, created classic opportunities for the Court to arbitrate between the often competing demands of federal and state powers.

Each of the bank tax cases involved a state statute which taxed the capital, stock shares, or deposits of either state or national banks. Usually the tax covered a bank's holdings which were invested in United States securities or certificates. In their assault upon such taxes, the banks regularly staked their attacks on the half-century-old doctrine of *McCulloch* v. *Maryland,* which prohibited a state from taxing the instrumentalities of the federal government. In most of the cases which came after the Civil War, however, the Supreme Court eschewed constitutional theory, relying instead on statutory construction. That is, when a federal law specifically exempted securities from taxation, the Court held the state laws invalid; but in the absence of such legislation, the Court proved willing to allow a generous scope to a state's sovereign power of taxation.

During the war the Court had ruled in *Bank of Commerce* v. *New York City* that states could not tax the credit or obligations of the federal government.[29] This doctrine held in the subsequent line of postwar decisions. For example, in the *Bank Tax Case* of 1865, the Court struck down a New York tax on state banks. The tax was laid on the banks, but it was based on valuation equal to capital holdings, which consisted in large part of United States securities. Although the state insisted that the statute involved only a corporate franchise tax, the Court refused to recognize the distinction. A congressional act in 1862 prohibited state taxation of federal bonds and the justices simply accepted the federal law as a matter of policy.[30] Yet the Court was not prepared to accept overly fine arguments of bankers against state tax laws. In *Society for Savings* v. *Coite* the Court sustained a state tax on a bank's business as measured by deposits even though the deposits were invested in United States securities.[31]

[29] 2 Black (67 U.S.) 620 (1863).

[30] 2 Wallace (69 U.S.) 200 (1865). Also see *Van Allen* v. *The Assessors,* 3 Wallace (70 U.S.) 573 (1866).

[31] 6 Wallace (73 U.S.) 594 (1868). Chase, Grier, and Miller dissented without opinion. In a companion case, the Court applied its holding to a state tax on the

In this period, the Court somewhat circumscribed the full implications of Marshall's dicta in *McCulloch* v. *Maryland*. The National Bank Act of 1864 permitted state taxation of the shares of a national bank. But in *National Bank* v. *Kentucky*, the bank contended that its federal charter and its capital investments in United States securities and bonds made it immune from state regulation. In an unanimous opinion, Justice Miller rejected these arguments, interpreting the *McCulloch* doctrine to mean simply that states could not regulate federal instrumentalities by impairing their efficiency, and not that the latter were immune altogether. State laws were unconstitutional only when they prevented the bank from performing its federal functions, Miller said; any other rule would be "an unauthorized and unjustifiable invasion of the rights of the states."[32]

The cases concerning state taxation of railroads involved similar principles. The challenge under *McCulloch*, however, seemed even sharper, as railroad charters and operations had a more intimate relationship to the federal government. In these cases, moreover, the state tax often had to be considered with respect to the burdens it placed upon interstate commerce and whether it interfered with the federal government's power to regulate such commerce. Issues involving state taxation of railroads, state taxation of commodities involved in interstate commerce, and state regulation of corporations all raised commerce clause considerations.

By the end of the Civil War, the meaning of the commerce clause was no clearer than it had been when the Constitution was drafted in 1787. Despite John Marshall's classic commentary in *Gibbons* v. *Ogden* in 1824, a number of questions still remained open. Primarily, they revolved around the nature of federalism; that is, to what extent could the states impose artificial restraints and barriers on a possible concern or interest of the federal government?[33] While no memorable doctrine emerged from the Chase Court's opinions in this area, its decisions involved the federal judiciary in important market place considerations.

capital stock of a private non-banking corporation, part of which was invested in United States securities. (*Hamilton Co.* v. *Massachusetts*, 6 Wallace [73 U.S.] 632 [1868]).

[32] 9 Wallace (76 U.S.) 353, 360–62 (1870). Cf. *The Banks* v. *The Mayor*, 7 Wallace (74 U.S.) 16 (1869); *Bank* v. *Supervisors, ibid.*, 26.

[33] 9 Wheaton (22 U.S.) 1 (1824). See Felix Frankfurter, *The Commerce Clause under Marshall, Taney, and Waite* (Chapel Hill: University of North Carolina Press, 1937), p. 21.

During the 1860's, the states increasingly taxed the property, gross receipts, and franchises of those railroads doing business within their boundaries. The principles arising from the litigation over these laws were similar to those in the bank tax cases. The Court once again narrowly construed the *McCulloch* limitation and generally refused to consider the state taxation as an undue burden on interstate commerce.

In *Thompson* v. *Pacific R. R.*, for example, the Court had to consider the validity of a Kansas tax on the property of the Union Pacific Railroad. The railroad involved here was a state-chartered corporation, despite its subsidization by the federal government. Attorney General Ebenezer Rockwood Hoar appeared for the carrier before the Supreme Court and invoked the *McCulloch* analogy, arguing that the federal government had assisted in the construction and that the railroad was used for transportation of the mails, troops, and war material.[34]

Chief Justice Chase, in an unanimous opinion, rejected Hoar's position and sustained the state's right to tax a private corporation which incidentally provided certain services for the federal government. In this case, Chase spelled out the Court's view of state taxation: "No one questions that the power to tax all property, business and persons, within their respective limits, is original in the states and has never been surrendered." He, of course, qualified this with the *McCulloch* idea that the operations of the national government could not be hindered. Specifically, for this situation, he held that when Congress did not act to immunize a person or corporation in its employ, there could be no objection to state taxation.[35]

A few years later, in *Railroad Co.* v. *Peniston*, the Court sustained a similar tax even though levied against a federally-chartered branch of the Union Pacific. The majority held that the tax only "remotely" affected the operations of the federal government and again refused to invoke *McCulloch* or the commerce power. The limitations of the federal constitution could not be construed, Justice Strong said, so as to "destroy the necessary powers of the states or prevent their efficient exercise." The basic test of the tax's validity, he contended, was its "effect" upon federal agencies.[36] Justice Swayne, concurring,

[34] 9 Wallace (76 U.S.) 579, 583–86 (1870). The fact that the railroad was state-chartered is clarified in *Railroad Co.* v. *Peniston*, 18 Wallace (85 U.S.) 5 (1874).

[35] 9 Wallace (76 U.S.) 587–92.

[36] 18 Wallace (85 U.S.) 5, 30–31, 36.

agreed with the result, but insisted that Congress could exempt the Union Pacific's property from state taxation if it chose to do so.[37]

Justice Bradley, who probably was the most railroad-oriented member of the Court, vigorously objected to his colleagues' consistent approval of such state taxation. Following the *McCulloch* precedent, he found a parallel between the Union Pacific and the Bank of the United States, both being created by the federal government to serve a governmental purpose. Anticipating the doctrine which the Court adopted over a decade later in the *Wabash* case, Bradley maintained that an interstate carrier should be exempt not only from state taxation, but from all state regulation and control.[38]

Bradley's dissent strikingly reveals the Court's role as an economic umpire. What was involved here were basic questions regarding the control of public instrumentalities and the allocation of benefits and burdens of capital investment. At this time, and through the later so-called Granger Cases, the Court's response—despite Bradley and Field—was quite traditional. The majority was prepared to allow public control. In addition, while investors were protected from repudiation, the Court would not sustain their claim of exemption from the burdens of maintaining state governmental costs and services merely because they incidentally served some federal governmental function.

Chase and his colleagues certainly allowed the states to go to some lengths in imposing tax burdens on interstate commerce. For example, in the *Railway Gross Receipts Tax Case*, the Court sustained a Pennsylvania tax on gross receipts derived from interstate transportation by a state-chartered railroad.[39] It found that such a tax had only an indirect or remote effect on interstate commerce, that it was only an excise on the company's franchise, and that such tax power was necessary for the healthy existence of state governments. Shortly afterward, the Court upheld a Mobile, Alabama, city ordinance which imposed a license fee upon railroads doing business in the city. The law required a $500 fee for railroads involved in interstate business, while charging $100 to those which served Alabama

[37] *Ibid.*, 37–38.
[38] *Ibid.*, 39, 47–49. Field joined in Bradley's dissent. See *Wabash, St. Louis and Pacific Railway Co.* v. *Illinois*, 118 U.S. 557 (1886).
[39] 15 Wallace (82 U.S.) 284, 293–94 (1873). Cf., however, *State Tax on Foreign-Held Bonds Case*, 15 Wallace (82 U.S.) 300 (1873), where the Court struck down a state tax on out-of-state coupon-clippers of state-chartered corporations.

exclusively. Chase ignored the obvious discrimination, contending that the tax applied to business done in Mobile, and not on inter-state commerce. Chase mentioned that Congress had not acted on this matter and therefore the states might legislate, thus signifying some reservations by the Court.[40] In the bank cases, it may be remembered, the justices had held state tax laws invalid when the federal government provided exemption or legislative protection.

When the justices were satisfied that state taxation directly affected interstate commerce, they were less tolerant of the states' "sovereign right" of taxation. Nevertheless, they still refused to allow a positive thrust to the commerce clause, only vaguely imple-menting it as a foil against what they considered "discriminatory" taxes. These cases involved taxation of persons crossing state lines, commodities carried in interstate commerce, and persons engaged in interstate business.

Crandall v. *Nevada* involved the constitutionality of a state per capita tax on persons leaving the state. The state justified the levy as a franchise tax because it had to be paid by the transportation company. While the Court unanimously found the tax invalid, only Chase and Clifford considered it an undue interference with the commerce clause, "irrespective of any Congressional action."[41] Justice Miller, speaking for the majority, contended that the tax "does not itself institute any regulation of commerce of a national character, or which has a uniform operation over the whole country." But the Nevada tax, he maintained, inhibited a person's freedom of movement, which was one of the "privileges and immunities" of national citizenship. Moreover, he held that the tax could be burden-some to the national government by interfering with troop move-ments, or with a citizen's right to travel to federal governmental offices.[42]

A year later, the Court made an interesting choice between an ordinary and non-discriminatory right of local taxation and the protective cloak of the commerce clause. *Woodruff* v. *Parham* dealt with a municipal tax on auction sales. An auctioneer refused to pay the tax, claiming that the goods came from out-of-state and were in their original package. The plaintiff's argument against the tax

[40]16 Wallace (83 U.S.) 479, 481–82 (1873). Cf., however, *State Freight Tax Case,* 15 Wallace (82 U.S.) 232 (1873).
[41]6 Wallace (73 U.S.) 35, 49 (1868).
[42]*Ibid.,* 39, 43.

rested on John Marshall's opinion in the 1827 case of *Brown* v. *Maryland,* which held that imported goods in their original package were not liable for local taxation.[43] Justice Miller, however, swept aside the precedent, emphasizing the non-discriminatory nature of the tax. It was not, therefore, "an attempt to fetter commerce among the states, or to deprive the citizens of other states of any privilege or immunity possessed by citizens of Alabama." Indeed, he argued, to strike down the tax would discriminate in favor of merchants who bought goods from outside the state.[44] Once again, the Court refused to allow the national character of the economy to create special local tax exemptions in favor of a particular group.

When, however, the discrimination clearly emerged, the Court unhesitatingly struck down the local taxation to preserve a barrier-free national market. *Ward* v. *Maryland* in 1871 began a long series of "drummer" cases which involved state attempts to apply discriminatory taxation upon out-of-state concerns or salesmen. Justice Clifford, for the Court, found the tax violative of a citizen's "privileges and immunities" which, among other things, allowed one to go from state to state "for the purpose of engaging in lawful commerce, trade or business without molestation," and to be exempt from higher excise taxes than imposed by a state upon its own citizens. Clifford only hinted that an excise tax on goods produced out of the state might be so heavy that it would violate the commerce clause.[45] Bradley in a concurring opinion, however, insisted that the tax violated the commerce clause because it amounted to a duty on imports into the state.[46]

Perhaps the Court's most complete exposition of the commerce clause in these years came in the *State Freight Tax Case* in 1873. Again the conflict was between what the Court called "the limits of State sovereignty in imposing taxation, and the power and duty of the Federal government to protect and regulate interstate commerce." Pennsylvania had levied a tonnage tax on all railroad freight carried both within and out of the state; the railroad,

[43]12 Wheaton (25 U.S.) 419 (1827).

[44]8 Wallace (75 U.S.) 123, 139–40 (1869). In the companion case of *Hinson* v. *Lott,* Miller explicitly stated that a discriminatory tax would be invalid under the commerce clause (*ibid.,* 148, 152). See note by John F. Dillon in *American Law Register,* 9 (November–December, 1870): 40.

[45]12 Wallace (79 U.S.) 418, 426, 429, 430. Clifford noted that state tax discrimination was an evil ostensibly remedied by the adoption of the Constitution.

[46]*Ibid.,* 432.

however, refused to pay the tax on goods destined for out-of-state shipment.

Justice Strong, for the Supreme Court, acknowledged that the tax had been designed for revenue purposes, but its "effect" had to be considered as paramount. Transportation, he stated, was essential to interstate commerce, and no state could burden the free flow of goods. The transportation of goods was a "constituent of commerce"; a state freight tax was a regulation of interstate commerce and therefore unconstitutional. Moreover, a tax also applied to goods carried in intrastate commerce did not remedy the defect.[47] The Court found in this case an artificial state pattern which could not be reconciled to the needs and demands of the national economy. The transportation of people or goods through the various states required a uniform system of regulation because it involved, by its nature, a national concern. "We regard it as established," Strong concluded, "that no State can impose a tax upon freight transported from State to State, or upon the transportation because of such transportation."[48]

The Court's searching inquiries of burdensome state regulations of interstate commerce generally proceeded on a pragmatic basis. As Justice Strong had noted, the litmus test was the effect of state practices, and not abstract principles. The Court in this period seemed predisposed to allow wide latitude toward traditional state police powers as long as the effect was not unduly burdensome on the national system. The climax of this idea was to come a few years later in *Munn* v. *Illinois* and the accompanying cases involving legislation regulating railroads and grain warehouses.[49]

Similarly, in *Paul* v. *Virginia* the Court refused to invoke the commerce clause as a protective shield for the protection of insurance interests.[50] The case involved state regulation of insurance companies which, at the time, was a hotly contested issue. The companies had experienced a boom during the war years and were increasingly restless with multifarious state regulations confronting

[47]15 Wallace (82 U.S.) 232, 275–77 (1873). The railroad's counsel stressed, and apparently to good effect, the disruptive commercial warfare under the Articles of Confederation.
[48]*Ibid.,* 281–82. Swayne and Davis dissented, contending that the tax was a valid corporation tax merely measured by tonnage.
[49]94 U.S. 113 (1877) and following decisions. See *Railroad Company* v. *Fuller,* 17 Wallace (84 U.S.) 560 (1874), a case which somewhat anticipated *Munn* v. *Illinois.*
[50]8 Wallace (75 U.S.) 168 (1869).

them. This, and the burgeoning of national power, encouraged the companies to seek federal regulation on the grounds that insurance sales constituted interstate commerce. A bill to this effect was introduced in the House in 1865 but it died in committee. Nevertheless, the companies relentlessly pursued their objective and bombarded various committees with thousands of petitions urging federal action. The petitions were standard, protesting that state regulations were "dissimilar and tend to the detriment of trade"; that federal protection was necessary "to the prosecution and safety" of the insurance business; and that Congress, under its commerce clause authority, could regulate interstate insurance in order to establish "the greatest security for the interests protected by Policies, and promotive of the greatest good and convenience to all concerned in such transactions."[51]

Failing to secure relief from Congress, the companies turned to the federal courts, but with similar results. *Paul* v. *Virginia* involved a challenge to a typical state regulation. The state required nondomestic insurance companies to apply for a state license and deposit bonds valued at between $30,000 and $50,000 as a condition of doing business within Virginia. Paul, an agent of an out-of-state concern, was refused a license because he failed to make the required deposit. When he persisted in selling policies, he was convicted of violating the licensing statute.

On appeal to the Supreme Court, Paul's eminent counsel, ex-Justice Benjamin R. Curtis and J. M. Carlisle, attacked state regulation as violative of a citizen's privileges and immunities and as an interference with interstate commerce. They contended that a corporation was a citizen of the state in which it was chartered and therefore entitled to the same privileges in another state as the latter accorded its own citizens. They also argued that the sale of insurance contracts constituted commerce and, citing *Crandall* v. *Nevada,* they maintained that Virginia had burdened the free exercise of that trade.[52]

Justice Field, who wrote the Court's unanimous opinion, offered arguments which contradict his later views and his historical stereo-

[51]House Judiciary Committee, 39A–H 14.8; Ways and Means, 39A–H 25.19; Senate Commerce Committee, 39A–H 3, Legislative Section, National Archives. Also see Morton Keller, *The Life Insurance Enterprise, 1865–1910: A Study in the Limits of Corporate Power* (Cambridge, Mass.: Harvard University Press, 1963), pp. 235–36.
[52]8 Wallace (75 U.S.) 168, 170–73.

type. He denied the Curtis-Carlisle argument in every particular. Corporations, he said, were not "citizens" within the meaning of the privileges and immunities clause. Corporate status in one state is not a privilege which another must respect: "Special privileges enjoyed by citizens in their own state are not secured in other states by this provision." States, therefore, could impose conditions in granting foreign corporations the right to do business within their boundaries. For one who so often uttered the *argumentum ad horrendum* regarding *any* governmental regulation, here Field uncharacteristically pondered over the consequences of a state losing control of foreign corporations: "And if, when composed of citizens of one state, their corporate powers and franchises could be exercised in other states without restriction, . . . the principal business of every state would, in fact, be controlled by corporations created by other states." On the commerce point, Field admitted that the federal commerce power extended to business carried on by interstate corporations; but, he countered, "issuing a policy of insurance is not a transaction of commerce." Insurance contracts were "local transactions" and the citizenship of the contracting parties was immaterial.[53] Field thus summarily disposed of the companies' chief argument, and with it their hopes for relief.

Paul v. *Virginia* was a neglected opportunity to extend the scope of the commerce clause and federal authority. Seventeen years later in the *Wabash* case, the Court refused to sanction state attempts to regulate any phase of interstate railroad activity and thus, in a certain sense, stimulated passage of the Interstate Commerce Act of 1887. That legislation, while originally negative in its implications, set the stage for the modern use and understanding of the federal commerce power. Had the Court ruled otherwise in the insurance case, it is possible that Congress might have acted sooner to regulate the national character of business, industry, and transportation.

There were a number of occasions during the period when the Court had to review the positive thrust of federal power and its

[53]*Ibid.,* 177, 180–81, 182–83. Cf. the Court's later abortive attempt to alter the *Paul* doctrine. In 1944, the Court held that insurance sales constituted interstate commerce and that the companies were liable under the Sherman Anti-Trust Act. Congress, however, soon responded with a law affirming the validity of state regulation and backed away from an opportunity to subject the insurance companies to the anti-trust laws. See *United States* v. *Southeastern Underwriters Association,* 322 U.S. 533 (1944).

impact upon subjects traditionally left to state control. As before, the divergent, pragmatic character of the Court's decisions precluded the development of coherent, consistent judicial doctrine and policy.

The Court twice declared such congressional acts unconstitutional. First, in *United States* v. *Dewitt,* the justices refused to sustain a law prohibiting the sale of certain flammable illuminating oils under the authority of the commerce clause. Chase's opinion regarded the prohibition as an attempt to control trade within the limits of a state and therefore plainly was a "regulation of police" which properly belonged to state authorities. A few years later, in *United States* v. *Railroad Company,* the Court held the federal income tax inapplicable on a railroad's indebtedness to a municipality.[54]

On the other hand, the Chase Court managed some notably latitudinarian interpretations of federal power. While the Court had constricted the taxation power on occasion, in *Veazie Bank* v. *Fenno,* Chief Justice Chase wrote a landmark opinion which became the leading precedent for sustaining federal taxation for police and exclusionary purposes.[55] The case grew out of a wartime tax of ten per cent on state bank notes—a tax Congress avowedly imposed in order to drive such notes from circulation and to encourage use of the newly created greenbacks and national bank notes. Chase maintained that the Constitution had granted Congress the power to tax "in its fullest extent," except as to exports and subject only to specific limitations of uniformity and apportionment. He rejected the bank's argument that the tax fell on a state-authorized franchise which was immune from federal taxation. The tax, he said, was not on the franchise but rather on personal property created by the bank. Similarly, he dismissed a challenge that the tax was so excessive that it amounted to the destruction of property. The tax power, Chase concluded, was an "acknowledged power" of Congress which the Court would not limit. "The power to tax may be exercised oppressively," he conceded, "but the responsibility of the legislature is not to the courts but to the people by whom its members are

---

[54] 9 Wallace (76 U.S.) 41 (1870); 17 Wallace (84 U.S.) 322 (1873).

[55] 8 Wallace (75 U.S.) 533 (1870). The case won immediate acceptance as an authoritative interpretation and justification for the idea of destructive taxation. See, for example, the comments of Judge Thomas Cooley in his influential works, *A Treatise on the Constitutional Limitations . . .,* 2d ed. (Boston: Little, Brown & Co., 1871), p. 484, and *The General Principles of Constitutional Law . . .* (Boston: Little, Brown & Co., 1880), p. 57.

elected." In addition, he bolstered his position by referring to the equally broad monetary powers of Congress.[56]

Chase's opinion, of course, cannot be considered *in vacuo*. The Court promulgated significant restrictions of the taxation power in the above-mentioned railroad case and again, in 1871, in *Collector* v. *Day*. Moreover, a year after the *Veazie* case, Chase himself led the assault against the legal tender acts which somewhat negated his generous remarks concerning the monetary powers of Congress.[57] The bank note case, more than anything else perhaps, amounted to judicial agreement with a desirable fiscal policy.

The Court also gave a significant boost to the federal government's national currency program when it held legal tenders exempt from state taxation.[58] But the vagaries of judicial imagination were something to behold as on the same day the justices endorsed a state's right to refuse greenbacks as payment for state taxes. The decision in *Lane County* v. *Oregon,* which also was written by Chief Justice Chase, highlights the difficulty in applying arbitrary labels to judicial behavior.[59] The *Veazie* decision, to be sure, enthusiastically endorsed a bold national policy; the language in *Lane County,* however, was reminiscent of the familiar state-sovereignty theory which allegedly had been buried by the North's victory in 1865.

The wartime currency legislation made greenbacks "legal tender in payment of all debts, public and private." Federal taxes, specifically, were made payable in greenbacks. An Oregon statute, however, required payment of state taxes in specie and the state accordingly refused to accept greenbacks from one of its political subdivisions. Chase framed the issue in terms of federal relations and, specifically, the nature of state taxation power. The federal government, he said, was supreme within the scope of its invested powers, but the states retained "functions essential to [their] separate and independent existence." Despite national taxation powers, the states' authority to tax property, business, and persons within their boundaries, remained complete. Moreover, the extent and mode of its exercise

[56]8 Wallace (75 U.S.) 540–41, 543, 547–48. By the time the Court decided the *Veazie* case, the bank tax had effectively discouraged the circulation of state bank notes. See Michal R. Belknap, "Government by Taxation: The Expansion of Federal Power through Revenue Legislation, 1861–1865" (M.A. thesis, University of Wisconsin, 1966), p. 206.

[57]See *Collector* v. *Day* and the *Legal Tender Cases* discussed above.

[58]*Bank* v. *Supervisors,* 7 Wallace (74 U.S.) 26 (1869).

[59]7 Wallace (74 U.S.) 71 (1869).

were within the discretion of the state. "There is nothing in the Constitution which contemplates or authorizes any direct abridgment of this power by national legislation." Therefore, Chase concluded, Congress could not, and did not intend to, restrain a state's choice as to how tax payments should be made.[60]

The *Slaughter-House Cases* offer a fitting capstone to the Supreme Court cases involving problems of federalism. Few cases in the Court's history are as rich in their immediate ramifications and long-range implications as this one. No discussion of Reconstruction, of the Fourteenth Amendment and all its attendant clauses— "privileges and immunities," "due process of law," and "equal protection of the laws"—of federalism, of state police power, and of property rights can ignore the trenchant remarks and lively ideas expressed in the justices' divergent opinions.

The *Slaughter-House* litigation arose out of a statute passed by the military-backed government in Louisiana in 1869. In all probability, bribery and corruption figured in the act's passage. The law created a new corporation with the exclusive right to erect an *abattoir* and cattle landing within New Orleans, and forbade slaughtering at any other place in the area. There were fixed maximum charges that the corporation could charge for each animal landed. While there were penalties prescribed for slaughtering animals elsewhere, the designated company was subject to heavy penalties if it refused use of its premises to any other person. As the company had exclusive privileges for twenty-five years, the statute was widely denounced as creating a monopoly and denying the right of other butchers to exercise their lawful trade.[61]

Counsel for the aggrieved butchers, led by ex-Justice John A. Campbell, offered the momentous idea that the privileges and immunities clause of the Fourteenth Amendment guaranteed every citizen "the assurance of property and liberty" from arbitrary violation by the states. Wisconsin's Senator Matthew H. Carpenter, as opposing counsel, warned the Court that such an interpretation of the amendment would strike at the ability of the states to regulate their internal affairs, and he generally rejected Campbell's position

[60] *Ibid.*, 76–77, 78, 79, 81.
[61] 16 Wallace (83 U.S.) 36, 38–43 (1873). A recent interesting analysis of the case is Loren P. Beth, "The Slaughter-House Cases—Revisited," *Louisiana Law Review*, 23 (April, 1963): 487–505. Fairman's *Mr. Justice Miller*, chap. 8, remains as the starting-point for comprehension. The *Nation*, 16 (April 24, 1873): 280, suggested that there was corruption in the passage of the Louisiana law.

that the amendment created a system of economic laissez faire.[62] The case thus offered the Court a choice between the competing demands of state police power versus property rights, but it was a choice compounded by the interjection of the issue and rights of national citizenship.

Justice Miller, for the majority, noted that a police power always had been conceded to the states. There was a right of the states to make regulations for the health and well-being of the community. Though he conceded that the police power was incapable of exact limitation, he insisted that it was vital for the "very security of social order, the life and health of the citizen, the comfort of an existence in a thickly populated community, the enjoyment of private and social life, and the beneficial use of property." The regulation of slaughterhouses, Miller added, was "among the most necessary and frequent exercises" of the power.[63] Thus the majority sustained the legislation as a traditional exercise of police power and, in particular, maintained the inclusion of slaughterhouse regulation under that authority. The Fourteenth Amendment, Miller insisted, had changed nothing in this respect. It simply was inconceivable to the majority that the framers of the amendment had any intention of restricting "the exercise of legislative power by the States, in their most ordinary and usual functions." The Court expressly denied itself a role of "perpetual censor" on such legislation—something which the plaintiffs' argument and the dissenters' opinions virtually assumed. Finally, the majority spoke for maintenance of the traditional balance between federal and state powers, again denying the entreaties of the plaintiffs and the minority.[64]

Field entered a dissenting opinion, in which Chase, Bradley, and Swayne concurred; the latter two also filed separate statements. The minority primarily based their attack upon the state law as a deprivation of the right to pursue a lawful calling, a right which they believed now had additional protection from the national government by virtue of the Fourteenth Amendment, and one which the federal judiciary had an obligation to enforce. This idea of judicial power, while a minority view in this case, was a recurrent

[62] 16 Wallace (83 U.S.) 36, 45–57. Walton H. Hamilton, "The Path of Due Process," *Ethics,* 48 (April, 1938): 269–96.

[63] 16 Wallace (83 U.S.) 62–63.

[64] *Ibid.,* 78–82. For further discussion of Miller's opinion, see the concluding chapter below.

theme in the contemporary conception of the judicial function.

Justice Field conceded the "legitimate exercise" of state police power. But the vital question in this case was whether the state, acting under the "pretense" of that power, could encroach upon the just and constitutional rights of its citizens. Field insisted that the "pretense" of sanitary regulations in this case was "a shallow one," and that the law presented "a naked case, unaccompanied by any public considerations, where a right to pursue a lawful and necessary calling," was taken away from some men and exclusively vested in others. Field, to be sure, found constitutional sanction against such legislation, particularly in the various clauses of the recently enacted Fourteenth Amendment. Yet, he cited enough precedents to show clearly that laws such as Louisiana's were repugnant to his conception of a general scheme of liberty or, as he stated it, to the "fundamental idea upon which our institutions rest." Indeed, Field probably would have resorted to the "rights of man" if the amendment had not existed; the majority, he lamented, had sustained a law which violated "the right of free labor, one of the most sacred and imprescriptable rights of man."[65]

While acknowledging the force of the Fourteenth Amendment, Field softened the change it wrought in terms of federal-state relations. Bradley and Swayne, however, were much more alert to this and challenged Miller's willingness to maintain the status quo ante bellum.

Justice Bradley combined the Magna Charta, Blackstone, and the Declaration of Independence to find the Louisiana statute destructive of individual rights and liberties. Government, he said, was instituted to protect life, liberty, property, and the pursuit of happiness, rights which belonged to the citizens of every free government. Most basically, every citizen must be free to pursue a calling in order to best preserve, exercise, and enjoy those rights: "This right to choose one's calling is an essential part of that liberty which it is the object of government to protect; and a calling, when chosen, is a man's property and right." The New Orleans butchers, Bradley believed, had been deprived of their lawful calling in an arbitrary and capricious manner and, as he said in reference to the new amendment, without "due process of law" and the "equal protection of the laws." The Fourteenth Amendment, he concluded, guaran-

[65]*Ibid.*, 87–89, 110.

teed that the national government would protect its citizens from such state actions.[66]

Athough the *Slaughter-House* decision primarily involved the issue of state regulatory power and the Fourteenth Amendment, the clash of opinions also marked a significant development in the persistent tension between competing views of the judicial function. Justice Miller advocated the traditional notion of judicial restraint when he warned that the Court would become a "perpetual censor" of state legislation if a highly nationalistic interpretation of the new amendment were adopted. Justices Field and Bradley, however, had little hesitation in assuming an activist role for the Court, although perhaps for different reasons. Whether it be to insure one's right "to pursue certain callings" or in behalf of "the National will and National interest," Field and Bradley were willing to provide judicial intervention. In the light of future developments, the dissenters spotlighted the emerging dominant conception of the judicial function and the future course of judicial behavior.

The idea of "states' rights" has a perjorative ring. It has come to be identified with schemes to lessen the influence and prestige of the nation-state, with the attendant ideas of national power being exercised for national purposes. Such an idea, long dormant in American thought, perhaps was just coming into its own following the Civil War. Old habits, however, were not easily broken. The Supreme Court of the postwar decade accepted the states as vital political subdivisions, with important police functions to fulfill within their own spheres. It was a scheme of "states' powers"—with certain reservations—which interested the justices, and not some a priori concept of "rights." They were not abstract theorists as much as they were individuals pragmatically adjusting to certain needs and demands. Perhaps the Court's willingness to adhere to traditional ideas of state police power and a state's "sovereign" right to tax should be seen in a more positive light. Without this, the result might have been similar to the "twilight zone" situation of the late nineteenth century in which the Court regarded certain

[66]*Ibid.,* 116, 122, 124. Professor Beth remarks that Swayne's dissent was "the most eloquent" and was distinguished from the others by its prewar "abolitionist flavor." Swayne's opinion was ambivalent; what Professor Beth says is quite true, yet Swayne's remarks also were clearly of a piece with his oft-expressed views of vested property rights (see *Louisiana Law Review*, 23:487–505).

phrases of commercial activity as beyond the reach of either the national or state governments.

Yet it would be incorrect to view the Court's decisions as excessively weighted in favor of states', as opposed to national, powers. In matters of admiralty jurisdiction,[67] wartime licensing taxation,[68] and federal judicial supremacy over state courts,[69] the Chase Court justices looked with favor on national power. The *Veazie Bank* case offers significant evidence that the Court would tolerate a broad expression of national power when persuaded of the desirability of the policy involved. Similarly, *Ward* v. *Maryland* indicated a judicial awareness of the need for a national market to function without state hindrances. A prominent Republican politician of the period later recalled that Chase had shown him a dissenting opinion in which the Chief Justice had asserted his "favorite principle of State rights."[70] But Chase's views in *Veazie Bank* and *Crandall* v. *Nevada*, among others, were vital affirmations of national power and supremacy. So much for labels.

The greatest significance of these varied cases is the doubt they cast upon the notion of a quiescent and impotent judiciary during the postwar decade. In fact, the Supreme Court neither cringed at threats from vindictive congressmen nor abdicated its traditional functions. Indeed, the Court steadily expanded its power through an increased use of the judicial veto and through its role as arbiter between federal and state power. While the issues were not particularly spectacular, and the stakes often not very high, they signified the Court's persistent utility for legitimating power and policy in the American system. They also demonstrate once again the Court's institutional toughness which was more relevant in the long run than the ephemeral turmoil over particular rulings. Modestly but surely, the Reconstruction era justices heralded the unprecedented use of federal judicial power.

[67] *The Daniel Ball*, 10 Wallace (77 U.S.) 557 (1871).

[68] *License Tax Cases*, 5 Wallace (72 U.S.) 462 (1867). Also see *Pervear* v. *Massachusetts, ibid.,* 475; *McGuire* v. *Massachusetts,* 3 Wallace (70 U.S.) 387 (1886). The political and legal problems of the license taxes are discussed in Belknap, "Government by Taxation," chap. 4.

[69] *Tarble's Case*, 13 Wallace (80 U.S.) 397 (1872); *Provident Institution* v. *Massachusetts,* 6 Wallace (73 U.S.) 611 (1868); *Van Hoffman* v. *Quincy,* 4 Wallace (71 U.S.) 535 (1867); *Amy* v. *Supervisors,* 11 Wallace (78 U.S.) 136 (1871).

[70] George W. Julian *Political Recollections, 1840 to 1872* (Chicago: Jansen, McClurg, 1884), p. 350. Chase probably referred to his *Tarble's Case* dissent (13 Wallace [80 U.S.] 397, 412 [1872]).

8

The Expansion of Power:
New Jurisdiction

It is apparent that the congressional threat to the federal judiciary during the Reconstruction era has been grossly exaggerated. While some Republicans mistrusted and feared the Supreme Court, they never succeeded in permanently damaging it. On the contrary, there was a healthy, vital respect for the federal judiciary and its powers. What is more, the dominant Republicans regularly turned to the judicial system for protection and enforcement of particular legislation and for fulfillment of their nationalist impulses.

During the Civil War and Reconstruction period Congress significantly enlarged federal jurisdiction. The fifteen years following the outbreak of Civil War, indeed, witnessed the greatest legislative expansion of jurisdiction since 1789. In a variety of ways, such as additional federal court power to issue writs of habeas corpus, new jurisdiction in admiralty and bankruptcy, and a broader scope for Supreme Court review by writs of error, the federal system was given authority to assume a more dominant position over the state courts.[1] The most far-reaching example involved the removal of causes from state to federal courts, and it is worth some detailed examination.

This removal legislation affords an excellent opportunity to

[1]A detailed treatment of the expansion of federal jurisdiction in the postwar era is in William M. Wiecek, "The Reconstruction of Federal Judicial Power: 1863–1875" (M.A. thesis, University of Wisconsin, 1966). My understanding of these problems has been most aided by Wiecek's work; Henry M. Hart, Jr., and Herbert Wechsler, *The Federal Courts and the Federal System* (Brooklyn: Foundation Press 1953); and by Felix Frankfurter and James M. Landis, *The Business of the Supreme Court: A Study in the Federal Judicial System* (New York: Macmillan, 1928), chaps. 1 and 2.

witness the accretive character of legal and constitutional change. While Congress seldom verbalized its broader aims, the cumulative effect of its legislation was a tremendous alteration of federal power. The removal laws ranged from supportive measures for the enforcement of substantive legislation to the climactic Jurisdiction and Removal Act of 1875 which fulfilled the scope of federal judicial power probably intended by the Constitution. In that statute, Congress provided that any suit asserting rights under the Constitution, laws, or treaties of the United States could be begun in a federal court, or removed from a state court, regardless of the citizenship of either party.

The course of removal legislation begins with the Judiciary Act of 1789. Article III, Section 2 of the Constitution had provided for federal judicial power in all cases arising under the Constitution, the laws, or treaties of the United States. In addition, it had empowered Congress to give the federal courts jurisdiction in diversity of citizenship controversies. The 1789 law, which established the federal judicial system, was a bundle of compromises and certainly did not reflect the Federalists' complete views of national judicial power. In that act, among other things, the federal courts were given jurisdiction in diversity of citizenship suits only in cases between a citizen of the state where the suit was brought and a citizen of another state. They were not given original cognizance in suits involving a question arising under the Constitution or laws of the United States.

The 1789 act also granted limited authority for removal of causes to the federal courts. Section 12 stipulated that civil cases could be removed before trial in state courts by a non-resident or alien defendant when the amount in dispute totaled more than five hundred dollars. Jurisdiction again was limited to cases where one party resided in the forum state, except where the defendant was an alien. Furthermore, land title cases could be removed if either party claimed title from a state other than that in which the suit had been brought, so long as the adverse party derived title from the forum state. Congress here followed a specific constitutional grant of federal judicial power, and one strongly urged by Alexander Hamilton in *The Federalist*.[2] The first legislation was designed to cope with

[2] 1 Stat. 73; Jacob E. Cooke, ed., *The Federalist* (Cleveland: World, 1961), pp. 538, 540. Charles Warren, "New Light on the History of the Federal Judiciary Act of

the problem of allegedly hostile state courts in diversity of citizenship cases, a problem very much on the minds of the Constitution's framers.

The Federalists finally expressed their most advanced views of national judicial power in their waning days of power. In the short-lived Judiciary Act of 1801, which is best known for its "court-packing" aspects, they substantially increased federal jurisdiction, partly by new removal provisions. Now suits arising under the Constitution, laws or treaties of the United States were to be removable regardless of the citizenship of the parties. In certain alien or diversity suits where the defendant did not appear, moreover, he could remove the cause to the federal courts after trial had begun. The Federalists acted from a mixture of economic considerations, especially concern for disputed land titles, and as a reflection of their nationalist drives. As Attorney General Edmund Randolph had suggested nearly a decade earlier, the federal courts were to be the "steady asserter of the federal rights."[3]

Although the Jeffersonian Republicans repealed the 1801 act a year later, the statute was a portent for future developments. While it no longer seems fashionable to draw comparisons between the Federalists and the Reconstruction Republicans, the latter's 1875 Removal Act almost precisely duplicated the language and motives of the Federalists.

From 1801 until the Civil War there were only a few provisions made for removal. Each instance was an *ad hoc* response to meet a specific need of the national government. For example, because of widespread smuggling during the War of 1812, Congress strengthened the powers of customs officials. Section 8 of the Revenue Act of 1815 provided for removal of actions brought against these officials for acts committed during performance of their duties. The specific removal statute served as a model for much of the later Civil War legislation, being a means to protect federal officers against local hostility and thus to protect and insure enforcement of

1789," *Harvard Law Review*, 37 (1924): 49, 53, illustrates how the Federalists compromised their nationalistic views on judicial power. For an early judicial interpretation of the 1789 removal procedures, see *Miller* v. *Lynde* (1796), Jesse Root, *Reports of Cases Adjudged in the* [Connecticut] *Superior Court . . .*, 2 vols. (Hartford: Hudson and Goodwin, 1798, 1802), 2:444.

[3] 2 Stat. 89; Kathryn Turner, "Federalist Policy and the Judiciary Act of 1801," *William and Mary Quarterly*, 22 (January, 1965): 3–32. This outstanding essay devotes equal attention to the jurisdictional and political questions surrounding the Act of 1801 and supersedes previous work.

particular federal laws. A similar situation grew out of the nullification controversy in 1833. As part of its counter-offensive against the federal government, South Carolina had made it a penal offense for federal customs officers to collect duties within the state. Congress, among other tactics, responded with a removal remedy, along with provision for a writ of habeas corpus *cum causa* which allowed removal of both cause and defendant to the federal circuit court.[4] The idea of rescuing governmental officers from hostile local courts followed the pre-Revolutionary practice of the British as, for example, in the 1774 Administration of Justice Act.

The 1833 legislation provoked a wide-ranging congressional debate on federal judicial power. Most southerners, even those supporting the Jackson administration's coercive program against South Carolina, deplored the expansion and intrusion of federal court authority. Yet, in 1855, southern congressmen enthusiastically supported similar measures to protect and enforce the fugitive slave laws. To be sure, southern concern for federal officers amounted to a parody of the Federalists' fears of aggressive and hostile state courts. Northern Republicans made the farce complete. Charles Sumner, William P. Fessenden, Benjamin Wade, and Salmon P. Chase offered a classic exposé of the "whose-ox-is-gored" thesis of constitutional rationale and interpretation. Chase, who later as Chief Justice held different views on removal legislation, deplored the 1855 bill as an "overthrow of State rights." It would, he said, "establish a great central, consolidated Federal Government. It is a step, let me say a stride rather, towards despotism." Some southerners and their northern supporters waxed eloquent on the principles of national power. Judah P. Benjamin of Louisiana, however, accurately described the removal idea in its historical context as a device to enforce federal power in the face of local hostility. While the bill overwhelmingly passed the Senate, it died in the House. Nevertheless, it illustrated the pragmatic character of removal and the South's willingness to utilize national institutions to protect its peculiar concerns.[5]

[4]Act of February 4, 1815, 3 Stat. 195, 198; Act of March 2, 1833, 4 Stat. 632, 633. The provisions of the 1833 act formed the basis for some of the specific removal acts of the 1860's. See *Gay* v. *Ruff,* 292 U.S. 25 (1933) for a review of the history of those removal sections. The Habeas Corpus Act of 1842 originated as a comprehensive removal bill (see Bill File, 27 Cong., 2 sess., National Archives).

[5]The debates on the 1833 and 1855 bills offer fascinating insights into attitudes toward judicial power. The 1855 debates, in particular, illustrate the tenuous

The federal government's widespread, sometimes unpopular, legislation and activities during the Civil War necessitated a supporting body of enforcement procedures. Accordingly, Congress often provided for removal in order to protect federal officers performing their official duties. In addition, Congress made some bold, new departures which significantly enlarged the scope of federal judicial power, however inadvertently.

The first of twelve removal measures passed during the Civil War and Reconstruction period came with the Habeas Corpus Act of 1863. Congress originally had planned to indemnify all persons arrested while acting under color of authority of federal law. The Senate Judiciary Committee, however, substituted a removal procedure exactly as had been stipulated in the 1815 revenue law. Federal officers *or* any other person could remove suits against them for wrongs done under authority of the President or federal law, even after judgment had been given. The cause could be taken to the United States Supreme Court on writ of error regardless of the amount of judgment.

This act primarily confirmed and authorized President Lincoln's suspension of the writ of habeas corpus and thus aroused prolonged, mostly partisan, debate in both houses of Congress. Democrats, many of whom had supported the 1855 bill, now bitterly assailed the expansion of federal power. Some of the conservative Republicans, led by Senator Orville H. Browning of Illinois, sought to narrow the scope of the removal provisions. While conceding the propriety of removal of pending cases, Browning objected to the section which allowed removal after final judgment and decision and *de novo* review in the federal courts. Browning, who long had evinced mounting concern about federal aggrandizement, warned that the removal provisions "might ultimately lead to an absorption of all the powers of the States by the General and central Government."[6]

The subsequent judicial reaction to the 1863 removal provisions revealed an ambivalent attitude on the part of the Supreme Court. First, in *The Mayor* v. *Cooper,* in 1867, the justices unanimously approved the congressional grant of removal jurisdiction after a

character of southern notions of state sovereignty (See *Debates in Congress*, 9:243 ff. [1833]; *Cong. Globe*, 33 Cong., 2 sess., Appendix, pp. 211 ff. [February 23, 1855]).
    [6]Act of March 3, 1863, 12 Stat. 756–57; *Cong. Globe*, 37 Cong., 3 sess., pp. 539, 559, 1087, *passim*.

lower federal court had declared the relevant sections of the 1863 act, and an 1866 amendment, unconstitutional and void. Justice Swayne, speaking for the Court, recited the origins of removal legislation in the Judiciary Act of 1789, and the subsequent additions before the Civil War, and he found that no federal court had ever doubted their validity; indeed, he commented, "the acquiescence is now universal." Swayne took a broad view of federal jurisdictional authority in general. It was not necessary, he said, for all questions in a case to be of a federal character for removal: "if there be a single such ingredient in the mass, it is sufficient." Yet, two years later, the Court found one limitation on removal when it held that facts determined by a state court jury could not be re-examined in the federal courts.[7]

The postwar removal legislation in part continued the pattern of pragmatic response to facilitate enforcement of particular federal laws. As such, Congress provided for removal as part of its internal revenue, civil rights, and voting rights legislation.

The removal provisions of the Internal Revenue Act of July 13, 1866, only tightened existing forms. In addition, Congress took steps to prevent state courts from determining the constitutionality of the internal revenue legislation when it provided for removal in all cases affecting the validity of the act.[8]

The Civil Rights Act of 1866 contained provisions for removal of suits originating under that statute or the Freedmens' Bureau Act in the manner prescribed by the Habeas Corpus Act of 1863. Appeals lay to the Supreme Court on all questions of law arising under the statute. The congressional debate centered on Section 1 which defined citizenship, and the removal provisions were mentioned only as part of a general Democratic assault on encroaching national power. In his veto message, Andrew Johnson attacked the bill in part because it authorized judicial powers which went beyond the bounds of constitutional mandate. To transfer civil rights cases to the federal courts, he charged, "would be an exercise of authority well calculated to excite distrust and alarm on the part of all the

[7] *The Mayor* v. *Cooper*, 6 Wallace (73 U.S.) 247, 252, 254 (1867); *The Justices* v. *Murray*, 9 Wallace (76 U.S.) 274 (1870). Also see *McKee* v. *Rains*, 10 Wallace (77 U.S.) 22 (1869), and *Bigelow* v. *Forrest*, 9 Wallace (76 U.S.) 339 (1869).

[8] 14 Stat. 171–72. The removal provisions were upheld in *Tennessee* v. *Davis*. Justice Strong, speaking for the Court, declared that "it ought . . . to be considered as settled that the constitutional powers of Congress . . . authorize . . . removal" (100 U.S. 257, 271 [1879]).

States."[9] It is strange, however, that Johnson never rejected other removal legislation, particularly when it was almost the exclusive concern of a statute.

The Civil Rights Act's removal provisions had an interesting aftermath. One Reynolds, a Negro, had been charged with the murder of a white man in Virginia. After the state supreme court overturned a first conviction, and he was found guilty in a second trial, he removed his cause to Judge Alexander Rives's federal circuit court for the Western District of Virginia. Reynolds contended that his civil rights were violated because Negroes were excluded from the jury. After Rives allowed the removal, one house of the Virginia General Assembly promptly censured the judge. The state then instituted proceedings to challenge the removal provisions and to compel Rives to surrender the defendant.[10]

In *Virginia* v. *Rives* in 1880, the Supreme Court found the removal provisions inapplicable in this case since the state had not excluded Negroes from juries by statute. Therefore Reynolds had to seek his remedy in the state courts as long as there was no violation of federal law. On the same day, however, in *Strauder* v. *West Virginia*, the relevant federal removal procedures were held constitutional when the state had deliberately limited jury duty to white persons.[11]

The 1871 Enforcement Act for voting rights marked the last congressional response to utilize removal procedures in order to enforce specific legislation. As usual, Congress acted to protect federal officials who were sued or prosecuted for acts committed under color of law. One innovation, though, was that the state courts were almost entirely circumvented; in his petition to the federal court, the defendant merely had to include certification by his counsel that the facts in the petition were true. Removal was by writ of certiorari or habeas corpus *cum causa*. Finally, all post-removal

[9]14 Stat. 27; *Cong. Globe,* 39 Cong., 1 sess., pts. 1 and 2, *passim.* The removal provisions of the 1866 act are still in effect in slightly different form (28 U.S.C. 1443 [1964]). See *People* v. *Galamison,* 342 Fed. 255 (C.A. 2d, 1965) for a recent summary of the provisions' history.

[10]Allan B. Magruder, "Removal of Suits to Federal Courts," *American Law Review,* 13 (April, 1879):434, 436 ff.; *Virginia* v. *Rives,* 100 U.S. 313 (1880).

[11]*Virginia* v. *Rives,* 100 U.S. 303 (1880.) The West Virginia case actually was decided on the basis of the Fourteenth Amendment, not the Civil Rights Act. Cf. *Neal* v. *Delaware,* 103 U.S. 370 (1880). Also see the *Nation,* 30 (March 4, 1880): 165–66. For recent Supreme Court statements on removal and civil rights, see *Georgia* v. *Rachel* (removal granted) and *Greenwood* v. *Peacock* (removal denied), 384 U.S. 780; *ibid.,* 808 (1966).

proceedings in the state court were void, and persons participating in such proceedings were subject to a misdemeanor charge. The Democrats this time sharply attacked the removal provisions, but the bill passed on almost solidly partisan lines.[12]

Following the war, Congress' interest in removal legislation continued to reflect its desire to protect federal officials from southern harassment. Yet, by design or otherwise, the scope of much of the removal legislation encompassed more than just southern policy. In some of their removal statutes, the Republicans fundamentally altered traditional federal-state relations which, ultimately, affected non-southern and non-reconstruction issues.

An act passed in May, 1866, amending the Habeas Corpus Act of 1863, provided that state court proceedings after removal were void and, if they were continued, the aggrieved party could secure damages and double costs. The act also extended the period in which removal could occur. The defendant now had the right to remove even after he appeared and filed his plea in the state court. Furthermore, any state court proceedings after removal made the other party and the state officials liable for damages and double costs. The congressional Democrats complained that the bill subverted the powers of the states, that it further marked "the destruction of all the landmarks of . . . Government," and that it would make justice expensive and distant for the average citizen. The Republican purpose, however, was clear. Trumbull justified the proposal as necessary to protect loyal men against suits arising from their "obedience to orders in putting down the rebellion." The Republicans clearly were angered at the persistence of prosecutions in the border and southern states. The bill's manager, Senator Daniel Clark of New Hampshire, summed up the majority's frustration: "We have had about enough of this State authority to teach it to yield respect and obedience to the laws of the United States." The bill easily passed both houses. Less than a year later, Congress further provided that defendants removing suits could secure a writ of habeas corpus *cum causa* if held in state custody.[13]

---

[12]16 Stat. 439–40. The refusal of a state court to permit removal was an old and persistent problem. *Gordon* v. *Longest,* 16 Peters (41 U.S.) 97 (1842). For debates on the 1871 act, see *Cong. Globe,* 41 Cong., 3 sess., pp. 1633 ff. (February 24, 1871).

[13]Act of May 11, 1866, 14 Stat. 46–47; *Cong. Globe,* 39 Cong,. 1 sess., pp. 1389, 1423, 1880–81, 1983, 2052–66 (March 14, 15, April 11, 17, 20, 1866); Act of February 5, 1867, 14 Stat. 385. The latter is not to be confused with the Habeas Corpus Act of the same date, which later played a prominent part in the McCardle

Senator Clark's frank outburst indicated growing Republican impatience with state harassment of national policy. In turn, the party's frustration led to further attempts to protect its, and thus the nation's, interests; and these additional efforts included latent possibilities which extended beyond the immediate issue of southern reconstruction policy.

The Removal Act of July 27, 1866, for example, represented a significant increment to federal jurisdictional authority and a half-way house toward the legislation of 1875. The signal achievement of this 1866 act was that Congress provided for removal of "separable controversies." The Republicans were responding to southern ploys to circumvent federal court jurisdiction. In southern state courts, residents alleging wrongs committed against them by a citizen of another state, particularly a carpetbagger, would join the defendants with a resident of the plaintiff's state, thus compelling the alien to have his cause tried in the state court. The 1866 act now permitted an out-of-state defendant to remove his part of the suit to the federal courts. The rest of the cause and the local defendants remained in the state court. While based on the diversity of citizenship ideas of the Constitution and the Judiciary Act of 1789, Congress boldly innovated with federal jurisdiction by splitting causes of action.[14] Later, in the 1875 act, the Republicans expanded the idea further by allowing removal of the entire case, thus giving the federal courts jurisdiction over citizens of the same state, even if a federal question were lacking in the controversy between them.

The Removal Act of 1866 was a momentous event yet, once again, provoked only minimal opposition. There was no debate in the Senate, the bill being introduced and passed within one day. In the House a few hours later, some Democrats protested, but to no avail. There was a brief flurry between Boutwell, the bill's manager, and

affair. The Act of May 11, 1866, was upheld in *The Mayor* v. *Cooper*, 6 Wallace (73 U.S.) 247 (1867). Protests against state harassment particularly came from the Provost Marshal–General's Bureau in the War Department. While a number of suits occurred in the border and ex-rebel states, the head of the Bureau also complained of similar troubles in certain northern states (James B. Fry to Edwin M. Stanton, January 6, 1866; William S. Rankin to General G. Clay Smith, January 18, 1866, House Committee on the Judiciary Papers, HR 39A–F 13.7, National Archives).

[14]14 Stat. 306–7. The phrase "separable controversies" was employed by the bench and bar and does not appear in the statute. Also see J.L.E., "The Constitutionality of Federal Removal Jurisdiction over Separable Controversies Involving Citizens of the Same State," *University of Pennsylvania Law Review*, 94 (January, 1946): 239.

Representative Lawrence S. Trimble, a Kentucky Democrat. Boutwell emphasized the southern motivation, but Trimble prophetically complained that "this bill goes further."[15]

Concurrent with the Reconstruction Acts of 1867, Congress allowed further options for removal. Passed as an amendment to the Removal Act of July 27, 1866, a new law provided that the plaintiff or defendant could transfer a cause upon an affidavit "stating that he has reason to, and does believe that, from prejudice or local influence, he will not be able to obtain justice in a [a] . . . state court." The "Local Prejudice Act," as it came to be known, was only briefly explained in both houses, then passed without debate and, finally, signed by President Johnson on the last day of the session. Johnson's support was curious. Here, as in the July, 1866, act, Congress audaciously expanded federal influence, yet Johnson, who regularly deplored the breakdown of traditional federalism, offered no objection or protest.

This Act of March 2, 1867, was an obvious device to protect federal officials, carpetbaggers, and freedmen from hostile southern courts. The bill originally presented by the Judiciary Committee actually limited the measure to the rebellious states, but that restriction was deleted on the floor and the act was made applicable in all states. The same change had been made in the Removal Act of 1866. Certainly, then, there were some congressmen who envisioned a larger design and were influential enough to secure the concurrence of their colleagues.[16]

The "separable controversy" and "local prejudice" acts were

[15]*Cong. Globe,* 39 Cong., 1 sess., pp. 4162, 4203 (July 26, 1866). For commentary on the "separable controversy" idea, see the opposed views of W. F. Cooper "Removal of Causes from State to Federal Courts," *Southern Law Review,* n.s., 3 [April, 1877]: 1, who believed the act unconstitutional unless it applied to controversies wholly between citizens of separate states; and, R. M. Smith ("Removal of Causes from State to Federal Courts," *ibid.* [June, 1877], 277), who strongly supported the legislation. Also see the concurring opinion by Justice Bradley in the *Removal Cases,* 100 U.S. 457, 470 (1879). A draft of the July, 1866, act may have been prepared in the War Department. Secretary Edwin M. Stanton at one point submitted a memorandum to the House Judiciary Committee which, among other items, urged provision for removal even after appearance had been made in the state court by the defendant. Support for the bill also came from the Internal Revenue Service and the Provost Marshal–General's Bureau (House Committee on the Judiciary Papers, HR 39A–F 13.5 and F 13.7, National Archives).

[16]14 Stat. 558–59; *Cong. Globe,* 39 Cong., 2 sess., pp. 1865–66, 1787, 2005 (February 27, March 2, 1867). Cf. S. 562, Senate Bill File, National Archives. For differing views on the purpose of this act, see I[saac] F. R[edfield], "Note," *American Law Register,* 13 (1874): 143, and Justice Field's opinion in *Gaines* v.

bold departures from traditional jurisdictional limitations. With the former, the Republicans had moved a good distance beyond John Marshall's inclinations. In *Strawbridge* v. *Curtiss,* in 1806, where all but one of the parties were from the same state, Marshall had held that this was not adequate diversity of citizenship to permit federal jurisdiction. "Each distinct interest," he said "should be represented by persons, all of whom are entitled to sue, or may be sued in the federal courts."[17]

Interestingly enough, the postwar Supreme Court reacted timorously to the new jurisdictional authority and reaffirmed Marshall's restrictive holding. In the *Sewing Machine Companies Case* of 1873 it construed the statutes of 1866 and 1867 as allowing removal only when there was common citizenship on each side of the controversy. Whatever the purpose of the 1866 act, the Court held that Congress did not intend the 1867 act to allow removal on grounds of local prejudice when co-plaintiffs or co-defendants were citizens of the same state as some of the adverse parties.[18] The Court maintained, in short, that the recent legislation was only declaratory of existing practice. But the legislative history of the 1866 act indicates that the Court clearly restricted congressional intent, if only to avoid a serious constitutional question.

The Removal Act of 1866 originated in a bill sponsored by Senator Ira Harris of New York. Harris was a member of the Judiciary Committee and played an active part in the writing of judicial legislation during the period. This bill, however, was a stronger substitute for one Harris earlier had proposed and which must have been modified in committee. Harris's original bill established the

---

Fuentes, 92 U.S. 10, 19 (1875). The act was held valid in *Railway Company* v. *Whitton's Administrator,* 13 Wallace (80 U.S.) 270 (1872).

[17]*Strawbridge* v. *Curtiss,* 3 Cranch (7 U.S.) 267 (1806). Marshall's ruling also was upheld in *Coal Company* v. *Blatchford,* 11 Wallace (78 U.S.) 172 (1871).

[18]18 Wallace (85 U.S.) 553 (1873). Justices Bradley and Miller dissented vigorously. In an earlier circuit court case, Miller offered a simple justification for this kind of removal. He compared it to state laws which allowed change of venue from one county to another. "The Federal courts," he concluded, "are not courts for non-residents more than for residents, and no injustice is done to the latter to be compelled there to litigate controversies which they may have with citizens of other states" *(Farmers' Trust Co.* v. *Maquillan,* cited in John F. Dillon, *Removal of Suits from State Courts to Federal Courts,* 2d ed. [St. Louis: Central Law Journal Co., 1877], pp. 25–26). Dillon was one of the newly created Circuit Judges under the 1869 act and served as such until 1879. Thereafter, he participated in some of the notable removal cases, such as the *Pacific Railroad Removal Cases,* discussed below. He was an enthusiastic advocate for federal jurisdictional authority.

"separable controversy" idea, but with a definite, qualifying proviso: "That the removals prescribed by this act shall apply only to such cases, and carry along only such parties as could, under the Constitution and existing laws, be brought in the [federal courts]."[19] This clause, along with limiting the act's force to those states "lately in insurrection," was rejected by Congress, signifying a desire for some broader change. In other words, a congressional majority had something other in mind than a mere declaration of existing practice. But it was not the first or the last time that a minority congressional view found favor in the Supreme Court.

At best, the Court seemed bewildered by the new legislation. Then, too, the overburdened justices probably were anxious to avoid increasing an already staggering case load. But perhaps their reluctance is best explained by the Court's adherence to traditional concepts of federalism. *The Sewing Machine Case* followed *Slaughter-House* by one year and certainly the two fit within the same ideological framework.

The Supreme Court, however, does not alone affect the legal process. Congressional persistence and prodding can and do force shifts and change despite a negative judicial reaction. Naturally, an alteration of the Court's membership changes the judicial environment and previously rejected legislation can receive more hospitable treatment. The combination of these two conditions operated upon the revolutionary Jurisdiction and Removal Act of 1875, which contained a clearer expression of congressional intentions and which received judicial approval.

The 1875 act began as an attempt to clarify the Removal Acts of July 27, 1866, and March 2, 1867, by expanding diversity jurisdiction and overcoming the Court's objections in *The Sewing Machine Case*. Section 1 of the original bill, sponsored by Representative Luke P. Poland, a Vermont Republican, simply authorized an out-of-state defendant to remove his cause even though other defendants lived in the state where the suit was brought. Poland admitted that he originally had opposed the idea, but "gentlemen" from "other portions of the country" who were "somewhat differently affected" than New England, convinced him otherwise. Representative Ebenezer Rockwood Hoar, Republican from Massachusetts, who successfully had argued *The Sewing Machine Case*, repeated his

[19]S. 562, Senate Bill File, National Archives. Harris dropped this bill on the same day as the other (S. 606) passed.

arguments that removal of this type violated the Constitution. The House Republicans replied only half-heartedly to the constitutional objections. Hoar seemed to speak so authoritatively that he may have discouraged his fellow partisans. Other Republicans, moreover, stressed that the federal courts already were overtaxed by litigation. Hoar's opposition proved crucial, for he apparently persuaded enough other Republicans to support a Democratic attempt to strike Section 1 entirely. The House thereupon passed minor revisions for removal procedure.[20]

The Senate Republicans, however, acted more decisively. Led by Matthew H. Carpenter of Wisconsin, they restored the clarification which the House had deleted and added substantially more jurisdictional authority. In its final form, the bill granted original cognizance to the federal courts and permitted removal in all suits arising under the Constitution, federal laws, or treaties; suits in which the United States was a plaintiff; suits between citizens and aliens; and suits between citizens of different states. Within this last category, the "separable controversy" idea achieved fruition, as the act provided for removal of the entire suit, regardless of whether the separable aspect was the principal one. The act departed from the 1789 limitations by allowing any suit asserting a right under the Constitution or federal law to be begun in the federal courts, or to be removed if the action had originated in the state court. In conference during the next session, the insistent senators secured House concurrence in their bill.[21]

The Senate debate centered on procedural mechanics, with little attention devoted to substantive matters. At one point, however, Democratic Senator Thomas F. Bayard accused the Republicans of subverting the "wisdom" of the Judiciary Act of 1789. He contended that the 1789 law had required one of the parties to be a resident of the district in which the suit was brought, but the Republicans proposed now that the parties simply be citizens of the different states in order to bring the case into federal court. Bayard frankly admitted that the first judiciary act may not have comprehended all the jurisdictional authority intended in Article III of the Constitution, but the restriction had been "wise" and "tested

---

[20]*Congressional Record*, 43 Cong., 1 sess., pp. 4301–4 (May 27, 1874). A year earlier, there was an unsuccessful attempt to clarify this type of removal action (42 Cong., 3 sess., H.R. 3283, House Committee on the Judiciary, H42A–F14.9, National Archives).

[21]18 Stat. 470–71; *Congressional Record*, 43 Cong., 2 sess., p. 2275 (March 3, 1875).

by the experience of time." Carpenter boldly countered that the
1789 act was "substantially in contravention of the Constitution."
Following Justice Joseph Story's 1816 assertion that the 1789 law
did not entirely fulfill the constitutional grant of judicial power,
Carpenter emphasized his party's purpose to utilize and make paramount the federal judicial system.[22]

In a series of cases over the next few years, the Supreme Court
finally acknowledged the congressional intent. At first, however, it
seemed as if judicial traditionalism would hold sway. Chief Justice
Morrison R. Waite, in the 1879 *Removal Cases*, in a very restricted
opinion, held that as long as *all* citizens on one side of a suit were
from different states than those of the other, the suit could be removed. Because the adverse parties in this case had followed such a
form, the majority refused to pass on the separability provisions.
But Bradley's concurring opinion seemed to indicate that the
majority was not disposed to alter its previous view very significantly.[23]

A few months later, however, the Court switched directions, and
in *Barney* v. *Latham*, Justice John Marshall Harlan accepted the full
implications of the "separable controversy" idea. For Harlan, the
1875 statute not only preserved the principles of the Removal Act of
July 27, 1866, but also made "radical changes." In short, Harlan
concluded, Congress had determined that removal of the separable
controversy should comprehend transfer of the whole suit to the
federal courts: "That such was the intention of Congress is a proposition which seems too obvious to require enforcement by argument."[24] It is interesting, however, that Harlan made no effort to
satisfy any constitutional misgivings and doubts involved in such
broad removal legislation. Furthermore, he did not expressly over-
rule Marshall's *Strawbridge* opinion.

What was so obvious for Harlan, usually a strong-minded nationalist, apparently was not so clear for some of his colleagues. *Barney*
v. *Latham* sustained an essential feature of the 1875 law only by a
narrow 4–3 margin. Diverse personalities and ideologues such as
Waite, Miller, and Field joined in dissent. Actually the decision may

[22]*Ibid.*, 43 Cong., 1 sess., pp. 4978–87 (June 15, 1874); *Martin* v. *Hunter's Lessee;*
1 Wheaton (14 U.S.) 304, 328 (1816). Carpenter later changed his allegiances and
became identified with anti-corporation sentiment (E. Bruce Thompson, *Matthew
Hale Carpenter* [Madison: University of Wisconsin Press, 1954], pp. 220 ff.).

[23]100 U.S. 457 (1879). Justice Swayne joined in Bradley's opinion, while Strong
separately concurred in the result.

[24]103 U.S. 205, 212–13 (1880).

have been dictated more by physical than ideological considerations. Justices Clifford and Hunt were ill and missed the whole term. It is certain that Clifford would have disagreed with Harlan and probable that Hunt would also. Waite's qualifications in the recent *Removal Cases* undoubtedly represented the true majority idea at that time.

In 1885, however, almost all judicial doubts were resolved, for the Court upheld the broader removal provisions of the 1875 law in the *Pacific Railroad Removal Cases* and, incidentally, offered a clue to the full implications of removal legislation. Justice Bradley, in a 7–2 decision held that a suit against a federally chartered corporation could be removed to the circuit court "on the ground that such suits are suits 'arising under the laws of the United States.' "[25] Bradley's opinion opened the floodgates for a staggering number of tort and corporate cases onto an already overburdened federal docket.

The Supreme Court thus accepted the responsibilities imposed on the federal judicial system by Congress and, accordingly, widened the scope of federal authority. The Republicans' removal legislation can be viewed as part of their southern policy and as a reflection of the nationalizing character of the Reconstruction era. But the *Pacific Railroad Removal Cases* also indicate the economic consequences of the jurisdictional changes. Felix Frankfurter and James M. Landis have suggested that the increasing attacks on railroad interests in the state courts largely prompted the 1875 act. It is clear that the removal legislation involved something more than countering southern obstructionism. For example, the original bills in 1866 and 1867 applied only to the former states of the Confederacy but were altered to include the whole nation. Representative Poland's remarks in 1874 pointed to difficulties in the state courts in "other portions" of the country, a probable reference to the "Granger" laws and litigation in the Midwest. Finally, Senator Carpenter, himself a leading railroad attorney, justified increasing federal court powers because of the sprawling, national character of com-

---

[25]115 U.S. 1. (1885). Waite and Miller dissented without opinion. Also see *Ames* v. *Kansas*, 111 U.S. 449 (1884). Incidentally, there were enough membership changes in the Court since the *Removal Cases* and *Barney* v. *Latham* to give the "nationalist-minded" side a clear majority—at least on this issue. For an example of pressures by "monied men" to get the "right" kind of appointments to the Supreme Court, see the fascinating material on Justice Stanley Matthews in C. Peter Magrath, *Morrison R. Waite: The Triumph of Character* (New York: Macmillan, 1963), pp. 239–42.

merce and industry. The 1789 law had been wise enough for a small nation, he admitted, but the thirteen states had become thirty-seven and the American people had "become totally changed in their methods of doing business . . . . The whole circumstances of the people, the necessities of our business, our situation, have totally and entirely changed."[26]

Justice Bradley's *Pacific Railroad Removal Cases* opinion did not offer much of a commentary linking the corporate purpose to national authority. But in his concurring remarks in the 1879 *Removal Cases*, Bradley had criticized the then majority for its reluctance to recognize such an implication in the congressional legislation. In brief, he had construed the 1875 act as granting federal jurisdiction so long as *some* diversity existed. He pointed out that the "absurdity" of regarding every stockholder in a corporation as a party to a controversy had forced the Court to acknowledge corporations as citizens of states which had chartered them. And now, Bradley contended, if the Court permitted a non-diverse party on one side to spoil federal jurisdiction, it would violate the very objective of removal, that is, to secure an impartial tribunal for citizens from different states.

In view of some pending, important cases involving interstate railroad receiverships, Bradley particularly urged a broad construction of the 1875 act. The old railroad lawyer remained faithful: "No cases are more appropriate to this jurisdiction or more urgently call for its exercise than those which relate to the foreclosure and sale of railroads extending into two or more states, and winding up the affairs of the companies that own them." Bradley had no qualms regarding the burden placed on the federal docket: "If the judicial force is not sufficient to meet the exigency, let it be increased. If the courts are not held at sufficiently convenient places, that difficulty can be easily removed."[27] And, indeed, as the business of the federal courts increased—in large part because of the congressional legislation— Congress ultimately accommodated the judicial system and litigants with more courts and more judges.

---

[26]Frankfurter and Landis, *The Business of the Supreme Court,* pp. 64–65; *Congressional Record,* 43 Cong., 1 sess., p. 4986 (June 15, 1874). In the 1820's Henry Clay sought to shift cases involving the Bank of the United States from the state to the federal courts, believing such a move advantageous for the Bank (see James F. Hopkins and Mary W. M. Hargreaves, eds., *The Papers of Henry Clay,* 3 vols. to date (Lexington: 1959–63), 2:720–23, 3:532–33, 548–50, 646–47.
[27]100 U.S. 457, 480, 482 (1879).

The postwar removal legislation certainly indicates a positive aspect of Republican attitudes toward the federal judiciary. Those laws reflected the party's nationalistic drives and its willingness to utilize the instruments of national administration. There was a conscious awareness of the federal judiciary's usefulness to further party aims, whether they were political or economic. The Court's activity in judicial review cases reflected self-created vigor and energy; yet, the congressional expansion of federal jurisdiction illustrates that the vitality of the federal judicial system was not a one-sided affair. Just as with the reorganization of judicial circuits in 1862 and 1866, Congress creatively and imaginatively experimented with the judicial system to serve the Republican party, as well as the national purpose.

Finally, the Act of 1875 poses an interesting counterpoint to the better-known Civil Rights Act of the same year and has a special symbolic importance of its own. Both laws, in fact, were enacted in the closing days of the Forty-third Congress, and just before control of the House of Representatives passed into Democratic hands. Both, too, may be seen as an ultimate expression of Republican reconstruction policies. One recognized a national obligation to confer and guarantee first-class citizenship to the freedmen. The other marked an expression of the party's nationalizing impulse and complementary concern for the national market.

Yet, in the late nineteenth century, the Civil Rights Act proved hollow and ultimately meaningless. It had passed only after bitter divisions among the Republicans themselves, partly as a galvanic reaction to the death of Charles Sumner, but probably more from nostalgia and party tradition. After the Supreme Court invalidated much of the law in 1883,[28] the very idea of civil rights legislation lapsed into a constitutional limbo for three-quarters of a century.

The Jurisdiction and Removal Act, however, persisted in meaning and application long beyond the Reconstruction era. Indeed, in terms of its Republican support, the statute symbolized a bridge between ideas and views advanced by older Republicans and those represented by the party's new breed which prevailed after 1875. The act seems truly transitional between the Republican drives during Reconstruction and those of the period conveniently labeled *laissez nous faire*. The means were the same; the objectives and purposes, however, differed. And as vast numbers of railroad and

[28]*Civil Rights Cases*, 109 U.S. 3 (1883).

corporate cases poured into the friendlier environs of the federal courts, secure from aggresive and hostile state laws and courts, the Republican design became abundantly clear. In fact, by the 1890's, the relationship between removal and receivership cases became a particular grievance and protest of the Populists.[29] Seventy-five years afterward, the Republicans' jurisdictional legislation proved to be an elaboration on the Federalists' motivation, as well as their technique.

---

[29]Alan F. Westin, "The Supreme Court, the Populist Movement, and the Campaign of 1896," *Journal of Politics*, 15 (February, 1953): 17–19.

9

The Supreme Court in the Reconstruction Era

The history of the Supreme Court in the nineteenth century usually is divided into chronological periods, designated to indicate either personal leadership or other special considerations. Thus we have the Marshall Court, the Taney Court, the Reconstruction (or Chase) Court, and the Waite-Fuller Court of the late nineteenth century, often (albeit carelessly) described as the Era of Judicial Supremacy. A typical chart of the Court's power, influence, and prestige for the century would indicate a pattern of steady growth, except for a marked setback lasting from 1857 to about 1873. The standard explanation of this anomaly is that the Dred Scott decision discredited the Court and thus impaired its effectiveness during the Civil War and Reconstruction. Linked to this view is the notion that the justices, confronted by aggressive and vindictive Radical Republicans, timidly retreated and acquiesced in the constitutionality of Congress' reconstruction program. The Court, it is said, played only a passive role in this period. This concept, however persistent, is open to challenge.

To be sure, the Supreme Court encountered almost unprecedented hostility in the fifteen years following Dred Scott. Not since the days of Thomas Jefferson's struggle with the Federalist-dominated judiciary had the Court's political standing been so precarious. In view of this situation, the Court's ongoing functions, its institutional toughness, and the vitality and enlargement of its powers are all the more impressive. Furthermore, the diversity of the criticism of the Dred Scott decision has been overlooked. The widespread expression that the Court had erred should not lead us to believe that the criticism was general in tone. Very much opposition focused entirely on the particular decision. For example, one Boston editor described the decision as a "horribly wicked" one, delivered by a "packed and partial" Supreme Court. Yet he regarded the institutional attacks as even more insidious. The Supreme Court, he maintained, exercised a beneficial role in American government and to repudiate its standing would be, he insisted, a "great evil."[1]

This readily admitted need for a judicial arbiter ultimately accounted for the dominant tendency in Republican party thinking. Beginning with Lincoln's attacks upon the Dred Scott decision in his 1858 campaign debates with Douglas, most Republicans recognized that southern domination of the judiciary, and not the Court's functional capacities, had to be changed. This is what Lincoln suggested when he said that his party intended to reverse the decision: "We mean," he explained, "to do what we can to have the court decide the other way."[2] When the Republicans achieved power, they acted responsibly and in a traditional manner. They did nothing to impair the Supreme Court's power and role in the national governmental apparatus. But the judicial reorganization legislation in 1862 enabled Lincoln decisively to alter the Court's predominantly southern character. While certainly not without partisan and sectional motivation, the reorganization was justifiable in terms of local needs and judicial business. Indeed, the Republican action had more validity than similar Democratic "reforms" in 1802 and 1837.

The Republicans, whatever their disappointment with the Dred Scott decision, recognized the Court as a desirable prize. Their concern with judicial appointments as well as their satisfaction with wartime decisions sustaining the North's war-making capacity, sprang from their respect for the Court's operational relevance to the constitutional and governmental system. They were concerned with the Court as an instrument of power—and this is significant for dispensing with an all too simple idea that the post-1857 Court operated in an atmosphere of suspicion and hostility. Furthermore, once Lincoln's appointments had altered the Court's sectional and partisan cast, the Republicans eagerly anticipated a judicial imprimatur for *their* policies.

Despite periodic apprehension, Republicans displayed a continuing respect for the Court during the postwar period. Admittedly,

---

[1]*Zion's Herald,* March 18, 1857. See chap. 2, *above.*

[2]Roy P. Basler, ed., *The Collected Works of Abraham Lincoln,* 9 vols. (New Brunswick: Rutgers University Press, 1953–55), 2:495.

notions of legislative supremacy along with some talk of annihilating the Court circulated among certain Republican elements after 1865; such ideas, however, never dominated the broad spectrum of party opinion. The Republicans during Reconstruction represented a congeries of factions and ideas, and clearly there was no overriding consensus to "do something" about the Court when it appeared potentially aggressive or antagonistic toward party policy. The Republican party, moreover, should be measured by what it actually did, not by what a few of its members said or proposed. With regard to the Supreme Court there was a great deal of sound and fury, but it signified only the disaffection and dissatisfaction of a limited group within the party. The majority rebuffed repeated attempts to punish the Court or curtail its powers.

The temporary withdrawal of jurisdiction in the *McCardle* case stands as the only exception to this behavior. The congressional action cannot be justified; it can, however, be understood. And it must be comprehended within the context of the terrible pressures operating upon the Republican party. The military reconstruction legislation was obtained at the cost of great internal stress and strain. However reluctantly many party members voted for that program, they found themselves, for better or worse, committed to it as a matter of party policy. It became, in a manner of speaking, the chief prop in the Republicans' appeal for political support, in the North as well as the South. Accordingly, the party stood ready to defend its program with whatever measures seemed necessary. These included the most extreme of all: impeachment and trial of a president who, the Republicans believed, had deliberately obstructed their avowed aims.

The Republican reaction to the possibility of judicial emasculation of their program was less drastic, yet more misguided. As the *McCardle* case moved to the Supreme Court, a rising chorus of opinion maintained that the justices would invalidate the Reconstruction Acts. With alarming regularity, the Republicans heard or read supposedly authoritative reports indicating such judicial action. The Democrats' hopefully self-fulfilling prophecy—that the laws were unconstitutional and that the Court would rule accordingly— became indistinguishable from fact. As for the Republicans, their pride as well as their program was at stake. While some party members realized the dubious nature of their handiwork, nearly all distinguished between wisdom and validity. Constitutional regularity *did* matter to the Republicans, and nothing irritated them more than presidential and Democratic lectures on "constitutionality." Ultimately, the Democratic-inspired rumors had a galvanic effect upon the Republicans. Convinced that the Court would void their program, they reluctantly used a constitutional power to prevent judicial action.

There is, of course, an ethical and policy question here, for Congress used its authority to affect specific litigation and not to define the general bounds of federal jurisdiction as probably intended by the Constitution's framers. Driven as they were to an extremist response, as in the impeachment of Andrew Johnson, the Republicans again played havoc with the substance of the separation of powers, while remaining within the bounds of constitutional procedure.

The irony is that the Republicans' precipitate response may have been misconceived. For it seems far from certain that the Supreme Court intended to invalidate the Reconstruction Acts. We can only guess at the extent to which the judicial recognition of political reality dictated prudence on their part. If such a consideration figured in their thinking, then the Chase Court justices were no different from their predecessors or successors. The best available evidence indicates that the justices divided equally on the substantive constitutional issues. Given this, they reacted with intelligence and caution to their division and refrained from rendering a constitutional opinion. Moreover, their responses and tactics in cases such as *Ex parte Milligan, Georgia* v. *Stanton,* and *Ex parte Yerger* should dispel long-prevailing notions of judicial timidity and cowardice.

The Republicans' desperate counterplay in the *McCardle* case nevertheless again indicated a certain respect for the potentialities of judicial power and the Court's vitality. Contemporary Republicans, unlike later historians, were quite aware that the judiciary was not in total eclipse. The idea of judicial inertia proceeds directly from the assumptions of congressional intimidation and judicial timidity. But while the practical limits of judicial power and an emotionally charged, polarized political situation inhibited the justices regarding the Reconstruction legislation, the Chase Court acted vigorously in other areas. In cases involving federalism and intergovernmental affairs (aside from Reconstruction), economic interests and operations in the national market, and its own authority in the governmental apparatus, the Court's decisions had a widespread impact on the nation. Unspectacular as the cases may have been, the issues demonstrated the Court's continuing utility. It might not be too much of an exaggeration to find in this period a firm establishment of the Court's political role of determining the legitimacy and meaning of power and policy, with its myriad of side-effects.[3] In addition, a consideration of the Supreme Court from this angle illustrates again the superficiality of the hostility to it. The dramatic highlights, the heated controversies have simply obscured the institutional toughness and the persistence of judicial activity.

Later, when the nation's interest and energy had flagged, and the inevitable reaction against Reconstruction had set in, the Supreme Court articulated the new national mood. First, in the *Slaughter-House Cases,* just prior to Chief Justice Chase's death in 1873, the Court aborted the more ambitious aspirations of Republican nationalism and laid the foundation for the legal subversion of Negro hopes for full equality. A closely divided bench held that the Fourteenth Amendment offered no positive sanction to national power and had not effected any fundamental change in the federal structure. Then, in a series of decisions over the next decades, the Court served as the instrument for national abandonment of the Negro's cause when it restricted federal attempts to protect Negro rights and condoned repressive state legislation.

Justice Miller, speaking for the majority in *Slaughter-House,* emphatically denied that the postwar constitutional changes had altered the "main features of the general [federal] system" as it had existed before the Civil War. Congress designed the Fourteenth Amendment, he said, to secure the freedom granted to Negroes by the Thirteenth Amendment. Furthermore, Congress sought protection for the freedman "from the oppressions of those who had formerly exercised unlimited dominion over him." Interestingly, in subsequent cases which actually involved Negroes and the Fourteenth Amendment (unlike *Slaughter-House*), neither Miller nor his colleagues reiterated this theme.[4]

Despite his alleged concern for the Negro, Miller fundamentally

[3]See Willard Hurst's suggestions in "Judicial Review and the Distribution of National Powers," in Edmond Cahn, ed., *Supreme Court and Supreme Law* (Bloomington: Indiana University Press, 1954), pp. 140–69.

[4]16 Wallace (83 U.S.) 36, 82, 71–72 (1873). Charles Fairman, *Mr. Justice Miller and the Supreme Court, 1862–1890* (Cambridge, Mass.: Harvard University Press, 1939), p. 186.

treated the new amendment as a tautology when he objected to transferring the protection of all civil rights from the states to the national government. The Fourteenth Amendment, Miller said, did not impose national authority over the whole domain of civil rights. Such a construction would, he believed, enable Congress to restrict state legislative power in its "most ordinary and usual functions." He feared, too, that it would establish the Court as a "perpetual censor" on state legislation and the civil rights of a state's citizens. Finally, Miller contended that such an interpretation would "fetter and degrade" the state governments and "radically" change the theory of relations between national and state powers.[5] Quite simply, the Court held that the postwar amendments notwithstanding, the nation presupposed the maintenance of the states with all their powers for local government, including the regulation of civil rights.

The Court's decision had devastating effects for the freedmen. Miller's arguments against federal power and for the continuance of state sovereignty over civil rights became the Court's most potent weapon in its later support of racialism. The *Slaughter-House* doctrines marked a barrier to positive national legislation in behalf of Negro civil rights and an opening wedge for the constitutional and judicial sanction of segregation, with all of its supporting legal apparatus.[6] In this way, then, the Court ultimately undermined one aspect of Reconstruction. By that time, however, judicial thinking was fully in accord with the prevailing national sentiment.

We often hear that the North tired of its crusading zeal, that it abandoned the Negro. Probably so; but not necessarily because of a surfeit of cynicism. In the 1870's, as well as the 1920's, there was a nostalgic yearning for "normalcy"—normalcy in the sense of a reversion to traditional ideas of a limited and negativist government. Whatever historical confusion exists concerning the original intent of the Fourteenth Amendment, the reaction to the *Slaughter-House* doctrines of national power and federal-state relations is instructive. Democrats naturally were elated, but the decision also had a favorable reception within the legal community and within certain Republican circles. There was a widespread belief that the Supreme

[5] 16 Wallace (83 U.S.) 36, 78. Of the four dissenters, Justice Swayne most effectively answered Miller on the changes in the federal system contemplated by the Fourteenth Amendment.

[6] For federal power, see *Civil Rights Cases*, 109 U.S. 3 (1883); for the segregation decisions, *Plessy* v. *Ferguson*, 163 U.S. 537 (1896), is basic.

Court had fulfilled its proper historical mission of arbitrating and determining powers and rights within the constitutional system.[7] Once again, the Court's recognized utility proved more powerful than the dissatisfaction and distrust generated by a particular decision in a particular controversy.

Much of the recent writing on Reconstruction suffers from viewing the subject as an isolated phenomenon and from an excessive concentration on the Negro problem and civil rights. In the light of current developments, of course, the Negro issue has a special attraction, and its place in the Reconstruction story is certainly important. To focus almost exclusively upon it, however, distorts the larger meaning of the period. The concern for the Negro manifested itself politically as part of a wider constitutional and legal problem. That concern more properly might be viewed as a by-product of the Republicans' conscious and well-articulated desires to reconstruct the nation—that is, to *re*construct the nation in order to insure constitutional and political hegemony for the physically dominant section and, correspondingly, to expand the authority and policy functions of the federal government, which that section would control.

"Our last Congresses have not been word-mongers, but Constitution-makers," boasted the *Chicago Tribune* in 1866. "Their votes, their laws, their organic changes in the Constitution, and the great events for which they legislated, will live for centuries."[8] Modern American legal history properly begins with the premises developed, however precariously, during the Civil War and Reconstruction era. The period witnessed the most fundamental reordering of the constitutional and federal framework since 1787. Significantly enough, the congressional Republicans did not ignore the judiciary. Their concern for the third branch of government reflected the broader constitutional implications of Reconstruction. The reorganization schemes of 1862, 1863, and 1866, the creation of intermediate courts of appeal, and the expansion of federal jurisdiction in a number of areas, all indicated a positive thrust, a desire and a willingness to incorporate the judiciary into the Republicans' vision of national

[7]Charles Warren, *The Supreme Court in United States History*, 3 vols. (Boston: Little, Brown & Co., 1922), 3:265–68, amply illustrates the full range of reaction to the decision.

[8]*Chicago Tribune*, July 28, 1866.

development. A silent, almost imperceptible revolution occurred in the bases of federal judicial power. Measured by their efforts and the results, the Republicans of the 1860's and 1870's were the staunchest supporters of the judicial system since the Federalists. In short, the judiciary as a power phenomenon in the federal system underwent a noteworthy transformation. The change was all too evident and painful for some. In the midst of a Senate debate on federal removal power, Willard Saulsbury of Delaware, an old-line, states'-rights Democrat, cried: "We are in revolutionary times; we are revolutionizing the law."[9] He was right.

The Supreme Court's power and influence over governmental and economic affairs in later years is a familiar story. Much of this developed after the Reconstruction period had come to a close; yet the Court's history between 1857 and 1873 need not be treated as an aberration from its steady upward pattern of institutional and power development. The Court's continuing functions, its tenacity, and its accretion of powers, either granted or assumed, together with Congress' acceptance of the judiciary's role, form a more meaningful backdrop for the later applications of judicial power. And there is one final, ironic twist: in our own day, the Supreme Court has undertaken to express and redeem most faithfully the Republican Reconstruction program—in all its aspects.

[9] *Cong. Globe,* 39 Cong., 1 sess., p. 1883 (April 11, 1866). It cannot be proven absolutely that the Republican framers of the Fourteenth Amendment envisioned a judicial interpretation and enforcement of the amendment so as to protect business interests. Yet Professor Hurst, in summing up the literature on the "conspiracy theory" of the Fourteenth Amendment, makes what I believe is the valid suggestion that the framers "may have foreseen" such a result (James Willard Hurst, *The Growth of American Law: The Law Makers* [Boston: Little, Brown & Co., 1950], pp. 227–28). I think that the Republicans' willingness to use the judiciary as an instrument of power, as evidenced by their general expansion of federal court jurisdiction during the period, adds another dimension to such a possibility.

BIBLIOGRAPHICAL ESSAY

This bibliographical note is not an exhaustive treatment of the sources and literature. It is intended essentially to illustrate the historiographical problems encountered and the nature of the most useful sources.

The rewriting of Reconstruction history, as I have said in my introductory chapter, is one of the most exciting events in current American historical scholarship. It is as if a previous generation of historians had left the period standing on its head, and a new group, influenced by a wholly different political and social environment, has set the story straight. Of course there are many historians today who disagree with the newer interpretations, or find them, at times, as unbalanced and distorted as their predecessors. Both groups perhaps have been too preoccupied with race and partisan politics, while giving short shrift to economic and legal aspects of Reconstruction. Historical bias aside, there nevertheless has been a significant conceptual shift. In his artful study of Andrew Johnson, Eric McKitrick has observed that current historians have covered the same terrain and sources as their predecessors; the difference has been in the degree and subtlety of exploitation. The "error" of earlier writers, it seems, has been mainly one of omission. They often failed, for example, to understand or recognize the complex character of political controversies in which there were varied shades of gray, as well as black and white.

The same may be said for the older treatment of the Supreme Court in the Reconstruction period. It seems that these historians consulted only Democratic statements in a congressional debate and ignored what the other side said. More important, they paid little or no attention to what was contained in the acts of Congress or in the opinions and decisions of the Supreme Court.

The older version, with its tale of unrelieved Republican villainy and Supreme Court impotence or cowardice (the charges vary and often they are illogically used interchangeably), is found in such scholarly works as William A. Dunning, *Essays on the Civil War and Reconstruction and Related Topics* (New York: Macmillan, 1898), and his *Reconstruction, Political, and Economic: 1865–1877* (New York: Harper's, 1907); John W. Burgess, *Reconstruction and the Constitution: 1866–1876* (New York: C. Scribner's Sons, 1903); James Ford Rhodes, *History of the United States from the Compromise of 1850*, vol. 6 (New York: Macmillan, 1906); and James G. Randall, *The Civil War and Reconstruction* (Boston: D. C. Heath, 1937). The biographies of Andrew Johnson and other Reconstruction figures, and the popular treatments of the period, such as that by Claude Bowers, have accepted and embellished these accounts of Reconstruction and the Supreme Court.

The overview of the traditional Reconstruction story has been under attack for nearly three decades. A number of critical articles have appeared, pointing out its shortcomings. The best is Bernard Weisberger's, "The Dark and Bloody Ground of Reconstruction Historiography," *Journal of Southern History* 25 (November 1959): 427–47. His observation that Reconstruction was not an isolated problem in federal-state relations helped to enlarge my view of other constitutional, legal, and judicial problems. Some of the other new works which proved suggestive in their approach, or contributed important information, are Eric L. McKitrick, *Andrew Johnson and Reconstruction* (Chicago: University of Chicago Press, 1960); John Hope Franklin, *Reconstruction after the Civil War* (Chicago: University of Chicago Press, 1961); La Wanda and John H. Cox, *Politics, Principle, and Prejudice, 1865–66* (Glencoe, Ill.: Free Press, 1963); W. R. Brock, *An American Crisis: Congress and Reconstruction, 1865–1867* (New York: St. Martin's Press, 1963); David Donald, *The Politics of Reconstruction* (Baton Rouge: Louisiana State University Press, 1965); and Harold M. Hyman's introductory essay in *The Radical Republicans and Reconstruction: 1861–1870* (Indianapolis: Bobbs-Merrill, 1967). Both McKitrick's and Hyman's works have excellent bibliographical surveys.

Recent standard works on constitutional and Supreme Court history have based their account of judicial activities on the older version of Reconstruction. They are, however, less marked by emotionalism and purposeful bias. While they sometimes recognize that the period also marked an expansion of judicial power, they unreservedly accept the idea that the Court was in danger of political annihilation. See, for example, Carl B. Swisher, *American Constitutional Development* (2d ed.; Boston: Houghton Mifflin Co., 1954); Alfred H. Kelly and Winfred A. Harbison, *The American Constitution: Its Origins and Development* (3d ed.; New York: W. W.

Norton, 1963); and C. Herman Prichett, *The American Constitution* (New York: McGraw-Hill, 1959). Charles Warren, *The Supreme Court in United States History* (3 vols.; Boston: Little, Brown & Co., 1922), offered a new dimension and authority to the established view of Republican chicanery, and it has served as a standard source for legal and constitutional historians. Warren's awareness of important legal changes in the period was unfortunately marred by a bias which distorted their larger political and economic meaning. Benjamin F. Wright, *The Growth of American Constitutional Law* (New York: Reynal & Hitchock, 1942), although somewhat brief, has a number of helpful insights on judicial activity.

The relevant judicial biographies vary widely in quality. Charles Fairman's *Mr. Justice Miller and the Supreme Court, 1862–1890* (Cambridge, Mass.: Harvard University Press, 1939) is in a class by itself. Each chapter is a veritable mine of information. Willard King, *Lincoln's Manager: David Davis* (Cambridge, Mass.: Harvard University Press, 1960) and Carl B. Swisher, *Stephen J. Field: Craftsman of the Law* (Washington: The Brookings Institution, 1930), also are useful, but they devote less attention to this period. David F. Hughes's unpublished doctoral dissertation, "Salmon P. Chase: Chief Justice" (Princeton University, 1963) recognizes the complexity of the judicial history for the period, yet mostly accepts the traditional views regarding the relationship between the Court and Congress. Harold M. Hollingsworth's "The Confirmation of Judicial Review under Taney and Chase" (Ph.D. dissertation, University of Tennessee, 1966), is quite similar in viewpoint. Hollingsworth clearly notes, however, the significant growth of judicial power during Chase's tenure.

Two outstanding M.A. theses which it was my pleasure to direct contributed greatly to my knowledge of particular legal and political problems. See Michal R. Belknap, "Government by Taxation: The Expansion of Federal Power Through Revenue Legislation, 1861–1865" (University of Wisconsin, 1966), and William M. Wiecek, "The Reconstruction of Federal Judicial Power: 1863–75" (University of Wisconsin, 1966).

The congressional debates and the Supreme Court reports obviously represent the chief primary sources for this study. But these printed, public materials must be supplemented with additional congressional and judicial files in the National Archives. Working papers, petitions, and dockets of the committees are crucial to understanding the legislative process. The Bill File is invaluable for noting the changes made in various legislative drafts and also for seeing what did not pass. The Minutes and Docket Books for the

Supreme Court occasionally were useful, particularly for the cases dealing with the Reconstruction Acts.

While manuscript collections for the Reconstruction period are exceedingly rich, they are very disappointing for this particular phase of it. The papers of congressional figures who were prominently involved in judicial affairs yielded little information or insight that could not be derived from the public documents. The papers of Representative James F. Wilson of Iowa, Chairman of the House Judiciary Committee, offer a vivid example. Perhaps no man in Congress was more intimately involved with legislation concerning the judiciary and legal change than Wilson, yet his private papers, which are available in the Fairfield, Iowa, Public Library, are a total disappointment for these aspects of the Reconstruction period.

The papers of some of the Supreme Court justices naturally proved more worthwhile. The richest by far, because of his trenchant political comments, are those of David Davis, collected by Willard King and housed in the Chicago Historical Society. Historians of this period are greatly in debt to Mr. King for discovering many new materials and for making them generally available. Chief Justice Chase's papers are scattered in the Library of Congress, the Historical Society of Pennsylvania, the Huntington Library, and the Cincinnati Historical Society. At the Historical Society of Pennsylvania, there is a "Legal File" in the Chase papers which yielded about as much "inside" and "new" information as one could expect. The papers of Justice Clifford, in the Maine Historical Society, are excellent, but most of the documents pertinent to this study are also in the Davis and Chase collections. Stephen J. Field's correspondence with Federal Judge Matthew Deady, while valuable for judicial matters of later years, contained little that was useful for this work. These papers are in the Oregon Historical Society. Relevant letters by the other justices are available in the Davis, Chase, and Clifford collections.

The numerous published diaries, memoirs, and collections of letters for this period proved useful to me in varying degrees. Special mention should be made of Justice Field's, *Personal Reminiscences of Early Days in California* (Washington: privately printed, 1893). It is a self-serving, self-righteous, partisan document. But those very characteristics make Field's comments on the Reconstruction period all the more revealing and surprising. Howard K. Beale's editions of the diaries of Attorney General Edward Bates and Secretary of the Navy Gideon Welles were occasionally revealing. I would, however, emphatically endorse McKitrick's judgment that Welles's *Diary* (3 vols.; New York: W. W. Norton, 1960) has been overrated as a source for the period. His comments on judicial matters have served me most as a counterpoint to the reality of affairs. The same can be said for Theodore C. Pease and James G. Randall, eds., *Diary of Orville Hickman Browning* (2 vols.; Springfield: Illinois State Historical Library, 1933). James G. Blaine, *Twenty Years of Congress* (Norwich, Conn.: 1884), George S. Boutwell, *Reminiscences of Sixty Years in Public Affairs* (2 vols.; New York: McClure, Phillips, 1902), B. R. Curtis, *A Memoir of Benjamin Robbins Curtis* (2 vols.; Boston: Little, Brown & Co., 1879), and George W. Julian, *Political Recollections, 1840 to 1872* (Chicago: Jansen, McClurg, 1884), were also helpful.

Newspaper and periodical comment in this period was sharp and highly partisan. Most prominent in providing partisan and regional points of view were the *Boston Daily Advertiser*, the *Chicago Tribune*, the *Detroit Free Press*, the *New York Tribune*, the *Nation* and *Harper's Weekly*. The popular organs, then as now, were quite limited and often superficial in their discussion of legal and judicial matters. Their interest naturally focused on the dramatic cases of constitutional law and showed little awareness of the complexity and subtlety of legal change. For these matters, the few contemporary law journals were valuable, especially the *Albany Law Journal*, *American Law Register*, *American Law Review*, and the *Chicago Legal News*.

Finally, there is a large body of writing on legal history scattered in the numerous law reviews. I have found them helpful for particular information and for technique, and they are appropriately cited throughout my notes. The writings of Howard Jay Graham and James Willard Hurst perhaps are not as visible in my citations as they might be, but they significantly enlarged my understanding of certain themes. Graham's articles on the Fourteenth Amendment illustrate the political problems surrounding legal change. Hurst's works, some of which are noted in my concluding chapter, are always useful when dealing with the nature of legal institutions and public policy.

INDEX